DICTIONARY
THEME-BASED

British English Collection

ENGLISH-ROMANIAN

The most useful words
To expand your lexicon and sharpen
your language skills

9000 words

Theme-based dictionary British English-Romanian - 9000 words

By Andrey Taranov

T&P Books vocabularies are intended for helping you learn, memorize and review foreign words. The dictionary is divided into themes, covering all major spheres of everyday activities, business, science, culture, etc.

The process of learning words using T&P Books' theme-based dictionaries gives you the following advantages:

- Correctly grouped source information predetermines success at subsequent stages of word memorization
- Availability of words derived from the same root allowing memorization of word units (rather than separate words)
- Small units of words facilitate the process of establishing associative links needed for consolidation of vocabulary
- Level of language knowledge can be estimated by the number of learned words

T&P Books Publishing
www.tpbooks.com

This book is also available in E-book formats.
Please visit www.tpbooks.com or the major online bookstores.

ROMANIAN THEME-BASED DICTIONARY
British English collection

T&P Books vocabularies are intended to help you learn, memorize, and review foreign words. The vocabulary contains over 9000 commonly used words arranged thematically.

- Vocabulary contains the most commonly used words
- Recommended as an addition to any language course
- Meets the needs of beginners and advanced learners of foreign languages
- Convenient for daily use, revision sessions, and self-testing activities
- Allows you to assess your vocabulary

Special features of the vocabulary

- Words are organized according to their meaning, not alphabetically
- Words are presented in three columns to facilitate the reviewing and self-testing processes
- Words in groups are divided into small blocks to facilitate the learning process
- The vocabulary offers a convenient and simple transcription of each foreign word

The vocabulary has 256 topics including:

Basic Concepts, Numbers, Colors, Months, Seasons, Units of Measurement, Clothing & Accessories, Food & Nutrition, Restaurant, Family Members, Relatives, Character, Feelings, Emotions, Diseases, City, Town, Sightseeing, Shopping, Money, House, Home, Office, Working in the Office, Import & Export, Marketing, Job Search, Sports, Education, Computer, Internet, Tools, Nature, Countries, Nationalities and more …

TABLE OF CONTENTS

PEOPLE. LIFE EVENTS

PRONUNCIATION GUIDE

T&P phonetic alphabet	Romanian example	English example
[a]	arbust [ar'bust]	shorter than in 'ask'
[e]	a merge [a 'merdʒe]	elm, medal
[ə]	brăţară [brə'tsarə]	Schwa, reduced 'e'
[i]	impozit [im'pozit]	shorter than in 'feet'
[ɨ]	cuvânt [ku'vɨnt]	big, America
[o]	avocat [avo'kat]	pod, John
[u]	fluture ['fluture]	book
[b]	bancă ['bankə]	baby, book
[d]	durabil [du'rabil]	day, doctor
[dʒ]	gemeni ['dʒemenʲ]	joke, general
[f]	frizer [fri'zer]	face, food
[g]	gladiolă [gladi'olə]	game, gold
[ʒ]	jucător [ʒukə'tor]	forge, pleasure
[h]	pahar [pa'har]	home, have
[k]	actor [ak'tor]	clock, kiss
[l]	clopot ['klopot]	lace, people
[m]	mobilă ['mobilə]	magic, milk
[n]	nuntă ['nuntə]	name, normal
[p]	profet [pro'fet]	pencil, private
[r]	roată [ro'atə]	rice, radio
[s]	salată [sa'latə]	city, boss
[ʃ]	cleştişor [kleʃti'ʃor]	machine, shark
[t]	statuie [sta'tue]	tourist, trip
[ts]	forţă ['fortsə]	cats, tsetse fly
[tʃ]	optzeci [opt'zetʃi]	church, French
[v]	valiză [va'lizə]	very, river
[z]	zmeură ['zmeurə]	zebra, please
[j]	foios [fo'jos]	yes, New York
[ʲ]	zori [zorʲ]	palatalization sign

ABBREVIATIONS
used in the dictionary

English abbreviations

ab.	-	about
adj	-	adjective
adv	-	adverb
anim.	-	animate
as adj	-	attributive noun used as adjective
e.g.	-	for example
etc.	-	et cetera
fam.	-	familiar
fem.	-	feminine
form.	-	formal
inanim.	-	inanimate
masc.	-	masculine
math	-	mathematics
mil.	-	military
n	-	noun
pl	-	plural
pron.	-	pronoun
sb	-	somebody
sing.	-	singular
sth	-	something
v aux	-	auxiliary verb
vi	-	intransitive verb
vi, vt	-	intransitive, transitive verb
vt	-	transitive verb

Romanian abbreviations

f	-	feminine noun
f pl	-	feminine plural
m	-	masculine noun
m pl	-	masculine plural
n	-	neuter
n pl	-	neuter plural
pl	-	plural

BASIC CONCEPTS

Basic concepts. Part 1

1. Pronouns

I, me	**eu**	[eu]
you	**tu**	[tu]
he	**el**	[el]
she	**ea**	[ˈia]
we	**noi**	[noj]
you (to a group)	**voi**	[ˈvoj]
they (masc.)	**ei**	[ˈej]
they (fem.)	**ele**	[ˈele]

2. Greetings. Salutations. Farewells

Hello! (fam.)	**Bună ziua!**	[ˈbunə ˈziwa]
Hello! (form.)	**Bună ziua!**	[ˈbunə ˈziwa]
Good morning!	**Bună dimineața!**	[ˈbunə dimiˈnʲaʦa]
Good afternoon!	**Bună ziua!**	[ˈbunə ˈziwa]
Good evening!	**Bună seara!**	[ˈbunə ˈsʲara]
to say hello	**a se saluta**	[a se saluˈta]
Hi! (hello)	**Salut!**	[saˈlut]
greeting (n)	**salut** (n)	[saˈlut]
to greet (vt)	**a saluta**	[a saluˈta]
How are you?	**Ce mai faci?**	[ʧie maj ˈfaʧi]
What's new?	**Ce mai e nou?**	[ʧe maj e ˈnou]
Bye-Bye! Goodbye!	**La revedere!**	[la reveˈdere]
See you soon!	**Pe curând!**	[pe kuˈrind]
Farewell! (to a friend)	**Rămâi cu bine!**	[rəˈmij ku ˈbine]
Farewell! (form.)	**Rămâneți cu bine!**	[rəmiˈneʦ ku ˈbine]
to say goodbye	**a-și lua rămas bun**	[aʃ luˈa rəˈmas bun]
Cheers!	**Pa!**	[pa]
Thank you! Cheers!	**Mulțumesc!**	[mulʦuˈmesk]
Thank you very much!	**Mulțumesc mult!**	[mulʦuˈmesk mult]
My pleasure!	**Cu plăcere**	[ku pləˈʧere]
Don't mention it!	**Pentru puțin**	[ˈpentru puˈʦin]
It was nothing	**Pentru puțin**	[ˈpentru puˈʦin]
Excuse me! (fam.)	**Scuză-mă!**	[ˈskuzəmə]
Excuse me! (form.)	**Scuzați-mă!**	[skuˈzaʦimə]

to excuse (forgive)	a scuza	[a sku'za]
to apologize (vi)	a cere scuze	[a 'ʧere 'skuze]
My apologies	Cer scuze	[ʧer 'skuze]
I'm sorry!	Lertaţi-mă!	[er'taʦimə]
to forgive (vt)	a ierta	[a er'ta]
please (adv)	vă rog	[və rog]

Don't forget!	Nu uitaţi!	[nu uj'taʦ^j]
Certainly!	Desigur!	[de'sigur]
Of course not!	Desigur ca nu!	[de'sigur kə nu]
Okay! (I agree)	Sunt de acord!	[sunt de a'kord]
That's enough!	Ajunge!	[a'ʒundʒe]

3. How to address

mister, sir	Domnule	['domnule]
madam	Doamnă	[do'amnə]
miss	Domnişoară	[domniʃo'arə]
young man	Tinere	['tinere]
young man (little boy)	Băiatule	[bə'jatule]
miss (little girl)	Fetiţo	[fe'tiʦo]

4. Cardinal numbers. Part 1

0 zero	zero	['zero]
1 one	unu	['unu]
2 two	doi	[doj]
3 three	trei	[trej]
4 four	patru	['patru]

5 five	cinci	[ʧinʧ]
6 six	şase	['ʃase]
7 seven	şapte	['ʃapte]
8 eight	opt	[opt]
9 nine	nouă	['nowə]

10 ten	zece	['zeʧe]
11 eleven	unsprezece	['unsprezeʧe]
12 twelve	doisprezece	['dojsprezeʧe]
13 thirteen	treisprezece	['trejsprezeʧe]
14 fourteen	paisprezece	['pajsprezeʧe]

15 fifteen	cincisprezece	['ʧinʧsprezeʧe]
16 sixteen	şaisprezece	['ʃajsprezeʧe]
17 seventeen	şaptesprezece	['ʃaptesprezeʧe]
18 eighteen	optsprezece	['opʦsprezeʧe]
19 nineteen	nouăsprezece	['nowəsprezeʧe]

20 twenty	douăzeci	[dowə'zeʧi]
21 twenty-one	douăzeci şi unu	[dowə'zeʧi ʃi 'unu]
22 twenty-two	douăzeci şi doi	[dowə'zeʧi ʃi doj]
23 twenty-three	douăzeci şi trei	[dowə'zeʧi ʃi trej]

30 thirty	**treizeci**	[trej'zetʃi]
31 thirty-one	**treizeci şi unu**	[trej'zetʃi ʃi 'unu]
32 thirty-two	**treizeci şi doi**	[trej'zetʃi ʃi doj]
33 thirty-three	**treizeci şi trei**	[trej'zetʃi ʃi trej]
40 forty	**patruzeci**	[patru'zetʃi]
41 forty-one	**patruzeci şi unu**	[patru'zetʃi ʃi 'unu]
42 forty-two	**patruzeci şi doi**	[patru'zetʃi ʃi doj]
43 forty-three	**patruzeci şi trei**	[patru'zetʃi ʃi trej]
50 fifty	**cincizeci**	[tʃintʃ'zetʃ]
51 fifty-one	**cincizeci şi unu**	[tʃintʃ'zetʃ ʃi 'unu]
52 fifty-two	**cincizeci şi doi**	[tʃintʃ'zetʃ ʃi doj]
53 fifty-three	**cincizeci şi trei**	[tʃintʃ'zetʃ ʃi trej]
60 sixty	**şaizeci**	[ʃaj'zetʃi]
61 sixty-one	**şaizeci şi unu**	[ʃaj'zetʃi ʃi 'unu]
62 sixty-two	**şaizeci şi doi**	[ʃaj'zetʃi ʃi doj]
63 sixty-three	**şaizeci şi trei**	[ʃaj'zetʃi ʃi trej]
70 seventy	**şaptezeci**	[ʃapte'zetʃi]
71 seventy-one	**şaptezeci şi unu**	[ʃapte'zetʃi ʃi 'unu]
72 seventy-two	**şaptezeci şi doi**	[ʃapte'zetʃi ʃi doj]
73 seventy-three	**şaptezeci şi trei**	[ʃapte'zetʃi ʃi trej]
80 eighty	**optzeci**	[opt'zetʃi]
81 eighty-one	**optzeci şi unu**	[opt'zetʃi ʃi 'unu]
82 eighty-two	**optzeci şi doi**	[opt'zetʃi ʃi doj]
83 eighty-three	**optzeci şi trei**	[opt'zetʃi ʃi trej]
90 ninety	**nouăzeci**	[nowə'zetʃi]
91 ninety-one	**nouăzeci şi unu**	[nowə'zetʃi ʃi 'unu]
92 ninety-two	**nouăzeci şi doi**	[nowə'zetʃi ʃi doj]
93 ninety-three	**nouăzeci şi trei**	[nowə'zetʃi ʃi trej]

5. Cardinal numbers. Part 2

100 one hundred	**o sută**	[o 'sutə]
200 two hundred	**două sute**	['dowə 'sute]
300 three hundred	**trei sute**	[trej 'sute]
400 four hundred	**patru sute**	['patru 'sute]
500 five hundred	**cinci sute**	[tʃintʃ 'sute]
600 six hundred	**şase sute**	['ʃase 'sute]
700 seven hundred	**şapte sute**	['ʃapte 'sute]
800 eight hundred	**opt sute**	[opt 'sute]
900 nine hundred	**nouă sute**	['nowə 'sute]
1000 one thousand	**o mie**	[o 'mie]
2000 two thousand	**două mii**	['dowə mij]
3000 three thousand	**trei mii**	[trej mij]
10000 ten thousand	**zece mii**	['zetʃe mij]
one hundred thousand	**o sută de mii**	[o 'sutə de mij]
million	**milion** (n)	[mi'ljon]
billion	**miliard** (n)	[mi'ljard]

6. Ordinal numbers

first (adj)	primul	['primul]
second (adj)	al doilea	[al 'dojlʲa]
third (adj)	al treilea	[al 'trejlʲa]
fourth (adj)	al patrulea	[al 'patrulʲa]
fifth (adj)	al cincilea	[al 'tʃintʃilʲa]

sixth (adj)	al şaselea	[al 'ʃaselʲa]
seventh (adj)	al şaptelea	[al 'ʃaptelʲa]
eighth (adj)	al optulea	[al 'optulʲa]
ninth (adj)	al nouălea	[al 'nowəlʲa]
tenth (adj)	al zecelea	[al 'zetʃelʲa]

7. Numbers. Fractions

fraction	fracţie (f)	['fraktsie]
one half	o doime	[o 'doime]
one third	o treime	[o 'treime]
one quarter	o pătrime	[o pə'trime]

one eighth	o optime	[o op'time]
one tenth	o zecime	[o ze'tʃime]
two thirds	două treimi	['dowə 'treimʲ]
three quarters	trei pătrimi	[trej pə'trimʲ]

8. Numbers. Basic operations

subtraction	scădere (f)	[skə'dere]
to subtract (vi, vt)	a scădea	[a skə'dʲa]
division	împărţire (f)	[impər'tsire]
to divide (vt)	a împărţi	[a impər'tsi]

addition	adunare (f)	[adu'nare]
to add up (vt)	a aduna	[a adu'na]
to add (vi)	a adăuga	[a adəu'ga]
multiplication	înmulţire (f)	[inmul'tsire]
to multiply (vt)	a înmulţi	[a inmul'tsi]

9. Numbers. Miscellaneous

digit, figure	cifră (f)	['tʃifrə]
number	număr (n)	['numər]
numeral	numeral (n)	[nume'ral]
minus sign	minus (n)	['minus]
plus sign	plus (n)	[plus]
formula	formulă (f)	[for'mulə]
calculation	calcul (n)	['kalkul]
to count (vi, vt)	a calcula	[a kalku'la]

to count up	a socoti	[a soko'ti]
to compare (vt)	a compara	[a kompa'ra]
How much?	Cât?	[kit]
How many?	Câţi? Câte?	[kits], ['kite]
sum, total	sumă (f)	['sumə]
result	rezultat (n)	[rezul'tat]
remainder	rest (n)	[rest]
a few (e.g., ~ years ago)	câţiva, câteva	[kits'va], [kite'va]
little (I had ~ time)	puţin	[pu'tsin]
the rest	rest (n)	[rest]
one and a half	unu şi jumătate	['unu ʃi ʒumə'tate]
dozen	duzină (f)	[du'zinə]
in half (adv)	în două	[in 'dowə]
equally (evenly)	în părţi egale	[in pərtsi e'gale]
half	jumătate (f)	[ʒumə'tate]
time (three ~s)	dată (f)	['datə]

10. The most important verbs. Part 1

to advise (vt)	a sfătui	[a sfətu'i]
to agree (say yes)	a fi de acord	[a fi de a'kord]
to answer (vi, vt)	a răspunde	[a rəs'punde]
to apologize (vi)	a cere scuze	[a 'tʃere 'skuze]
to arrive (vi)	a sosi	[a so'si]
to ask (~ oneself)	a întreba	[a intre'ba]
to ask (~ sb to do sth)	a cere	[a 'tʃere]
to be (vi)	a fi	[a fi]
to be afraid	a se teme	[a se 'teme]
to be hungry	a fi foame	[a fi fo'ame]
to be interested in …	a se interesa	[a se intere'sa]
to be needed	a fi necesar	[a fi netʃe'sar]
to be surprised	a se mira	[a se mi'ra]
to be thirsty	a fi sete	[a fi 'sete]
to begin (vt)	a începe	[a in'tʃepe]
to belong to …	a aparţine	[a apar'tsine]
to boast (vi)	a se lăuda	[a se ləu'da]
to break (split into pieces)	a rupe	[a 'rupe]
to call (~ for help)	a chema	[a ke'ma]
can (v aux)	a putea	[a pu'tʲa]
to catch (vt)	a prinde	[a 'prinde]
to change (vt)	a schimba	[a skim'ba]
to choose (select)	a alege	[a a'ledʒe]
to come down (the stairs)	a coborî	[a kobo'ri]
to compare (vt)	a compara	[a kompa'ra]
to complain (vi, vt)	a se plânge	[a se 'plindʒe]
to confuse (mix up)	a încurca	[a inkur'ka]

to continue (vt)	a continua	[a kontinu'a]
to control (vt)	a controla	[a kontro'la]
to cook (dinner)	a găti	[a gə'ti]
to cost (vt)	a costa	[a kos'ta]
to count (add up)	a calcula	[a kalku'la]
to count on ...	a conta pe ...	[a kon'ta pe]
to create (vt)	a crea	[a 'krʲa]
to cry (weep)	a plânge	[a 'plindʒe]

11. The most important verbs. Part 2

to deceive (vi, vt)	a minţi	[a min'tsi]
to decorate (tree, street)	a împodobi	[a impodo'bi]
to defend (a country, etc.)	a apăra	[a apə'ra]
to demand (request firmly)	a cere	[a 'tʃere]
to dig (vt)	a săpa	[a sə'pa]
to discuss (vt)	a discuta	[a disku'ta]
to do (vt)	a face	[a 'fatʃe]
to doubt (have doubts)	a se îndoi	[a se indo'i]
to drop (let fall)	a scăpa	[a skə'pa]
to enter (room, house, etc.)	a intra	[a in'tra]
to exist (vi)	a exista	[a ekzis'ta]
to expect (foresee)	a prevedea	[a preve'dʲa]
to explain (vt)	a explica	[a ekspli'ka]
to fall (vi)	a cădea	[a kə'dʲa]
to fancy (vt)	a plăcea	[a plə'tʃa]
to find (vt)	a găsi	[a gə'si]
to finish (vt)	a termina	[a termi'na]
to fly (vi)	a zbura	[a zbu'ra]
to follow ... (come after)	a urma	[a ur'ma]
to forget (vi, vt)	a uita	[a uj'ta]
to forgive (vt)	a ierta	[a er'ta]
to give (vt)	a da	[a da]
to give a hint	a face aluzie	[a 'fatʃe a'luzie]
to go (on foot)	a merge	[a 'merdʒe]
to go for a swim	a se scălda	[a se skəl'da]
to go out (for dinner, etc.)	a ieşi	[a e'ʃi]
to guess (the answer)	a ghici	[a gi'tʃi]
to have (vt)	a avea	[a a'vʲa]
to have breakfast	a lua micul dejun	[a lu'a 'mikul de'ʒun]
to have dinner	a cina	[a tʃi'na]
to have lunch	a lua prânzul	[a lu'a 'prinzul]
to hear (vt)	a auzi	[a au'zi]
to help (vt)	a ajuta	[a aʒu'ta]
to hide (vt)	a ascunde	[a as'kunde]
to hope (vi, vt)	a spera	[a spe'ra]

to hunt (vi, vt)	a vâna	[a vi'na]
to hurry (vi)	a se grăbi	[a se grə'bi]

12. The most important verbs. Part 3

to inform (vt)	a informa	[a infor'ma]
to insist (vi, vt)	a insista	[a insis'ta]
to insult (vt)	a jigni	[a ʒig'ni]
to invite (vt)	a invita	[a invi'ta]
to joke (vi)	a glumi	[a glu'mi]
to keep (vt)	a păstra	[a pəs'tra]
to keep silent, to hush	a tăcea	[a tə'tʃa]
to kill (vt)	a omorî	[a omo'ri]
to know (sb)	a cunoaşte	[a kuno'aʃte]
to know (sth)	a şti	[a ʃti]
to laugh (vi)	a râde	[a 'ride]
to liberate (city, etc.)	a elibera	[a elibe'ra]
to look for ... (search)	a căuta	[a kəu'ta]
to love (sb)	a iubi	[a ju'bi]
to make a mistake	a greşi	[a gre'ʃi]
to manage, to run	a conduce	[a kon'dutʃe]
to mean (signify)	a însemna	[a insem'na]
to mention (talk about)	a menţiona	[a mentsio'na]
to miss (school, etc.)	a lipsi	[a lip'si]
to notice (see)	a observa	[a obser'va]
to object (vi, vt)	a contrazice	[a kontra'zitʃe]
to observe (see)	a observa	[a obser'va]
to open (vt)	a deschide	[a des'kide]
to order (meal, etc.)	a comanda	[a koman'da]
to order (mil.)	a ordona	[a ordo'na]
to own (possess)	a poseda	[a pose'da]
to participate (vi)	a participa	[a partitʃi'pa]
to pay (vi, vt)	a plăti	[a plə'ti]
to permit (vt)	a permite	[a per'mite]
to plan (vt)	a planifica	[a planifi'ka]
to play (children)	a juca	[a ʒu'ka]
to pray (vi, vt)	a se ruga	[a se ru'ga]
to prefer (vt)	a prefera	[a prefe'ra]
to promise (vt)	a promite	[a pro'mite]
to pronounce (vt)	a pronunţa	[a pronun'tsa]
to propose (vt)	a propune	[a pro'pune]
to punish (vt)	a pedepsi	[a pedep'si]

13. The most important verbs. Part 4

to read (vi, vt)	a citi	[a tʃi'ti]
to recommend (vt)	a recomanda	[a rekoman'da]

to refuse (vi, vt)	a refuza	[a refu'za]
to regret (be sorry)	a regreta	[a regre'ta]
to rent (sth from sb)	a închiria	[a inkiri'ja]

to repeat (say again)	a repeta	[a repe'ta]
to reserve, to book	a rezerva	[a rezer'va]
to run (vi)	a alerga	[a aler'ga]
to save (rescue)	a salva	[a sal'va]

to say (~ thank you)	a spune	[a 'spune]
to scold (vt)	a certa	[a tʃer'ta]
to see (vt)	a vedea	[a ve'dʲa]
to sell (vt)	a vinde	[a 'vinde]

to send (vt)	a trimite	[a tri'mite]
to shoot (vi)	a trage	[a 'tradʒə]
to shout (vi)	a striga	[a stri'ga]
to show (vt)	a arăta	[a arə'ta]
to sign (document)	a semna	[a sem'na]

to sit down (vi)	a se aşeza	[a se aʃə'za]
to smile (vi)	a zâmbi	[a zim'bi]
to speak (vi, vt)	a vorbi	[a vor'bi]
to steal (money, etc.)	a fura	[a fu'ra]
to stop (for pause, etc.)	a se opri	[a se o'pri]

to stop (please ~ calling me)	a înceta	[a antʃe'ta]
to study (vt)	a studia	[a studi'a]
to swim (vi)	a înota	[a ino'ta]
to take (vt)	a lua	[a lu'a]
to think (vi, vt)	a se gândi	[a se gin'di]

to threaten (vt)	a ameninţa	[a amenin'tsa]
to touch (with hands)	a atinge	[a a'tindʒe]
to translate (vt)	a traduce	[a tra'dutʃe]
to trust (vt)	a avea încredere	[a a'vʲa in'kredere]
to try (attempt)	a încerca	[a intʃer'ka]

to turn (e.g., ~ left)	a întoarce	[a into'artʃe]
to underestimate (vt)	a subaprecia	[a subapretʃi'a]
to understand (vt)	a înţelege	[a intse'ledʒe]
to unite (vt)	a uni	[a u'ni]
to wait (vt)	a aştepta	[a aʃtep'ta]

to want (wish, desire)	a vrea	[a vrʲa]
to warn (vt)	a avertiza	[a averti'za]
to work (vi)	a lucra	[a lu'kra]
to write (vt)	a scrie	[a 'skrie]
to write down	a nota	[a no'ta]

14. Colours

| colour | culoare (f) | [kulo'are] |
| shade (tint) | nuanţă (f) | [nu'antsə] |

hue	**ton** (n)	[ton]
rainbow	**curcubeu** (n)	[kurku'beu]
white (adj)	**alb**	[alb]
black (adj)	**negru**	['negru]
grey (adj)	**sur**	['sur]
green (adj)	**verde**	['verde]
yellow (adj)	**galben**	['galben]
red (adj)	**roşu**	['roʃu]
blue (adj)	**albastru închis**	[al'bastru i'nkis]
light blue (adj)	**albastru deschis**	[al'bastru des'kis]
pink (adj)	**roz**	['roz]
orange (adj)	**portocaliu**	[portoka'lju]
violet (adj)	**violet**	[vio'let]
brown (adj)	**cafeniu**	[kafe'nju]
golden (adj)	**de culoarea aurului**	[de kulo'arʲa 'auruluj]
silvery (adj)	**argintiu**	[ardʒin'tju]
beige (adj)	**bej**	[beʒ]
cream (adj)	**crem**	[krem]
turquoise (adj)	**turcoaz**	[turko'az]
cherry red (adj)	**vişiniu**	[viʃi'nju]
lilac (adj)	**lila**	[li'la]
crimson (adj)	**de culoarea zmeurei**	[de kulo'arʲa 'zmeurej]
light (adj)	**de culoare deschisă**	[de kulo'are des'kisə]
dark (adj)	**de culoare închisă**	[de kulo'are i'nkisə]
bright, vivid (adj)	**aprins**	[a'prins]
coloured (pencils)	**colorat**	[kolo'rat]
colour (e.g. ~ film)	**color**	[ko'lor]
black-and-white (adj)	**alb-negru**	[alb 'negru]
plain (one-coloured)	**monocrom**	[mono'krom]
multicoloured (adj)	**multicolor**	[multiko'lor]

15. Questions

Who?	**Cine?**	['tʃine]
What?	**Ce?**	[tʃe]
Where? (at, in)	**Unde?**	['unde]
Where (to)?	**Unde?**	['unde]
From where?	**De unde?**	[de 'unde]
When?	**Când?**	[kind]
Why? (What for?)	**Pentru ce?**	['pentru tʃe]
Why? (~ are you crying?)	**De ce?**	[de tʃe]
What for?	**Pentru ce?**	['pentru tʃe]
How? (in what way)	**Cum?**	[kum]
What? (What kind of ...?)	**Care?**	['kare]
Which?	**Care?**	['kare]
To whom?	**Cui?**	[kuj]

About whom?	**Despre cine?**	['despre 'tʃine]
About what?	**Despre ce?**	['despre tʃe]
With whom?	**Cu cine?**	[ku 'tʃine]

How many?	**Cât? Câtă?**	[kit], ['kitə]
How much?	**Câţi? Câte?**	[kits], ['kite]
Whose?	**Al cui?**	['al kuj]
Whose? (fem.)	**A cui?**	[a kuj]
Whose? (pl)	**Ai cui?, Ale cui?**	[aj kuj], ['ale kuj]

16. Prepositions

with (accompanied by)	**cu**	[ku]
without	**fără**	[fərə]
to (indicating direction)	**la**	[la]
about (talking ~ …)	**despre**	['despre]
before (in time)	**înainte de**	[ina'inte de]
in front of …	**înaintea**	[ina'intʲa]

under (beneath, below)	**sub**	[sub]
above (over)	**deasupra**	[dʲa'supra]
on (atop)	**pe**	[pe]
from (off, out of)	**din**	[din]
of (made from)	**din**	[din]

in (e.g. ~ ten minutes)	**peste**	['peste]
over (across the top of)	**prin**	[prin]

17. Function words. Adverbs. Part 1

Where? (at, in)	**Unde?**	['unde]
here (adv)	**aici**	[a'itʃi]
there (adv)	**acolo**	[a'kolo]

somewhere (to be)	**undeva**	[unde'va]
nowhere (not in any place)	**nicăieri**	[nikə'erʲ]

by (near, beside)	**lângă …**	['lingə]
by the window	**lângă fereastră**	['lingə fe'rʲastrə]

Where (to)?	**Unde?**	['unde]
here (e.g. come ~!)	**aici**	[a'itʃi]
there (e.g. to go ~)	**acolo**	[a'kolo]
from here (adv)	**de aici**	[de a'itʃi]
from there (adv)	**de acolo**	[de a'kolo]

close (adv)	**aproape**	[apro'ape]
far (adv)	**departe**	[de'parte]

near (e.g. ~ Paris)	**alături**	[a'ləturʲ]
nearby (adv)	**alături**	[a'ləturʲ]
not far (adv)	**aproape**	[apro'ape]

left (adj)	**stâng**	[stiŋg]
on the left	**din stânga**	[din 'stiŋga]
to the left	**în stânga**	[in 'stiŋga]
right (adj)	**drept**	[drept]
on the right	**din dreapta**	[din 'drʲapta]
to the right	**în dreapta**	[in 'drʲapta]
in front (adv)	**în faţă**	[in 'faʦə]
front (as adj)	**din faţă**	[din 'faʦə]
ahead (the kids ran ~)	**înainte**	[ina'inte]
behind (adv)	**în urmă**	[in 'urmə]
from behind	**din spate**	[din 'spate]
back (towards the rear)	**înapoi**	[ina'poj]
middle	**mijloc** (n)	['miʒlok]
in the middle	**la mijloc**	[la 'miʒlok]
at the side	**dintr-o parte**	['dintro 'parte]
everywhere (adv)	**peste tot**	['peste tot]
around (in all directions)	**în jur**	[in ʒur]
from inside	**dinăuntru**	[dinə'untru]
somewhere (to go)	**undeva**	[unde'va]
straight (directly)	**direct**	[di'rekt]
back (e.g. come ~)	**înapoi**	[ina'poj]
from anywhere	**de undeva**	[de unde'va]
from somewhere	**de undeva**	[de unde'va]
firstly (adv)	**în primul rând**	[in 'primul rind]
secondly (adv)	**în al doilea rând**	[in al 'dojlʲa rind]
thirdly (adv)	**în al treilea rând**	[in al 'trejlʲa rind]
suddenly (adv)	**deodată**	[deo'datə]
at first (in the beginning)	**la început**	[la inʧe'put]
for the first time	**prima dată**	['prima 'datə]
long before ...	**cu mult timp înainte de ...**	[ku mult timp ina'inte de]
anew (over again)	**din nou**	[din 'nou]
for good (adv)	**pentru totdeauna**	['pentru totdʲa'una]
never (adv)	**niciodată**	[niʧio'datə]
again (adv)	**iarăşi**	['jarəʃ]
now (at present)	**acum**	[a'kum]
often (adv)	**des**	[des]
then (adv)	**atunci**	[a'tunʧi]
urgently (quickly)	**urgent**	[ur'dʒent]
usually (adv)	**de obicei**	[de obi'ʧej]
by the way, ...	**apropo**	[apro'po]
possibly	**posibil**	[po'sibil]
probably (adv)	**probabil**	[pro'babil]
maybe (adv)	**poate**	[po'ate]
besides ...	**în afară de aceasta, ...**	[in a'farə de a'ʧasta]
that's why ...	**de aceea**	[de a'ʧeja]

in spite of ...	deşi ...	[de'ʃi]
thanks to ...	datorită ...	[dato'ritə]
what (pron.)	ce	[t͡ʃe]
that (conj.)	că	[kə]
something	ceva	[t͡ʃe'va]
anything (something)	ceva	[t͡ʃe'va]
nothing	nimic	[ni'mik]
who (pron.)	cine	['t͡ʃine]
someone	cineva	[t͡ʃine'va]
somebody	cineva	[t͡ʃine'va]
nobody	nimeni	['nimenⁱ]
nowhere (a voyage to ~)	nicăieri	[nikə'erⁱ]
nobody's	al nimănui	[al nimə'nuj]
somebody's	al cuiva	[al kuj'va]
so (I'm ~ glad)	aşa	[a'ʃa]
also (as well)	de asemenea	[de a'semenⁱa]
too (as well)	la fel	[la fel]

18. Function words. Adverbs. Part 2

Why?	De ce?	[de t͡ʃe]
for some reason	nu se ştie de ce	[nu se 'ʃtie de t͡ʃe]
because ...	pentru că ...	['pentru kə]
for some purpose	cine ştie pentru ce	['t͡ʃine 'ʃtie 'pentru t͡ʃe]
and	şi	[ʃi]
or	sau	['sau]
but	dar	[dar]
for (e.g. ~ me)	pentru	['pentru]
too (excessively)	prea	[prⁱa]
only (exclusively)	numai	['numaj]
exactly (adv)	exact	[e'gzakt]
about (more or less)	vreo	['vrⁱo]
approximately (adv)	aproximativ	[aproksima'tiv]
approximate (adj)	aproximativ	[aproksima'tiv]
almost (adv)	aproape	[apro'ape]
the rest	restul	['restul]
each (adj)	fiecare	[fie'kare]
any (no matter which)	oricare	[ori'kare]
many, much (a lot of)	mult	[mult]
many people	mulţi	[mult͡s]
all (everyone)	toţi	[tot͡s]
in return for ...	în schimb la ...	[in 'skimb la]
in exchange (adv)	în schimbul	[in 'skimbul]
by hand (made)	manual	[manu'al]
hardly (negative opinion)	puţin probabil	[pu'tsin pro'babil]

probably (adv)	**probabil**	[pro'babil]
on purpose (intentionally)	**intenționat**	[inten͡tsio'nat]
by accident (adv)	**întâmplător**	[intimplə'tor]

very (adv)	**foarte**	[fo'arte]
for example (adv)	**de exemplu**	[de e'gzemplu]
between	**între**	['intre]
among	**printre**	['printre]
so much (such a lot)	**atât**	[a'tit]
especially (adv)	**mai ales**	[maj a'les]

Basic concepts. Part 2

19. Opposites

rich (adj)	**bogat**	[bo'gat]
poor (adj)	**sărac**	[sə'rak]
ill, sick (adj)	**bolnav**	[bol'nav]
well (not sick)	**sănătos**	[sənə'tos]
big (adj)	**mare**	['mare]
small (adj)	**mic**	[mik]
quickly (adv)	**repede**	['repede]
slowly (adv)	**încet**	[in'ʧet]
fast (adj)	**rapid**	[ra'pid]
slow (adj)	**lent**	[lent]
glad (adj)	**vesel**	['vesel]
sad (adj)	**trist**	[trist]
together (adv)	**împreună**	[impre'unə]
separately (adv)	**separat**	[sepa'rat]
aloud (to read)	**cu voce tare**	[ku 'voʧe 'tare]
silently (to oneself)	**în gând**	[in gind]
tall (adj)	**înalt**	[i'nalt]
low (adj)	**scund**	[skund]
deep (adj)	**adânc**	[a'dink]
shallow (adj)	**de adâncime mică**	[de adin'ʧime 'mikə]
yes	**da**	[da]
no	**nu**	[nu]
distant (in space)	**îndepărtat**	[indepər'tat]
nearby (adj)	**apropiat**	[apropi'jat]
far (adv)	**departe**	[de'parte]
nearby (adv)	**aproape**	[apro'ape]
long (adj)	**lung**	[lung]
short (adj)	**scurt**	[skurt]
good (kindhearted)	**bun**	[bun]
evil (adj)	**rău**	['rəu]

married (adj)	căsătorit	[kəsəto'rit]
single (adj)	celibatar (m)	[tʃeliba'tar]
to forbid (vt)	a interzice	[a inter'zitʃe]
to permit (vt)	a permite	[a per'mite]
end	sfârşit (n)	[sfir'ʃit]
beginning	început (n)	[intʃe'put]
left (adj)	stâng	[sting]
right (adj)	drept	[drept]
first (adj)	primul	['primul]
last (adj)	ultimul	['ultimul]
crime	crimă (f)	['krimə]
punishment	pedeapsă (f)	[pe'dʲapsə]
to order (vt)	a ordona	[a ordo'na]
to obey (vi, vt)	a se supune	[a se su'pune]
straight (adj)	drept	[drept]
curved (adj)	strâmb	[strimb]
paradise	rai (n)	[raj]
hell	iad (n)	[jad]
to be born	a se naşte	[a se 'naʃte]
to die (vi)	a muri	[a mu'ri]
strong (adj)	puternic	[pu'ternik]
weak (adj)	slab	[slab]
old (adj)	bătrân	[bə'trin]
young (adj)	tânăr	['tinər]
old (adj)	vechi	[vekʲ]
new (adj)	nou	['nou]
hard (adj)	tare	['tare]
soft (adj)	moale	[mo'ale]
warm (tepid)	cald	[kald]
cold (adj)	rece	['retʃe]
fat (adj)	gras	[gras]
thin (adj)	slab	[slab]
narrow (adj)	îngust	[in'gust]
wide (adj)	lat	[lat]
good (adj)	bun	[bun]
bad (adj)	rău	['rəu]
brave (adj)	curajos	[kura'ʒos]
cowardly (adj)	fricos	[fri'kos]

20. Weekdays

Monday	**luni** (f)	[lunʲ]
Tuesday	**marţi** (f)	['martsʲ]
Wednesday	**miercuri** (f)	['merkurʲ]
Thursday	**joi** (f)	[ʒoj]
Friday	**vineri** (f)	['vinerʲ]
Saturday	**sâmbătă** (f)	['simbətə]
Sunday	**duminică** (f)	[du'minikə]

today (adv)	**astăzi**	['astəzʲ]
tomorrow (adv)	**mâine**	['mijne]
the day after tomorrow	**poimâine**	[poj'mine]
yesterday (adv)	**ieri**	[jerʲ]
the day before yesterday	**alaltăieri**	[a'laltəerʲ]

day	**zi** (f)	[zi]
working day	**zi** (f) **de lucru**	[zi de 'lukru]
public holiday	**zi** (f) **de sărbătoare**	[zi de sərbəto'are]
day off	**zi** (f) **liberă**	[zi 'liberə]
weekend	**zile** (f pl) **de odihnă**	['zile de o'dihnə]

all day long	**toată ziua**	[to'atə 'ziwa]
the next day (adv)	**a doua zi**	['dowa zi]
two days ago	**cu două zile în urmă**	[ku 'dowə 'zile in 'urmə]
the day before	**în ajun**	[in a'ʒun]
daily (adj)	**zilnic**	['zilnik]
every day (adv)	**în fiecare zi**	[in fie'kare zi]

week	**săptămână** (f)	[səptə'minə]
last week (adv)	**săptămâna trecută**	[səptə'mina tre'kutə]
next week (adv)	**săptămâna viitoare**	[səptə'mina viito'are]
weekly (adj)	**săptămânal**	[səptəmi'nal]
every week (adv)	**în fiecare săptămână**	[in fie'kare səptə'minə]
twice a week	**de două ori pe săptămână**	[de 'dowə orʲ pe səptə'minə]
every Tuesday	**în fiecare marţi**	[in fie'kare 'martsʲ]

21. Hours. Day and night

morning	**dimineaţă** (f)	[dimi'nʲatsə]
in the morning	**dimineaţa**	[dimi'nʲatsa]
noon, midday	**amiază** (f)	[a'mjazə]
in the afternoon	**după masă**	['dupə 'masə]

evening	**seară** (f)	['sʲarə]
in the evening	**seara**	['sʲara]
night	**noapte** (f)	[no'apte]
at night	**noaptea**	[no'aptʲa]
midnight	**miezul** (n) **nopţii**	['mezul 'noptsij]

second	**secundă** (f)	[se'kundə]
minute	**minut** (n)	[mi'nut]
hour	**oră** (f)	['orə]

half an hour	jumătate de oră	[ʒumə'tate de 'orə]
a quarter-hour	un sfert de oră	[un sfert de 'orə]
fifteen minutes	cincisprezece minute	['tʃintʃsprezetʃe mi'nute]
24 hours	o zi (f)	[o zi]

sunrise	răsărit (n)	[rəsə'rit]
dawn	zori (m pl)	[zorⁱ]
early morning	zori (m pl) de zi	[zorⁱ de zi]
sunset	apus (n)	[a'pus]

early in the morning	dimineața devreme	[dimi'nⁱatsa de'vreme]
this morning	azi dimineață	[azⁱ dimi'nⁱatsə]
tomorrow morning	mâine dimineață	['mijne dimi'nⁱatsə]

this afternoon	această după-amiază	[a'tʃastə 'dupa ami'azə]
in the afternoon	după masă	['dupə 'masə]
tomorrow afternoon	mâine după-masă	['mijne 'dupə 'masə]

tonight (this evening)	astă-seară	['astə 'sⁱarə]
tomorrow night	mâine seară	['mijne 'sⁱarə]

at 3 o'clock sharp	la ora trei fix	[la 'ora trej fiks]
about 4 o'clock	în jur de ora patru	[in ʒur de 'ora 'patru]
by 12 o'clock	pe la ora douăsprezece	[pe la 'ora 'dowəsprezetʃe]

in 20 minutes	peste douăzeci de minute	['peste dowə'zetʃi de mi'nute]
in an hour	peste o oră	['peste o 'orə]
on time (adv)	la timp	[la timp]

a quarter to …	fără un sfert	['fərə un sfert]
within an hour	în decurs de o oră	[in de'kurs de o 'orə]
every 15 minutes	la fiecare cincisprezece minute	[la fie'kare 'tʃintʃsprezetʃe mi'nute]
round the clock	zi și noapte	[zi ʃi no'apte]

22. Months. Seasons

January	ianuarie (m)	[janu'arie]
February	februarie (m)	[febru'arie]
March	martie (m)	['martie]
April	aprilie (m)	[a'prilie]
May	mai (m)	[maj]
June	iunie (m)	['junie]

July	iulie (m)	['julie]
August	august (m)	['august]
September	septembrie (m)	[sep'tembrie]
October	octombrie (m)	[ok'tombrie]
November	noiembrie (m)	[no'embrie]
December	decembrie (m)	[de'tʃembrie]

spring	primăvară (f)	[primə'varə]
in spring	primăvara	[primə'vara]
spring (as adj)	de primăvară	[de primə'varə]

summer	**vară** (f)	['varə]
in summer	**vara**	['vara]
summer (as adj)	**de vară**	[de 'varə]

autumn	**toamnă** (f)	[to'amnə]
in autumn	**toamna**	[to'amna]
autumn (as adj)	**de toamnă**	[de to'amnə]

winter	**iarnă** (f)	['jarnə]
in winter	**iarna**	['jarna]
winter (as adj)	**de iarnă**	[de 'jarnə]

month	**lună** (f)	['lunə]
this month	**în luna curentă**	[in 'luna ku'rentə]
next month	**în luna următoare**	[in 'luna urməto'are]
last month	**în luna trecută**	[in 'luna tre'kutə]

a month ago	**o lună în urmă**	[o 'lunə in 'urmə]
in a month (a month later)	**peste o lună**	['peste o 'lunə]
in 2 months (2 months later)	**peste două luni**	['peste 'dowə lunʲ]
the whole month	**luna întreagă**	['luna in'trʲagə]
all month long	**o lună întreagă**	[o 'lunə in'trʲagə]

monthly (~ magazine)	**lunar**	[lu'nar]
monthly (adv)	**în fiecare lună**	[in fie'kare 'lunə]

every month	**fiecare lună**	[fie'kare 'lunə]
twice a month	**de două ori pe lună**	[de 'dowə orʲ pe 'lunə]

year	**an** (m)	[an]
this year	**anul acesta**	['anul a'ʧesta]

next year	**anul viitor**	['anul vii'tor]
last year	**anul trecut**	['anul tre'kut]

a year ago	**acum un an**	[a'kum un an]
in a year	**peste un an**	['peste un an]
in two years	**peste doi ani**	['peste doj anʲ]

the whole year	**tot anul**	[tot 'anul]
all year long	**un an întreg**	[un an in'treg]

every year	**în fiecare an**	[in fie'kare an]
annual (adj)	**anual**	[anu'al]

annually (adv)	**în fiecare an**	[in fie'kare an]
4 times a year	**de patru ori pe an**	[de 'patru orʲ pe an]

date (e.g. today's ~)	**dată** (f)	['datə]
date (e.g. ~ of birth)	**dată** (f)	['datə]
calendar	**calendar** (n)	[kalen'dar]

half a year	**jumătate** (f) **de an**	[ʒumə'tate de an]
six months	**jumătate** (f) **de an**	[ʒumə'tate de an]
season (summer, etc.)	**sezon** (n)	[se'zon]
century	**veac** (n)	[vʲak]

23. Time. Miscellaneous

time	timp (m)	[timp]
moment	clipă (f)	['klipə]
instant (n)	moment (n)	[mo'mənt]
instant (adj)	momentan	[momen'tan]
lapse (of time)	perioadă (f)	[perio'adə]
life	viață (f)	['vjaʦə]
eternity	veşnicie (f)	[veʃni'ʧie]
epoch	epocă (f)	[e'pokə]
era	eră (f)	['erə]
cycle	ciclu (n)	['ʧiklu]
period	perioadă (f)	[perio'adə]
term (short-~)	termen (n)	['termen]
the future	viitor (n)	[vii'tor]
future (as adj)	viitor	[vii'tor]
next time	data următoare	['data urməto'are]
the past	trecut (n)	[tre'kut]
past (recent)	trecut	[tre'kut]
last time	data trecută	['data tre'kutə]
later (adv)	mai târziu	[maj tir'zju]
after (prep.)	după	['dupə]
nowadays (adv)	acum	[a'kum]
now (at this moment)	acum	[a'kum]
immediately (adv)	imediat	[imedi'at]
soon (adv)	în curând	[in ku'rind]
in advance (beforehand)	în prealabil	[in prʲa'labil]
a long time ago	demult	[de'mult]
recently (adv)	recent	[re'ʧent]
destiny	soartă (f)	[so'artə]
recollections	memorie (f)	[me'morie]
archives	arhivă (f)	[ar'hivə]
during …	în timpul …	[in 'timpul]
long, a long time (adv)	îndelung	[inde'lung]
not long (adv)	puţin timp	[pu'ʦin 'timp]
early (in the morning)	devreme	[de'vreme]
late (not early)	târziu	[tir'zju]
forever (for good)	pentru totdeauna	['pentru totdʲa'una]
to start (begin)	a începe	[a in'ʧepe]
to postpone (vt)	a amâna	[a amʲ'na]
at the same time	concomitent	[konkomi'tent]
permanently (adv)	mereu	[me'reu]
constant (noise, pain)	permanent	[perma'nent]
temporary (adj)	temporar	[tempo'rar]
sometimes (adv)	uneori	[une'orʲ]
rarely (adv)	rar	[rar]
often (adv)	adesea	[a'desʲa]

24. Lines and shapes

square	pătrat (n)	[pə'trat]
square (as adj)	pătrat	[pə'trat]
circle	cerc (n)	[ʧerk]
round (adj)	rotund	[ro'tund]
triangle	triunghi (n)	[tri'ungʲ]
triangular (adj)	triunghiular	[trjungju'lar]
oval	oval (n)	[o'val]
oval (as adj)	oval	[o'val]
rectangle	dreptunghi (n)	[drep'tungʲ]
rectangular (adj)	dreptunghiular	[dreptungju'lar]
pyramid	piramidă (f)	[pira'midə]
rhombus	romb (n)	[romb]
trapezium	trapez (n)	[tra'pez]
cube	cub (n)	[kub]
prism	prismă (f)	['prizmə]
circumference	circumferință (f)	[ʧirkumfe'rinʦə]
sphere	sferă (f)	['sferə]
ball (solid sphere)	sferă (f)	['sferə]
diameter	diametru (n)	[di'ametru]
radius	rază (f)	['razə]
perimeter (circle's ~)	perimetru (n)	[peri'metru]
centre	centru (n)	['ʧentru]
horizontal (adj)	orizontal	[orizon'tal]
vertical (adj)	vertical	[verti'kal]
parallel (n)	paralelă (f)	[para'lelə]
parallel (as adj)	paralel	[para'lel]
line	linie (f)	['linie]
stroke	linie (f)	['linie]
straight line	dreaptă (f)	['drʲaptə]
curve (curved line)	curbă (f)	['kurbə]
thin (line, etc.)	subțire	[sub'ʦire]
contour (outline)	contur (n)	[kon'tur]
intersection	intersecție (f)	[inter'sekʦie]
right angle	unghi (n) drept	[ungʲ drept]
segment	segment (n)	[seg'ment]
sector (circular ~)	sector (n)	[sek'tor]
side (of a triangle)	latură (f)	['laturə]
angle	unghi (n)	[ungʲ]

25. Units of measurement

weight	greutate (f)	[greu'tate]
length	lungime (f)	[lun'ʤime]
width	lățime (f)	[lə'ʦime]
height	înălțime (f)	[inəl'ʦime]

depth	adâncime (f)	[adin'tʃime]
volume	volum (n)	[vo'lum]
area	suprafață (f)	[supra'fatsə]

gram	gram (n)	[gram]
milligram	miligram (n)	[mili'gram]
kilogram	kilogram (n)	[kilo'gram]
ton	tonă (f)	['tonə]
pound	funt (m)	[funt]
ounce	uncie (f)	['untʃie]

metre	metru (m)	['metru]
millimetre	milimetru (m)	[mili'metru]
centimetre	centimetru (m)	[tʃenti'metru]
kilometre	kilometru (m)	[kilo'metru]
mile	milă (f)	['milə]

inch	țol (m)	[tsol]
foot	picior (m)	[pi'tʃior]
yard	yard (m)	[jard]

| square metre | metru (m) pătrat | ['metru pə'trat] |
| hectare | hectar (n) | [hek'tar] |

litre	litru (m)	['litru]
degree	grad (n)	[grad]
volt	volt (m)	[volt]
ampere	amper (m)	[am'per]
horsepower	cal-putere (m)	[kal pu'tere]

quantity	cantitate (f)	[kanti'tate]
a little bit of ...	puțin ...	[pu'tsin]
half	jumătate (f)	[ʒumə'tate]
dozen	duzină (f)	[du'zinə]
piece (item)	bucată (f)	[bu'katə]

| size | dimensiune (f) | [dimensi'une] |
| scale (map ~) | proporție (f) | [pro'portsie] |

minimal (adj)	minim	['minim]
the smallest (adj)	cel mai mic	[tʃel maj mik]
medium (adj)	de, din mijloc	[de, din 'miʒlok]
maximal (adj)	maxim	['maksim]
the largest (adj)	cel mai mare	[tʃel maj 'mare]

26. Containers

canning jar (glass ~)	borcan (n)	[bor'kan]
tin, can	cutie (f)	[ku'tie]
bucket	găleată (f)	[gə'lʲatə]
barrel	butoi (n)	[bu'toj]

| wash basin (e.g., plastic ~) | lighean (n) | [li'gʲan] |
| tank (100L water ~) | rezervor (n) | [rezer'vor] |

hip flask	damigeană (f)	[dami'dʒanə]
jerrycan	canistră (f)	[ka'nistrə]
tank (e.g., tank car)	cisternă (f)	[tʃis'ternə]

mug	cană (f)	['kanə]
cup (of coffee, etc.)	ceaşcă (f)	['tʃaʃkə]
saucer	farfurioară (f)	[farfurio'arə]
glass (tumbler)	pahar (n)	[pa'har]
wine glass	cupă (f)	['kupə]
stock pot (soup pot)	cratiţă (f)	['kratitsə]

bottle (~ of wine)	sticlă (f)	['stiklə]
neck (of the bottle, etc.)	gâtul (n) sticlei	['gitul 'stiklej]

carafe (decanter)	garafă (f)	[ga'rafə]
pitcher	ulcior (n)	[ul'tʃior]
vessel (container)	vas (n)	[vas]
pot (crock, stoneware ~)	oală (f)	[o'alə]
vase	vază (f)	['vazə]

flacon, bottle (perfume ~)	flacon (n)	[fla'kon]
vial, small bottle	sticluţă (f)	[sti'klutsə]
tube (of toothpaste)	tub (n)	[tub]

sack (bag)	sac (m)	[sak]
bag (paper ~, plastic ~)	pachet (n)	[pa'ket]
packet (of cigarettes, etc.)	pachet (n)	[pa'ket]

box (e.g. shoebox)	cutie (f)	[ku'tie]
crate	ladă (f)	['ladə]
basket	coş (n)	[koʃ]

27. Materials

material	material (n)	[materi'al]
wood (n)	lemn (n)	[lemn]
wood-, wooden (adj)	de, din lemn	[de, din lemn]

glass (n)	sticlă (f)	['stiklə]
glass (as adj)	de, din sticlă	[de, din 'stiklə]

stone (n)	piatră (f)	['pjatrə]
stone (as adj)	de, din piatră	[de, din 'pjatrə]

plastic (n)	masă (f) plastică	['masə 'plastikə]
plastic (as adj)	de, din masă plastică	[de, din 'masə 'plastikə]

rubber (n)	cauciuc (n)	[kau'tʃuk]
rubber (as adj)	de, din cauciuc	[de, din kau'tʃiuk]

cloth, fabric (n)	ţesătură (f)	[tsesə'turə]
fabric (as adj)	de, din ţesătură	[de, din tsesə'turə]
paper (n)	hârtie (f)	[hir'tie]
paper (as adj)	de, din hârtie	[de, din hir'tie]

cardboard (n)	**carton** (n)	[kar'ton]
cardboard (as adj)	**de, din carton**	[de, din kar'ton]
polyethylene	**polietilenă** (f)	[polieti'lenə]
cellophane	**celofan** (n)	[tʃelo'fan]
plywood	**furnir** (n)	[fur'nir]
porcelain (n)	**porțelan** (n)	[portse'lan]
porcelain (as adj)	**de, din porțelan**	[de, din portse'lan]
clay (n)	**argilă** (f)	[ar'dʒilə]
clay (as adj)	**de lut**	[de 'lut]
ceramic (n)	**ceramică** (f)	[tʃe'ramikə]
ceramic (as adj)	**de, din ceramică**	[de, din tʃe'ramikə]

28. Metals

metal (n)	**metal** (n)	[me'tal]
metal (as adj)	**de, din metal**	[de, din me'tal]
alloy (n)	**aliaj** (n)	[a'ljaʒ]
gold (n)	**aur** (n)	['aur]
gold, golden (adj)	**de, din aur**	[de, din 'aur]
silver (n)	**argint** (n)	[ar'dʒint]
silver (as adj)	**de, din argint**	[de, din ar'dʒint]
iron (n)	**fier** (n)	[fier]
iron-, made of iron (adj)	**de, din fier**	[de, din 'fjer]
steel (n)	**oțel** (n)	[o'tsel]
steel (as adj)	**de, din oțel**	[de, din o'tsel]
copper (n)	**cupru** (n)	['kupru]
copper (as adj)	**de, din cupru**	[de, din 'kupru]
aluminium (n)	**aluminiu** (n)	[alu'miniu]
aluminium (as adj)	**de, din aluminiu**	[de, din alu'miniu]
bronze (n)	**bronz** (n)	[bronz]
bronze (as adj)	**de, din bronz**	[de, din bronz]
brass	**alamă** (f)	[a'lamə]
nickel	**nichel** (n)	['nikel]
platinum	**platină** (f)	['platinə]
mercury	**mercur** (n)	[mer'kur]
tin	**cositor** (n)	[kosi'tor]
lead	**plumb** (n)	[plumb]
zinc	**zinc** (n)	[zink]

HUMAN BEING

Human being. The body

29. Humans. Basic concepts

human being	**om** (m)	[om]
man (adult male)	**bărbat** (m)	[bər'bat]
woman	**femeie** (f)	[fe'meje]
child	**copil** (m)	[ko'pil]

girl	**fată** (f)	['fatə]
boy	**băiat** (m)	[bə'jat]
teenager	**adolescent** (m)	[adoles'tʃent]
old man	**bătrân** (m)	[bə'trin]
old woman	**bătrână** (f)	[bə'trinə]

30. Human anatomy

organism (body)	**organism** (n)	[orga'nizm]
heart	**inimă** (f)	['inimə]
blood	**sânge** (n)	['sindʒe]
artery	**arteră** (f)	[ar'terə]
vein	**venă** (f)	['venə]

brain	**creier** (m)	['krejer]
nerve	**nerv** (m)	[nerv]
nerves	**nervi** (m pl)	[nervi]
vertebra	**vertebră** (f)	[ver'tebrə]
spine (backbone)	**coloană** (f) **vertebrală**	[kolo'anə verte'bralə]

stomach (organ)	**stomac** (n)	[sto'mak]
intestines, bowels	**intestin** (n)	[intes'tin]
intestine (e.g. large ~)	**intestin** (n)	[intes'tin]
liver	**ficat** (m)	[fi'kat]
kidney	**rinichi** (m)	[ri'niki]

bone	**os** (n)	[os]
skeleton	**schelet** (n)	[ske'let]
rib	**coastă** (f)	[ko'astə]
skull	**craniu** (n)	['kranju]

muscle	**muşchi** (m)	[muʃki]
biceps	**biceps** (m)	['bitʃeps]
triceps	**triceps** (m)	['tritʃeps]
tendon	**tendon** (n)	[ten'don]
joint	**încheietură** (f)	[inkeje'turə]

lungs	plămâni (m pl)	[plə'minⁱ]
genitals	organe (n pl) genitale	[or'gane dʒeni'tale]
skin	piele (f)	['pjele]

31. Head

head	cap (n)	[kap]
face	față (f)	['faʦə]
nose	nas (n)	[nas]
mouth	gură (f)	['gurə]

eye	ochi (m)	[okⁱ]
eyes	ochi (m pl)	[okⁱ]
pupil	pupilă (f)	[pu'pilə]
eyebrow	sprânceană (f)	[sprin'tʃanə]
eyelash	geană (f)	['dʒanə]
eyelid	pleoapă (f)	[pleo'apə]

tongue	limbă (f)	['limbə]
tooth	dinte (m)	['dinte]
lips	buze (f pl)	['buze]
cheekbones	pomeți (m pl)	[po'meʦⁱ]
gum	gingie (f)	[dʒin'dʒie]
palate	palat (n)	[pa'lat]

nostrils	nări (f pl)	[nərⁱ]
chin	bărbie (f)	[bər'bie]
jaw	maxilar (n)	[maksi'lar]
cheek	obraz (m)	[o'braz]

forehead	frunte (f)	['frunte]
temple	tâmplă (f)	['timplə]
ear	ureche (f)	[u'reke]
back of the head	ceafă (f)	['tʃafə]
neck	gât (n)	[git]
throat	gât (n)	[git]

hair	păr (m)	[pər]
hairstyle	coafură (f)	[koa'furə]
haircut	tunsoare (f)	[tunso'are]
wig	perucă (f)	[pe'rukə]

moustache	mustăți (f pl)	[mus'təʦⁱ]
beard	barbă (f)	['barbə]
to have (a beard, etc.)	a purta	[a pur'ta]
plait	cosiță (f)	[ko'siʦə]
sideboards	favoriți (m pl)	[favo'riʦⁱ]

red-haired (adj)	roșcat	[roʃ'kat]
grey (hair)	cărunt	[kə'runt]
bald (adj)	chel	[kel]
bald patch	chelie (f)	[ke'lie]
ponytail	coadă (f)	[ko'adə]
fringe	breton (n)	[bre'ton]

32. Human body

| hand | mână (f) | ['minə] |
| arm | braţ (n) | [braʦ] |

finger	deget (n)	['dedʒet]
thumb	degetul (n) mare	['dedʒetul 'mare]
little finger	degetul (n) mic	['dedʒetul mik]
nail	unghie (f)	['ungie]

fist	pumn (m)	[pumn]
palm	palmă (f)	['palmə]
wrist	încheietura (f) mâinii	[inkeje'tura 'minij]
forearm	antebraţ (n)	[ante'braʦ]
elbow	cot (n)	[kot]
shoulder	umăr (m)	['umər]

leg	picior (n)	[pi'ʧior]
foot	talpă (f)	['talpə]
knee	genunchi (n)	[dʒe'nunkʲ]
calf	pulpă (f)	['pulpə]
hip	coapsă (f)	[ko'apsə]
heel	călcâi (n)	[kəl'kij]

body	corp (n)	[korp]
stomach	burtă (f)	['burtə]
chest	piept (n)	[pjept]
breast	sân (m)	[sin]
flank	coastă (f)	[ko'astə]
back	spate (n)	['spate]
lower back	regiune (f) lombară	[redʒi'une lom'barə]
waist	talie (f)	['talie]

navel (belly button)	buric (n)	[bu'rik]
buttocks	fese (f pl)	['fese]
bottom	şezut (n)	[ʃə'zut]

beauty spot	aluniţă (f)	[alu'nitsə]
birthmark (café au lait spot)	semn (n) din naştere	[semn din 'naʃtere]
tattoo	tatuaj (n)	[tatu'aʒ]
scar	cicatrice (f)	[ʧika'triʧe]

Clothing & Accessories

33. Outerwear. Coats

clothes	îmbrăcăminte (f)	[imbrəkə'minte]
outerwear	haină (f)	['hajnə]
winter clothing	îmbrăcăminte (f) de iarnă	[imbrəkə'minte de 'jarnə]
coat (overcoat)	palton (n)	[pal'ton]
fur coat	şubă (f)	['ʃubə]
fur jacket	scurtă (f) îmblănită	['skurtə imblə'nitə]
down coat	scurtă (f) de puf	['skurtə de 'puf]
jacket (e.g. leather ~)	scurtă (f)	['skurtə]
raincoat (trenchcoat, etc.)	trenci (f)	[trentʃi]
waterproof (adj)	impermeabil (n)	[imperme'abil]

34. Men's & women's clothing

shirt (button shirt)	cămaşă (f)	[kə'maʃə]
trousers	pantaloni (m pl)	[panta'lonʲ]
jeans	blugi (m pl)	[bluʤʲ]
suit jacket	sacou (n)	[sa'kou]
suit	costum (n)	[kos'tum]
dress (frock)	rochie (f)	['rokie]
skirt	fustă (f)	['fustə]
blouse	bluză (f)	['bluzə]
knitted jacket (cardigan, etc.)	jachetă (f) tricotată	[ʒa'ketə triko'tatə]
jacket (of a woman's suit)	jachetă (f)	[ʒa'ketə]
T-shirt	tricou (n)	[tri'kou]
shorts (short trousers)	şorturi (n pl)	['ʃorturʲ]
tracksuit	costum (n) sportiv	[kos'tum spor'tiv]
bathrobe	halat (n)	[ha'lat]
pyjamas	pijama (f)	[piʒa'ma]
jumper (sweater)	sveter (n)	['sveter]
pullover	pulover (n)	[pu'lover]
waistcoat	vestă (f)	['vestə]
tailcoat	frac (n)	[frak]
dinner suit	smoching (n)	['smoking]
uniform	uniformă (f)	[uni'formə]
workwear	haină (f) de lucru	['hajnə de 'lukru]
boiler suit	salopetă (f)	[salo'petə]
coat (e.g. doctor's smock)	halat (n)	[ha'lat]

35. Clothing. Underwear

underwear	lenjerie (f) de corp	[lenʒe'rie de 'korp]
vest (singlet)	maiou (n)	[ma'jou]
socks	şosete (f pl)	[ʃo'sete]
nightdress	cămaşă (f) de noapte	[kə'maʃə de no'apte]
bra	sutien (n)	[su'tjen]
knee highs (knee-high socks)	ciorapi (m pl)	[tʃio'rapʲ]
tights	ciorapi pantalon (m pl)	[tʃio'rapʲ panta'lon]
stockings (hold ups)	ciorapi (m pl)	[tʃio'rapʲ]
swimsuit, bikini	costum (n) de baie	[kos'tum de 'bae]

36. Headwear

hat	căciulă (f)	[kə'tʃiulə]
trilby hat	pălărie (f)	[pələ'rie]
baseball cap	şapcă (f)	['ʃapkə]
flatcap	chipiu (n)	[ki'pju]
beret	beretă (f)	[be'retə]
hood	glugă (f)	['glugə]
panama hat	panama (f)	[pana'ma]
knit cap (knitted hat)	căciulă (f) împletită	[kə'tʃiulə imple'titə]
headscarf	basma (f)	[bas'ma]
women's hat	pălărie (f) de damă	[pələ'rie de 'damə]
hard hat	cască (f)	['kaskə]
forage cap	bonetă (f)	[bo'netə]
helmet	coif (n)	[kojf]
bowler	pălărie (f)	[pələ'rie]
top hat	joben (n)	[ʒo'ben]

37. Footwear

footwear	încălţăminte (f)	[inkəltsə'minte]
shoes (men's shoes)	ghete (f pl)	['gete]
shoes (women's shoes)	pantofi (m pl)	[pan'tofʲ]
boots (e.g., cowboy ~)	cizme (f pl)	['tʃizme]
carpet slippers	şlapi (m pl)	[ʃlapʲ]
trainers	adidaşi (m pl)	[a'didaʃ]
trainers	tenişi (m pl)	['teniʃ]
sandals	sandale (f pl)	[san'dale]
cobbler (shoe repairer)	cizmar (m)	[tʃiz'mar]
heel	toc (n)	[tok]
pair (of shoes)	pereche (f)	[pe'reke]
lace (shoelace)	şiret (n)	[ʃi'ret]

to lace up (vt)	a şnurui	[a ʃnuru'i]
shoehorn	lingură (f) pentru pantofi	['lingurə 'pentru pan'tofʲ]
shoe polish	cremă (f) de ghete	['kremə de 'gete]

38. Textile. Fabrics

cotton (n)	bumbac (m)	[bum'bak]
cotton (as adj)	de, din bumbac	[de, din bum'bak]
flax (n)	in (n)	[in]
flax (as adj)	de, din in	[de, din in]

silk (n)	mătase (f)	[mə'tase]
silk (as adj)	de, din mătase	[de, din mə'tase]
wool (n)	lână (f)	['linə]
wool (as adj)	de, din lână	[de, din 'linə]

velvet	catifea (f)	[kati'fʲa]
suede	piele (f) întoarsă	['pjele into'arsə]
corduroy	ţesătură de bumbac catifelată (f)	[tsesə'turə de bum'bak katife'latə]

nylon (n)	nailon (n)	[naj'lon]
nylon (as adj)	de, din nailon	[de, din naj'lon]
polyester (n)	poliester (n)	[polies'ter]
polyester (as adj)	de, din poliester	[de, din polies'ter]

leather (n)	piele (f)	['pjele]
leather (as adj)	de, din piele	[de, din 'pjele]
fur (n)	blană (f)	['blanə]
fur (e.g. ~ coat)	de, din blană	[de, din 'blanə]

39. Personal accessories

gloves	mănuşi (f pl)	[mə'nuʃ]
mittens	mănuşi (f pl) cu un singur deget	[mə'nuʃ ku un 'singur 'dedʒet]

scarf (muffler)	fular (m)	[fu'lar]

glasses	ochelari (m pl)	[oke'larʲ]
frame (eyeglass ~)	ramă (f)	['ramə]
umbrella	umbrelă (f)	[um'brelə]
walking stick	baston (n)	[bas'ton]
hairbrush	perie (f) de păr	[pe'rie de pər]
fan	evantai (n)	[evan'taj]

tie (necktie)	cravată (f)	[kra'vatə]
bow tie	papion (n)	[papɪ'on]
braces	bretele (f pl)	[bre'tele]
handkerchief	batistă (f)	[ba'tistə]

comb	pieptene (m)	['pjeptene]
hair slide	agrafă (f)	[a'grafə]

hairpin	ac (n) de păr	[ak de pər]
buckle	cataramă (f)	[kata'ramə]
belt	cordon (n)	[kor'don]
shoulder strap	curea (f)	[ku'rʲa]
bag (handbag)	geantă (f)	['dʒantə]
handbag	poşetă (f)	[po'ʃətə]
rucksack	rucsac (n)	[ruk'sak]

40. Clothing. Miscellaneous

fashion	modă (f)	['modə]
in vogue (adj)	la modă	[la 'modə]
fashion designer	modelier (n)	[mode'ljer]
collar	guler (n)	['guler]
pocket	buzunar (n)	[buzu'nar]
pocket (as adj)	de buzunar	[de buzu'nar]
sleeve	mânecă (f)	['minekə]
hanging loop	gaică (f)	['gajkə]
flies (on trousers)	şliţ (n)	[ʃlits]
zip (fastener)	fermoar (n)	[fermo'ar]
fastener	capsă (f)	['kapsə]
button	nasture (m)	['nasture]
buttonhole	butonieră (f)	[buto'njerə]
to come off (ab. button)	a se rupe	[a se 'rupe]
to sew (vi, vt)	a coase	[a ko'ase]
to embroider (vi, vt)	a broda	[a bro'da]
embroidery	broderie (f)	[brode'rie]
sewing needle	ac (n)	[ak]
thread	aţă (f)	['atsə]
seam	cusătură (f)	[kusə'turə]
to get dirty (vi)	a se murdări	[a se murdə'ri]
stain (mark, spot)	pată (f)	['patə]
to crease, to crumple	a se şifona	[a se ʃifo'na]
to tear, to rip (vt)	a rupe	[a 'rupe]
clothes moth	molie (f)	['molie]

41. Personal care. Cosmetics

toothpaste	pastă (f) de dinţi	['pastə de dintsʲ]
toothbrush	periuţă (f) de dinţi	[peri'utsə de dintsʲ]
to clean one's teeth	a se spăla pe dinţi	[a se spə'la pe dintsʲ]
razor	brici (n)	['britʃi]
shaving cream	cremă (f) de bărbierit	['kremə de bərbie'rit]
to shave (vi)	a se bărbieri	[a se bərbie'ri]
soap	săpun (n)	[sə'pun]

shampoo	**şampon** (n)	[ʃam'pon]
scissors	**foarfece** (n)	[fo'arfetʃe]
nail file	**pilă** (f) **de unghii**	['pilə de 'ungij]
nail clippers	**cleştişor** (n)	[kleʃti'ʃor]
tweezers	**pensetă** (f)	[pen'setə]

cosmetics	**cosmetică** (f)	[kos'metikə]
face mask	**mască** (f)	['maskə]
manicure	**manichiură** (f)	[mani'kjurə]
to have a manicure	**a face manichiura**	[a 'fatʃe mani'kjura]
pedicure	**pedichiură** (f)	[pedi'kjurə]

make-up bag	**trusă** (f) **de cosmetică**	['trusə de kos'metikə]
face powder	**pudră** (f)	['pudrə]
powder compact	**pudrieră** (f)	[pudri'erə]
blusher	**fard de obraz** (n)	[fard de o'braz]

perfume (bottled)	**parfum** (n)	[par'fum]
toilet water (lotion)	**apă de toaletă** (f)	['apə de toa'letə]
lotion	**loţiune** (f)	[lotsi'une]
cologne	**colonie** (f)	[ko'lonie]

eyeshadow	**fard** (n) **de pleoape**	[fard 'pentru pleo'ape]
eyeliner	**creion** (n) **de ochi**	[kre'jon 'pentru okʲ]
mascara	**rimel** (n)	[ri'mel]

lipstick	**ruj** (n)	[ruʒ]
nail polish	**ojă** (f)	['oʒə]
hair spray	**gel** (n) **de păr**	[dʒel de pər]
deodorant	**deodorant** (n)	[deodo'rant]

cream	**cremă** (f)	['kremə]
face cream	**cremă** (f) **de faţă**	['kremə de 'fatsə]
hand cream	**cremă** (f) **pentru mâini**	['kremə 'pentru minʲ]
anti-wrinkle cream	**cremă** (f) **anti-rid**	['kremə 'anti rid]
day (as adj)	**de zi**	[de zi]
night (as adj)	**de noapte**	[de no'apte]

tampon	**tampon** (n)	[tam'pon]
toilet paper (toilet roll)	**hârtie** (f) **igienică**	[hir'tie idʒi'enikə]
hair dryer	**uscător** (n) **de păr**	[uskə'tor de pər]

42. Jewellery

jewellery, jewels	**giuvaeruri** (n pl)	[dʒiuva'erurʲ]
precious (e.g. ~ stone)	**preţios**	[pretsi'os]
hallmark stamp	**marcă** (f)	['markə]

ring	**inel** (n)	[i'nel]
wedding ring	**verighetă** (f)	[veri'getə]
bracelet	**brăţară** (f)	[brə'tsarə]

earrings	**cercei** (m pl)	[tʃer'tʃej]
necklace (~ of pearls)	**colier** (n)	[ko'ljer]

| crown | coroană (f) | [koro'anə] |
| bead necklace | mărgele (f pl) | [mər'dʒele] |

diamond	briliant (n)	[brili'ant]
emerald	smarald (n)	[sma'rald]
ruby	rubin (n)	[ru'bin]
sapphire	safir (n)	[sa'fir]
pearl	perlă (f)	['perlə]
amber	chihlimbar (n)	[kihlim'bar]

43. Watches. Clocks

watch (wristwatch)	ceas (n) de mână	[tʃas de 'minə]
dial	cadran (n)	[ka'dran]
hand (clock, watch)	acul (n) ceasornicului	['akul tʃasor'nikuluj]
metal bracelet	brăţară (f)	[brə'tsarə]
watch strap	curea (f)	[ku'rʲa]

battery	baterie (f)	[bate'rie]
to be flat (battery)	a se termina	[a se termi'na]
to change a battery	a schimba bateria	[a skim'ba bate'rija]
to run fast	a merge înainte	[a 'merdʒe ina'inte]
to run slow	a rămâne în urmă	[a rə'mine in 'urmə]

wall clock	pendulă (f)	[pen'dulə]
hourglass	clepsidră (f)	[klep'sidrə]
sundial	cadran (n) solar	[ka'dran so'lar]
alarm clock	ceas (n) deşteptător	[tʃas deʃteptə'tor]
watchmaker	ceasornicar (m)	[tʃasorni'kar]
to repair (vt)	a repara	[a repa'ra]

Food. Nutricion

meat	carne (f)	['karne]
chicken	carne (f) de găină	['karne de gə'inə]
poussin	carne (f) de pui	['karne de puj]
duck	carne (f) de rață	['karne de 'ratsə]
goose	carne (f) de gâscă	['karne de 'giskə]
game	vânat (n)	[vi'nat]
turkey	carne (f) de curcan	['karne de 'kurkan]
pork	carne (f) de porc	['karne de pork]
veal	carne (f) de vițel	['karne de vi'tsel]
lamb	carne (f) de berbec	['karne de ber'bek]
beef	carne (f) de vită	['karne de 'vitə]
rabbit	carne (f) de iepure de casă	['karne de 'epure de 'kasə]
sausage (bologna, etc.)	salam (n)	[sa'lam]
vienna sausage (frankfurter)	crenvurșt (n)	[kren'vurʃt]
bacon	costiță (f) afumată	[kos'titsə afu'matə]
ham	șuncă (f)	['ʃunkə]
gammon	pulpă (f)	['pulpə]
pâté	pateu (n)	[pa'teu]
liver	ficat (m)	[fi'kat]
mince (minced meat)	carne (f) tocată	['karne to'katə]
tongue	limbă (f)	['limbə]
egg	ou (n)	['ow]
eggs	ouă (n pl)	['owə]
egg white	albuș (n)	[al'buʃ]
egg yolk	gălbenuș	[gəlbe'nuʃ]
fish	pește (m)	['peʃte]
seafood	produse (n pl) marine	[pro'duse ma'rine]
caviar	icre (f pl) de pește	['ikre de 'peʃte]
crab	crab (m)	[krab]
prawn	crevetă (f)	[kre'vetə]
oyster	stridie (f)	['stridie]
spiny lobster	langustă (f)	[lan'gustə]
octopus	caracatiță (f)	[kara'katitsə]
squid	calmar (m)	[kal'mar]
sturgeon	carne (f) de nisetru	['karne de ni'setru]
salmon	somon (m)	[so'mon]
halibut	calcan (m)	[kal'kan]
cod	batog (m)	[ba'tog]
mackerel	macrou (n)	[ma'krou]

tuna	ton (m)	[ton]
eel	ţipar (m)	[tsi'par]
trout	păstrăv (m)	[pəs'trəv]
sardine	sardea (f)	[sar'dʲa]
pike	ştiucă (f)	['ʃtjukə]
herring	scrumbie (f)	[skrum'bie]
bread	pâine (f)	['pine]
cheese	caşcaval (n)	['brinzə]
sugar	zahăr (n)	['zahər]
salt	sare (f)	['sare]
rice	orez (n)	[o'rez]
pasta (macaroni)	paste (f pl)	['paste]
noodles	tăiţei (m)	[təi'tsej]
butter	unt (n)	['unt]
vegetable oil	ulei (n) vegetal	[u'lej vedʒe'tal]
sunflower oil	ulei (n) de floarea-soarelui	[u'lej de flo'arʲa so'areluj]
margarine	margarină (f)	[marga'rinə]
olives	olive (f pl)	[o'live]
olive oil	ulei (n) de măsline	[u'lej de məs'line]
milk	lapte (n)	['lapte]
condensed milk	lapte (n) condensat	['lapte konden'sat]
yogurt	iaurt (n)	[ja'urt]
soured cream	smântână (f)	[smin'tinə]
cream (of milk)	frişcă (f)	['friʃkə]
mayonnaise	maioneză (f)	[majo'nezə]
buttercream	cremă (f)	['kremə]
groats (barley ~, etc.)	crupe (f pl)	['krupe]
flour	făină (f)	[fə'inə]
tinned food	conserve (f pl)	[kon'serve]
cornflakes	fulgi (m pl) de porumb	['fuldʒʲ de po'rumb]
honey	miere (f)	['mjere]
jam	gem (n)	[dʒem]
chewing gum	gumă (f) de mestecat	['gumə de meste'kat]

45. Drinks

water	apă (f)	['apə]
drinking water	apă (f) potabilă	['apə po'tabilə]
mineral water	apă (f) minerală	['apə mine'ralə]
still (adj)	necarbogazoasă	[nekarbogazo'asə]
carbonated (adj)	carbogazoasă	[karbogazo'asə]
sparkling (adj)	gazoasă	[gazo'asə]
ice	gheaţă (f)	['gʲatsə]
with ice	cu gheaţă	[ku 'gʲatsə]

non-alcoholic (adj)	fără alcool	['fərə alko'ol]
soft drink	băutură (f) fără alcool	[bəu'turə fərə alko'ol]
refreshing drink	băutură (f) răcoritoare	[bəu'turə rəkorito'are]
lemonade	limonadă (f)	[limo'nadə]

spirits	băuturi (f pl) alcoolice	[bəu'turʲ alko'olitʃe]
wine	vin (n)	[vin]
white wine	vin (n) alb	[vin alb]
red wine	vin (n) roşu	[vin 'roʃu]

liqueur	lichior (n)	[li'kør]
champagne	şampanie (f)	[ʃam'panie]
vermouth	vermut (n)	[ver'mut]

whisky	whisky (n)	['wiski]
vodka	votcă (f)	['votkə]
gin	gin (n)	[dʒin]
cognac	coniac (n)	[ko'njak]
rum	rom (n)	[rom]

coffee	cafea (f)	[ka'fʲa]
black coffee	cafea (f) neagră	[ka'fʲa 'nʲagrə]
white coffee	cafea (f) cu lapte	[ka'fʲa ku 'lapte]
cappuccino	cafea (f) cu frişcă	[ka'fʲa ku 'friʃkə]
instant coffee	cafea (f) solubilă	[ka'fʲa so'lubilə]

milk	lapte (n)	['lapte]
cocktail	cocteil (n)	[kok'tejl]
milkshake	cocteil (n) din lapte	[kok'tejl din 'lapte]

juice	suc (n)	[suk]
tomato juice	suc (n) de roşii	[suk de 'roʃij]
orange juice	suc (n) de portocale	[suk de porto'kale]
freshly squeezed juice	suc (n) natural	[suk natu'ral]

beer	bere (f)	['bere]
lager	bere (f) blondă	['bere 'blondə]
bitter	bere (f) brună	['bere 'brunə]

tea	ceai (n)	[tʃaj]
black tea	ceai (n) negru	[tʃaj 'negru]
green tea	ceai (n) verde	[tʃaj 'verde]

46. Vegetables

vegetables	legume (f pl)	[le'gume]
greens	verdeaţă (f)	[ver'dʲatsə]

tomato	roşie (f)	['roʃie]
cucumber	castravete (m)	[kastra'vete]
carrot	morcov (m)	['morkov]
potato	cartof (m)	[kar'tof]
onion	ceapă (f)	['tʃapə]
garlic	usturoi (m)	[ustu'roj]

cabbage	varză (f)	['varzə]
cauliflower	conopidă (f)	[kono'pidə]
Brussels sprouts	varză (f) de Bruxelles	['varzə de bruk'sel]
broccoli	broccoli (m)	['brokoli]

beetroot	sfeclă (f)	['sfeklə]
aubergine	pătlăgea (f) vânătă	[pətlə'dʒʲa 'vinətə]
courgette	dovlecel (m)	[dovle'tʃel]
pumpkin	dovleac (m)	[dov'lʲak]
turnip	nap (m)	[nap]

parsley	pătrunjel (m)	[pətrun'ʒel]
dill	mărar (m)	[mə'rar]
lettuce	salată (f)	[sa'latə]
celery	ţelină (f)	['tseline]
asparagus	sparanghel (m)	[sparan'gel]
spinach	spanac (n)	[spa'nak]

pea	mazăre (f)	['mazəre]
beans	boabe (f pl)	[bo'abe]
maize	porumb (m)	[po'rumb]
kidney bean	fasole (f)	[fa'sole]

sweet paper	piper (m)	[pi'per]
radish	ridiche (f)	[ri'dike]
artichoke	anghinare (f)	[angi'nare]

47. Fruits. Nuts

fruit	fruct (n)	[frukt]
apple	măr (n)	[mər]
pear	pară (f)	['parə]
lemon	lămâie (f)	[lə'mie]
orange	portocală (f)	[porto'kalə]
strawberry (garden ~)	căpşună (f)	[kəp'ʃunə]

tangerine	mandarină (f)	[manda'rinə]
plum	prună (f)	['prunə]
peach	piersică (f)	['pjersikə]
apricot	caisă (f)	[ka'isə]
raspberry	zmeură (f)	['zmeurə]
pineapple	ananas (m)	[ana'nas]

banana	banană (f)	[ba'nanə]
watermelon	pepene (m) verde	['pepene 'verde]
grape	struguri (m pl)	['strugurʲ]
sour cherry	vişină (f)	['viʃinə]
sweet cherry	cireaşă (f)	[tʃi'rʲaʃə]
melon	pepene (m) galben	['pepene 'galben]

grapefruit	grepfrut (n)	['grepfrut]
avocado	avocado (n)	[avo'kado]
papaya	papaia (f)	[pa'paja]
mango	mango (n)	['mango]

pomegranate	**rodie** (f)	['rodie]
redcurrant	**coacăză** (f) **roşie**	[ko'akəzə 'roʃie]
blackcurrant	**coacăză** (f) **neagră**	[ko'akəzə 'nʲagrə]
gooseberry	**agrişă** (f)	[a'griʃə]
bilberry	**afină** (f)	[a'finə]
blackberry	**mură** (f)	['murə]
raisin	**stafidă** (f)	[sta'fidə]
fig	**smochină** (f)	[smo'kinə]
date	**curmală** (f)	[kur'malə]
peanut	**arahidă** (f)	[ara'hidə]
almond	**migdală** (f)	[mig'dalə]
walnut	**nucă** (f)	['nukə]
hazelnut	**alună** (f) **de pădure**	[a'lunə de pə'dure]
coconut	**nucă** (f) **de cocos**	['nukə de 'kokos]
pistachios	**fistic** (m)	['fistik]

48. Bread. Sweets

bakers' confectionery (pastry)	**produse** (n pl) **de cofetărie**	[pro'duse də kofetə'rie]
bread	**pâine** (f)	['pine]
biscuits	**biscuit** (m)	[bisku'it]
chocolate (n)	**ciocolată** (f)	[tʃioko'latə]
chocolate (as adj)	**de, din ciocolată**	[de, din tʃioko'latə]
candy (wrapped)	**bomboană** (f)	[bombo'anə]
cake (e.g. cupcake)	**prăjitură** (f)	[prəʒi'turə]
cake (e.g. birthday ~)	**tort** (n)	[tort]
pie (e.g. apple ~)	**plăcintă** (f)	[plə'tʃintə]
filling (for cake, pie)	**umplutură** (f)	[umplu'turə]
jam (whole fruit jam)	**dulceaţă** (f)	[dul'tʃatsə]
marmalade	**marmeladă** (f)	[marme'ladə]
wafers	**napolitane** (f pl)	[napoli'tane]
ice-cream	**îngheţată** (f)	[inge'tsatə]

49. Cooked dishes

course, dish	**fel** (n) **de mâncare**	[fel de mi'nkare]
cuisine	**bucătărie** (f)	[bukətə'rie]
recipe	**reţetă** (f)	[re'tsetə]
portion	**porţie** (f)	['portsie]
salad	**salată** (f)	[sa'latə]
soup	**supă** (f)	['supə]
clear soup (broth)	**supă** (f) **de carne**	['supə de 'karne]
sandwich (bread)	**tartină** (f)	[tar'tinə]
fried eggs	**omletă** (f)	[om'letə]
hamburger (beefburger)	**hamburger** (m)	['hamburger]

beefsteak	biftec (n)	[bif'tek]
side dish	garnitură (f)	[garni'turə]
spaghetti	spaghete (f pl)	[spa'gete]
mash	piure (n) de cartofi	[pju're de kar'tofʲ]
pizza	pizza (f)	['piʦa]
porridge (oatmeal, etc.)	caşă (f)	['kaʃə]
omelette	omletă (f)	[om'letə]

boiled (e.g. ~ beef)	fiert	[fiert]
smoked (adj)	afumat	[afu'mat]
fried (adj)	prăjit	[prə'ʒit]
dried (adj)	uscat	[us'kat]
frozen (adj)	congelat	[kondʒe'lat]
pickled (adj)	marinat	[mari'nat]

sweet (sugary)	dulce	['dulʧe]
salty (adj)	sărat	[sə'rat]
cold (adj)	rece	['reʧe]
hot (adj)	fierbinte	[fier'binte]
bitter (adj)	amar	[a'mar]
tasty (adj)	gustos	[gus'tos]

to cook in boiling water	a fierbe	[a 'fjerbe]
to cook (dinner)	a găti	[a gə'ti]
to fry (vt)	a prăji	[a prə'ʒi]
to heat up (food)	a încălzi	[a inkəl'zi]

to salt (vt)	a săra	[a sə'ra]
to pepper (vt)	a pipera	[a pipe'ra]
to grate (vt)	a da prin răzătoare	[a da prin rəzəto'are]
peel (n)	coajă (f)	[ko'aʒə]
to peel (vt)	a curăţa	[a kurə'ʦa]

50. Spices

salt	sare (f)	['sare]
salty (adj)	sărat	[sə'rat]
to salt (vt)	a săra	[a sə'ra]

black pepper	piper (m) negru	[pi'per 'negru]
red pepper (milled ~)	piper (m) roşu	[pi'per 'roʃu]
mustard	muştar (m)	[muʃ'tar]
horseradish	hrean (n)	[hrʲan]

condiment	condiment (n)	[kondi'ment]
spice	condiment (n)	[kondi'ment]
sauce	sos (n)	[sos]
vinegar	oţet (n)	[o'ʦet]

anise	anason (m)	[ana'son]
basil	busuioc (n)	[busu'jok]
cloves	cuişoare (f pl)	[kuiʃo'are]
ginger	ghimber (m)	[gim'ber]
coriander	coriandru (m)	[kori'andru]

cinnamon	**scorţişoară** (f)	[skortsiʃo'arə]
sesame	**susan** (m)	[su'san]
bay leaf	**foi** (f) **de dafin**	[foj de 'dafin]
paprika	**paprică** (f)	['paprikə]
caraway	**chimen** (m)	[ki'men]
saffron	**şofran** (m)	[ʃo'fran]

51. Meals

food	**mâncare** (f)	[min'kare]
to eat (vi, vt)	**a mânca**	[a min'ka]
breakfast	**micul dejun** (n)	['mikul de'ʒun]
to have breakfast	**a lua micul dejun**	[a lu'a 'mikul de'ʒun]
lunch	**prânz** (n)	[prinz]
to have lunch	**a lua prânzul**	[a lu'a 'prinzul]
dinner	**cină** (f)	['tʃinə]
to have dinner	**a cina**	[a tʃi'na]
appetite	**poftă** (f) **de mâncare**	['poftə de mi'nkare]
Enjoy your meal!	**Poftă bună!**	['poftə 'bunə]
to open (~ a bottle)	**a deschide**	[a des'kide]
to spill (liquid)	**a vărsa**	[a vər'sa]
to spill out (vi)	**a se vărsa**	[a se vər'sa]
to boil (vi)	**a fierbe**	[a 'fjerbe]
to boil (vt)	**a fierbe**	[a 'fjerbe]
boiled (~ water)	**fiert**	[fiert]
to chill, cool down (vt)	**a răci**	[a rə'tʃi]
to chill (vi)	**a se răci**	[a se rə'tʃi]
taste, flavour	**gust** (n)	[gust]
aftertaste	**aromă** (f)	[a'romə]
to slim down (lose weight)	**a slăbi**	[a slə'bi]
diet	**dietă** (f)	[di'etə]
vitamin	**vitamină** (f)	[vita'minə]
calorie	**calorie** (f)	[kalo'rie]
vegetarian (n)	**vegetarian** (m)	[vedʒetari'an]
vegetarian (adj)	**vegetarian**	[vedʒetari'an]
fats (nutrient)	**grăsimi** (f pl)	[grə'simiʲ]
proteins	**proteine** (f pl)	[prote'ine]
carbohydrates	**hidraţi** (m pl) **de carbon**	[hi'dratsʲ de kar'bon]
slice (of lemon, ham)	**felie** (f)	[fe'lie]
piece (of cake, pie)	**bucată** (f)	[bu'katə]
crumb (of bread, cake, etc.)	**firimitură** (f)	[firimi'turə]

52. Table setting

spoon	**lingură** (f)	['lingurə]
knife	**cuţit** (n)	[ku'tsit]

fork	furculiță (f)	[furku'litsə]
cup (e.g., coffee ~)	ceaşcă (f)	['tʃaʃkə]
plate (dinner ~)	farfurie (f)	[farfu'rie]
saucer	farfurioară (f)	[farfurio'arə]
serviette	şerveţel (n)	[ʃərve'tsel]
toothpick	scobitoare (f)	[skobito'are]

53. Restaurant

restaurant	restaurant (n)	[restau'rant]
coffee bar	cafenea (f)	[kafe'nʲa]
pub, bar	bar (n)	[bar]
tearoom	salon (n) de ceai	[sa'lon de tʃaj]

waiter	chelner (m)	['kelner]
waitress	chelneriță (f)	[kelne'ritsə]
barman	barman (m)	['barman]

menu	meniu (n)	[me'nju]
wine list	meniu (n) de vinuri	[menju de 'vinurʲ]
to book a table	a rezerva o masă	[a rezer'va o 'masə]

course, dish	mâncare (f)	[min'kare]
to order (meal)	a comanda	[a koman'da]
to make an order	a face comandă	[a 'fatʃe ko'mandə]

aperitif	aperitiv (n)	[aperi'tiv]
starter	gustare (f)	[gus'tare]
dessert, pudding	desert (n)	[de'sert]

bill	notă (f) de plată	['notə de 'platə]
to pay the bill	a achita nota de plată	[a aki'ta 'nota de 'platə]
to give change	a da rest	[a da 'rest]
tip	bacşiş (n)	[bak'ʃiʃ]

Family, relatives and friends

54. Personal information. Forms

name (first name)	**prenume** (n)	[pre'nume]
surname (last name)	**nume** (n)	['nume]
date of birth	**data** (f) **naşterii**	['data 'naʃterij]
place of birth	**locul** (n) **naşterii**	['lokul 'naʃterij]
nationality	**naţionalitate** (f)	[natsionali'tate]
place of residence	**locul** (n) **de reşedinţă**	['lokul de reʃə'dintsə]
country	**ţară** (f)	['tsarə]
profession (occupation)	**profesie** (f)	[pro'fesie]
gender, sex	**sex** (n)	[seks]
height	**înălţime** (f)	[inəl'tsime]
weight	**greutate** (f)	[greu'tate]

55. Family members. Relatives

mother	**mamă** (f)	['mamə]
father	**tată** (m)	['tatə]
son	**fiu** (m)	['fju]
daughter	**fiică** (f)	['fiikə]
younger daughter	**fiica** (f) **mai mică**	['fiika maj 'mikə]
younger son	**fiul** (m) **mai mic**	['fjul maj mik]
eldest daughter	**fiica** (f) **mai mare**	['fiika maj 'mare]
eldest son	**fiul** (m) **mai mare**	['fjul maj 'mare]
brother	**frate** (m)	['frate]
sister	**soră** (f)	['sorə]
cousin (masc.)	**văr** (m)	[vər]
cousin (fem.)	**vară** (f)	['varə]
mummy	**mamă** (f)	['mamə]
dad, daddy	**tată** (m)	['tatə]
parents	**părinţi** (m pl)	[pə'rintsʲ]
child	**copil** (m)	[ko'pil]
children	**copii** (m pl)	[ko'pij]
grandmother	**bunică** (f)	[bu'nikə]
grandfather	**bunic** (m)	[bu'nik]
grandson	**nepot** (m)	[ne'pot]
granddaughter	**nepoată** (f)	[nepo'atə]
grandchildren	**nepoţi** (m pl)	[ne'potsʲ]
uncle	**unchi** (m)	[unkʲ]
aunt	**mătuşă** (f)	[mə'tuʃə]

| nephew | nepot (m) | [ne'pot] |
| niece | nepoată (f) | [nepo'atə] |

mother-in-law (wife's mother)	soacră (f)	[so'akrə]
father-in-law (husband's father)	socru (m)	['sokru]
son-in-law (daughter's husband)	cumnat (m)	[kum'nat]
stepmother	mamă vitregă (f)	['mamə 'vitregə]
stepfather	tată vitreg (m)	['tatə 'vitreg]

infant	sugaci (m)	[su'gatʃi]
baby (infant)	prunc (m)	[prunk]
little boy, kid	pici (m)	[pitʃi]

wife	soție (f)	[so'tsie]
husband	soț (m)	[sots]
spouse (husband)	soț (m)	[sots]
spouse (wife)	soție (f)	[so'tsie]

married (masc.)	căsătorit	[kəsəto'rit]
married (fem.)	căsătorită	[kəsəto'ritə]
single (unmarried)	celibatar (m)	[tʃeliba'tar]
bachelor	burlac (m)	[bur'lak]
divorced (masc.)	divorțat	[divor'tsat]
widow	văduvă (f)	[vəduvə]
widower	văduv (m)	[vəduv]

relative	rudă (f)	['rudə]
close relative	rudă (f) apropiată	['rudə apropi'jatə]
distant relative	rudă (f) îndepărtată	['rudə indeper'tatə]
relatives	rude (f pl) de sânge	['rude de 'sindʒe]

orphan (boy or girl)	orfan (m)	[or'fan]
guardian (of a minor)	tutore (m)	[tu'tore]
to adopt (a boy)	a adopta	[a adop'ta]
to adopt (a girl)	a adopta	[a adop'ta]

56. Friends. Colleagues

friend (masc.)	prieten (m)	[pri'eten]
friend (fem.)	prietenă (f)	[pri'etenə]
friendship	prietenie (f)	[priete'nie]
to be friends	a prieteni	[a priete'ni]

pal (masc.)	amic (m)	[a'mik]
pal (fem.)	amică (f)	[a'mikə]
partner	partener (m)	[parte'ner]

chief (boss)	şef (m)	[ʃef]
superior (n)	director (m)	[di'rektor]
subordinate (n)	subordonat (m)	[subordo'nat]
colleague	coleg (m)	[ko'leg]

acquaintance (person)	**cunoscut** (m)	[kunos'kut]
fellow traveller	**tovarăş** (m) **de drum**	[to'varəʃ de drum]
classmate	**coleg** (m) **de clasă**	[ko'leg de 'klasə]
neighbour (masc.)	**vecin** (m)	[ve'tʃin]
neighbour (fem.)	**vecină** (f)	[ve'tʃinə]
neighbours	**vecini** (m pl)	[ve'tʃinʲ]

57. Man. Woman

woman	**femeie** (f)	[fe'meje]
girl (young woman)	**domnişoară** (f)	[domniʃo'arə]
bride	**mireasă** (f)	[mi'rʲasə]
beautiful (adj)	**frumoasă**	[frumo'asə]
tall (adj)	**înaltă**	[i'naltə]
slender (adj)	**zveltă**	['zveltə]
short (adj)	**scundă**	['skundə]
blonde (n)	**blondă** (f)	['blondə]
brunette (n)	**brunetă** (f)	[bru'netə]
ladies' (adj)	**de damă**	[de 'damə]
virgin (girl)	**virgină** (f)	[vir'dʒinə]
pregnant (adj)	**gravidă** (f)	[gra'vidə]
man (adult male)	**bărbat** (m)	[bər'bat]
blonde haired man	**blond** (m)	[blond]
dark haired man	**brunet** (m)	[bru'net]
tall (adj)	**înalt**	[i'nalt]
short (adj)	**scund**	[skund]
rude (rough)	**grosolan**	[groso'lan]
stocky (adj)	**robust**	[ro'bust]
robust (adj)	**tare**	['tare]
strong (adj)	**puternic**	[pu'ternik]
strength	**forță** (f)	['fortsə]
plump, fat (adj)	**gras**	[gras]
swarthy (dark-skinned)	**negricios**	[negri'tʃios]
slender (well-built)	**zvelt**	[zvelt]
elegant (adj)	**elegant**	[ele'gant]

58. Age

age	**vârstă** (f)	['virstə]
youth (young age)	**tinerețe** (f)	[tine'retse]
young (adj)	**tânăr**	['tinər]
younger (adj)	**mai mic**	[maj mik]
older (adj)	**mai mare**	[maj 'mare]
young man	**tânăr** (m)	['tinər]

| teenager | adolescent (m) | [adoles'tʃent] |
| guy, fellow | flăcău (m) | [flǝkǝu] |

| old man | bătrân (m) | [bǝ'trin] |
| old woman | bătrână (f) | [bǝ'trinǝ] |

| adult (adj) | adult (m) | [a'dult] |
| middle-aged (adj) | de vârstă medie | [de 'virstǝ 'medie] |

| elderly (adj) | în vârstă | [in 'virstǝ] |
| old (adj) | bătrân | [bǝ'trin] |

retirement	pensie (f)	['pensie]
to retire (from job)	a se pensiona	[a se pensio'na]
retiree, pensioner	pensionar (m)	[pensio'nar]

59. Children

child	copil (m)	[ko'pil]
children	copii (m pl)	[ko'pij]
twins	gemeni (m pl)	['dʒemenʲ]

cradle	leagăn (n)	['lʲagǝn]
rattle	sunătoare (f)	[sunǝto'are]
nappy	scutec (n)	['skutek]

| dummy, comforter | biberon (n) | [bibe'ron] |
| pram | cărucior (n) pentru copii | [kǝru'tʃior 'pentru ko'pij] |

| nursery | grădiniță (f) de copii | [grǝdi'nitsǝ de ko'pij] |
| babysitter | dădacă (f) | [dǝ'dakǝ] |

| childhood | copilărie (f) | [kopilǝ'rie] |
| doll | păpușă (f) | [pǝ'puʃǝ] |

| toy | jucărie (f) | [ʒukǝ'rie] |
| construction set (toy) | constructor (m) | [kon'struktor] |

well-bred (adj)	bine crescut	['bine kres'kut]
ill-bred (adj)	needucat	[needu'kat]
spoilt (adj)	răsfățat	[rǝsfǝ'tsat]

| to be naughty | a face pozne | [a 'fatʃe 'pozne] |
| mischievous (adj) | năzbâtios | [nǝzbiti'os] |

| mischievousness | năzbâtie (f) | [nǝz'bitie] |
| mischievous child | ştrengar (m) | [ʃtren'gar] |

| obedient (adj) | ascultător | [askultǝ'tor] |
| disobedient (adj) | neascultător | [neaskultǝ'tor] |

docile (adj)	inteligent	[inteli'dʒent]
clever (intelligent)	deştept	[deʃ'tept]
child prodigy	copil (m) minune	[ko'pil mi'nune]

60. Married couples. Family life

to kiss (vt)	a săruta	[a səru'ta]
to kiss (vi)	a se săruta	[a se səru'ta]
family (n)	familie (f)	[fa'milie]
family (as adj)	de familie	[de fa'milie]
couple	pereche (f)	[pe'reke]
marriage (state)	căsătorie (f)	[kəsəto'rie]
hearth (home)	cămin (n)	[kə'min]
dynasty	dinastie (f)	[dinas'tie]
date	întâlnire (f)	[intil'nire]
kiss	sărut (n)	[sə'rut]
love (for sb)	iubire (f)	[ju'bire]
to love (sb)	a iubi	[a ju'bi]
beloved	iubit	[ju'bit]
tenderness	gingăşie (f)	[dʒingə'ʃie]
tender (affectionate)	tandru	['tandru]
faithfulness	fidelitate (f)	[fideli'tate]
faithful (adj)	fidel	[fi'del]
care (attention)	grijă (f)	['griʒə]
caring (~ father)	grijuliu	[griʒu'lju]
newlyweds	tineri (m pl) căsătoriţi	['tineri kəsəto'rits]
honeymoon	lună (f) de miere	['lunə de 'mjere]
to get married (ab. woman)	a se mărita	[a se məri'ta]
to get married (ab. man)	a se căsători	[a se kəsəto'ri]
wedding	nuntă (f)	['nuntə]
golden wedding	nuntă (f) de aur	['nuntə de 'aur]
anniversary	aniversare (f)	[aniver'sare]
lover (masc.)	amant (m)	[a'mant]
mistress (lover)	amantă (f)	[a'mantə]
adultery	adulter (n)	[adul'ter]
to cheat on … (commit adultery)	a înşela	[a inʃə'la]
jealous (adj)	gelos	[dʒe'los]
to be jealous	a fi gelos	[a fi dʒe'los]
divorce	divorţ (n)	[di'vorts]
to divorce (vi)	a divorţa	[a divor'tsa]
to quarrel (vi)	a se certa	[a se tʃer'ta]
to be reconciled (after an argument)	a se împăca	[a se impə'ka]
together (adv)	împreună	[impre'unə]
зсх	зех (n)	[sɛks]
happiness	fericire (f)	[feri'tʃire]
happy (adj)	fericit	[feri'tʃit]
misfortune (accident)	nenorocire (f)	[nenoro'tʃire]
unhappy (adj)	nefericit	[neferi'tʃit]

Character. Feelings. Emotions

61. Feelings. Emotions

feeling (emotion)	sentiment (n)	[senti'ment]
feelings	sentimente (n pl)	[senti'mente]
hunger	foame (f)	[fo'ame]
to be hungry	a fi foame	[a fi fo'ame]
thirst	sete (f)	['sete]
to be thirsty	a fi sete	[a fi 'sete]
sleepiness	somnolenţă (f)	[somno'lentsə]
to feel sleepy	a fi somn	[a fi somn]
tiredness	oboseală (f)	[obo'siːalə]
tired (adj)	obosit	[obo'sit]
to get tired	a obosi	[a obo'si]
mood (humour)	dispoziţie (f)	[dispo'zitsie]
boredom	plictiseală (f)	[plikti'siːalə]
to be bored	a se plictisi	[a se plikti'si]
seclusion	singurătate (f)	[singurə'tate]
to seclude oneself	a se izola	[a se izo'la]
to worry (make anxious)	a nelinişti	[a nelinif'ti]
to be worried	a se nelinişti	[a se nelinif'ti]
worrying (n)	nelinişte (f)	[ne'linifte]
anxiety	nelinişte (f)	[ne'linifte]
preoccupied (adj)	preocupat	[preoku'pat]
to be nervous	a se enerva	[a se ener'va]
to panic (vi)	a panica	[a pani'ka]
hope	speranţă (f)	[spe'rantsə]
to hope (vi, vt)	a spera	[a spe'ra]
certainty	siguranţă (f)	[sigu'rantsə]
certain, sure (adj)	sigur	['sigur]
uncertainty	nesiguranţă (f)	[nesigu'rantsə]
uncertain (adj)	nesigur	[ne'sigur]
drunk (adj)	beat	[biːat]
sober (adj)	treaz	[triːaz]
weak (adj)	slab	[slab]
happy (adj)	norocos	[noro'kos]
to scare (vt)	a speria	[a speri'ja]
fury (madness)	turbare (f)	[tur'bare]
rage (fury)	furie (f)	[fu'rie]
depression	depresie (f)	[de'presie]
discomfort (unease)	disconfort (n)	[diskon'fort]

comfort	confort (n)	[kon'fort]
to regret (be sorry)	a regreta	[a regre'ta]
regret	regret (n)	[re'gret]
bad luck	ghinion (n)	[gini'on]
sadness	întristare (f)	[intri'stare]

shame (remorse)	ruşine (f)	[ru'ʃine]
gladness	veselie (f)	[vese'lie]
enthusiasm, zeal	entuziasm (n)	[entuzi'asm]
enthusiast	entuziast (m)	[entuzi'ast]
to show enthusiasm	a arăta entuziasm	[a arə'ta entuzi'asm]

62. Character. Personality

character	caracter (n)	[karak'ter]
character flaw	viciu (n)	['vitʃiu]
mind	minte (f)	['minte]
reason	raţiune (f)	[raʦi'une]

conscience	conştiinţă (f)	[konʃti'inʦə]
habit (custom)	obişnuinţă (f)	[obiʃnu'inʦə]
ability (talent)	talent (n)	[ta'lent]
can (e.g. ~ swim)	a putea	[a pu'tʲa]

patient (adj)	răbdător	[rəbdə'tor]
impatient (adj)	nerăbdător	[nerəbdə'tor]
curious (inquisitive)	curios	[kuri'os]
curiosity	curiozitate (f)	[kuriozi'tate]

modesty	modestie (f)	[modes'tie]
modest (adj)	modest	[mo'dest]
immodest (adj)	lipsit de modestie	[lip'sit de modes'tie]

laziness	lene (f)	['lene]
lazy (adj)	leneş	['leneʃ]
lazy person (masc.)	leneş (m)	['leneʃ]

cunning (n)	viclenie (f)	[vikle'nie]
cunning (as adj)	viclean	[vik'lʲan]
distrust	neîncredere (f)	[nein'kredere]
distrustful (adj)	neîncrezător	[neinkrezə'tor]

generosity	generozitate (f)	[dʒenerozi'tate]
generous (adj)	generos	[dʒene'ros]
talented (adj)	talentat	[talen'tat]
talent	talent (n)	[ta'lent]

courageous (adj)	îndrăzneţ	[indrəz'neʦ]
courage	îndrăzneală (f)	[indrəz'nʲalə]
honest (adj)	onest	[o'nest]
honesty	onestitate (f)	[onesti'tate]

| careful (cautious) | prudent | [pru'dent] |
| brave (courageous) | curajos | [kura'ʒos] |

serious (adj)	**serios**	[se'rjos]
strict (severe, stern)	**sever**	[se'ver]
decisive (adj)	**hotărât**	[hotə'rit]
indecisive (adj)	**nehotărât**	[nehotə'rit]
shy, timid (adj)	**sfios**	[sfi'os]
shyness, timidity	**sfială** (f)	[sfi'jalə]
confidence (trust)	**încredere** (f)	[in'kredere]
to believe (trust)	**a avea încredere**	[a a'vʲa in'kredere]
trusting (credulous)	**credul**	[kre'dul]
sincerely (adv)	**sincer**	['sintʃer]
sincere (adj)	**sincer**	['sintʃer]
sincerity	**sinceritate** (f)	[sintʃeri'tate]
open (person)	**deschis**	[des'kis]
calm (adj)	**liniştit**	[liniʃ'tit]
frank (sincere)	**sincer**	['sintʃer]
naïve (adj)	**naiv**	[na'iv]
absent-minded (adj)	**distrat**	[dis'trat]
funny (odd)	**hazliu**	[haz'lju]
greed, stinginess	**lăcomie** (f)	[ləko'mie]
greedy, stingy (adj)	**lacom**	['lakom]
stingy (adj)	**zgârcit**	[zgir'tʃit]
evil (adj)	**rău**	['rəu]
stubborn (adj)	**încăpăţânat**	[inkəpətsi'nat]
unpleasant (adj)	**neplăcut**	[neplə'kut]
selfish person (masc.)	**egoist** (m)	[ego'ist]
selfish (adj)	**egoist**	[ego'ist]
coward	**laş** (m)	[laʃ]
cowardly (adj)	**fricos**	[fri'kos]

63. Sleep. Dreams

to sleep (vi)	**a dormi**	[a dor'mi]
sleep, sleeping	**somn** (n)	[somn]
dream	**vis** (n)	[vis]
to dream (in sleep)	**a visa**	[a vi'sa]
sleepy (adj)	**somnoros**	[somno'ros]
bed	**pat** (n)	[pat]
mattress	**saltea** (f)	[sal'tʲa]
blanket (eiderdown)	**plapumă** (f)	['plapumə]
pillow	**pernă** (f)	['pernə]
sheet	**cearşaf** (n)	[tʃar'ʃaf]
insomnia	**insomnie** (f)	[insom'nie]
sleepless (adj)	**fără somn**	['fərə somn]
sleeping pill	**somnifer** (n)	[somni'fer]
to take a sleeping pill	**a lua somnifere**	[a lu'a somni'fere]
to feel sleepy	**a fi somn**	[a fi somn]

to yawn (vi)	a căsca	[a kəs'ka]
to go to bed	a merge la culcare	[a 'merdʒe la kul'kare]
to make up the bed	a face patul	[a 'fatʃe 'patul]
to fall asleep	a adormi	[a ador'mi]

nightmare	coşmar (n)	[koʃ'mar]
snore, snoring	sforăit (n)	[sforə'it]
to snore (vi)	a sforăi	[a sforə'i]

alarm clock	ceas (n) deşteptător	[tʃas deʃteptə'tor]
to wake (vt)	a trezi	[a tre'zi]
to wake up	a se trezi	[a se tre'zi]
to get up (vi)	a se ridica	[a se ridi'ka]
to have a wash	a se spăla	[a se spə'la]

64. Humour. Laughter. Gladness

humour (wit, fun)	umor (n)	[u'mor]
sense of humour	simţ (n)	[simts]
to enjoy oneself	a se veseli	[a se vese'li]
cheerful (merry)	vesel	['vesel]
merriment (gaiety)	veselie (f)	[vese'lie]

smile	zâmbet (n)	['zimbet]
to smile (vi)	a zâmbi	[a zim'bi]
to start laughing	a izbucni în râs	[a izbuk'ni in ris]
to laugh (vi)	a râde	[a 'ride]
laugh, laughter	râs (n)	[ris]

anecdote	anecdotă (f)	[anek'dotə]
funny (anecdote, etc.)	hazliu	[haz'lju]
funny (odd)	hazliu	[haz'lju]

to joke (vi)	a glumi	[a glu'mi]
joke (verbal)	glumă (f)	['glumə]
joy (emotion)	bucurie (f)	[buku'rie]
to rejoice (vi)	a se bucura	[a se buku'ra]
joyful (adj)	bucuros	[buku'ros]

65. Discussion, conversation. Part 1

communication	comunicare (f)	[komuni'kare]
to communicate	a comunica	[a komuni'ka]

conversation	convorbire (f)	[konvor'bire]
dialogue	dialog (n)	[dia'log]
discussion (discourse)	dezbatere (f)	[dez'batere]
dispute (debate)	polemică (f)	[po'lemikə]
to dispute, to debate	a revendica	[a revendi'ka]

interlocutor	interlocutor (m)	[interloku'tor]
topic (theme)	temă (f)	['temə]

point of view	punct (n) de vedere	[punkt de ve'dere]
opinion (point of view)	părere (f)	[pə'rere]
speech (talk)	discurs (n)	[dis'kurs]

discussion (of a report, etc.)	discuţie (f)	[dis'kutsie]
to discuss (vt)	a discuta	[a disku'ta]
talk (conversation)	conversaţie (f)	[konver'satsie]
to talk (to chat)	a conversa	[a konver'sa]
meeting (encounter)	întâlnire (f)	[intil'nire]
to meet (vi, vt)	a se întâlni	[a se intil'ni]

proverb	proverb (n)	[pro'verb]
saying	zicătoare (f)	[zikəto'are]
riddle (poser)	ghicitoare (f)	[gitʃito'are]
to pose a riddle	a ghici o ghicitoare	[a gi'tʃi o gitʃito'are]
password	parolă (f)	[pa'rolə]
secret	secret (n)	[se'kret]

oath (vow)	jurământ (n)	[ʒurə'mint]
to swear (an oath)	a jura	[a ʒu'ra]
promise	promisiune (f)	[promisi'une]
to promise (vt)	a promite	[a pro'mite]

advice (counsel)	sfat (n)	[sfat]
to advise (vt)	a sfătui	[a sfətu'i]
to listen to … (obey)	a asculta	[a askul'ta]

news	noutate (f)	[nou'tate]
sensation (news)	senzaţie (f)	[sen'zatsie]
information (report)	informaţii (f pl)	[infor'matsij]
conclusion (decision)	concluzie (f)	[kon'kluzie]
voice	voce (f)	['votʃe]
compliment	compliment (n)	[kompli'ment]
kind (nice)	amabil	[a'mabil]

word	cuvânt (n)	[ku'vint]
phrase	frază (f)	['frazə]
answer	răspuns (n)	[rəs'puns]

truth	adevăr (n)	[ade'vər]
lie	minciună (f)	[min'tʃiunə]

thought	gând (f)	[gind]
idea (inspiration)	gând (n)	[gind]
fantasy	imaginaţie (f)	[imadʒi'natsie]

66. Discussion, conversation. Part 2

respected (adj)	stimat	[sti'mat]
to respect (vt)	a respecta	[a respek'ta]
respect	respect (n)	[res'pekt]
Dear … (letter)	Stimate …	[sti'mate]
to introduce (sb to sb)	a prezenta	[a prezen'ta]
intention	intenţie (f)	[in'tentsie]

to intend (have in mind)	a intenționa	[a intentsio'na]
wish	urare (f)	[u'rare]
to wish (~ good luck)	a ura	[a u'ra]

surprise (astonishment)	mirare (f)	[mi'rare]
to surprise (amaze)	a mira	[a mi'ra]
to be surprised	a se mira	[a se mi'ra]

to give (vt)	a da	[a da]
to take (get hold of)	a lua	[a lu'a]
to give back	a restitui	[a restitu'i]
to return (give back)	a înapoia	[a inapo'ja]

to apologize (vi)	a cere scuze	[a 'tʃere 'skuze]
apology	scuză (f)	['skuzə]
to forgive (vt)	a ierta	[a er'ta]

to talk (speak)	a vorbi	[a vor'bi]
to listen (vi)	a asculta	[a askul'ta]
to hear out	a asculta	[a askul'ta]
to understand (vt)	a înțelege	[a intse'ledʒe]

to show (to display)	a arăta	[a arə'ta]
to look at …	a se uita	[a se uj'ta]
to call (yell for sb)	a chema	[a ke'ma]
to disturb (vt)	a deranja	[a deran'ʒa]
to pass (to hand sth)	a transmite	[a trans'mite]

demand (request)	rugăminte (f)	[rugə'minte]
to request (ask)	a ruga	[a ru'ga]
demand (firm request)	cerere (f)	['tʃerere]
to demand (request firmly)	a cere	[a 'tʃere]

to tease (call names)	a tachina	[a taki'na]
to mock (make fun of)	a-şi bate joc	[aʃ 'bate ʒok]
mockery, derision	derâdere (f)	[de'ridere]
nickname	poreclă (f)	[po'reklə]

insinuation	aluzie (f)	[a'luzie]
to insinuate (imply)	a face aluzie	[a 'fatʃe a'luzie]
to mean (vt)	a se subînțelege	[a se subintse'ledʒe]

| description | descriere (f) | [de'skriere] |
| to describe (vt) | a descrie | [a de'skrie] |

| praise (compliments) | laudă (f) | ['laudə] |
| to praise (vt) | a lăuda | [a ləu'da] |

disappointment	dezamăgire (f)	[dezamə'dʒire]
to disappoint (vt)	a dezamăgi	[a dezamə'dʒi]
to bc disappointed	a se dezamăgi	[a se dezamə'dʒi]

supposition	presupunere (f)	[presu'punere]
to suppose (assume)	a presupune	[a presu'pune]
warning (caution)	avertisment (n)	[avertis'ment]
to warn (vt)	a preveni	[a preve'ni]

67. Discussion, conversation. Part 3

to talk into (convince)	a convinge	[a kon'vindʒe]
to calm down (vt)	a linişti	[a liniʃ'ti]
silence (~ is golden)	tăcere (f)	[tə'tʃere]
to be silent (not speaking)	a tăcea	[a tə'tʃa]
to whisper (vi, vt)	a şopti	[a ʃop'ti]
whisper	şoaptă (f)	[ʃo'aptə]
frankly, sincerely (adv)	sincer	['sintʃer]
in my opinion …	după părerea mea …	['dupə pə'reri̯a mi̯a]
detail (of the story)	amănunt (n)	[amə'nunt]
detailed (adj)	amănunţit	[amənun'tsit]
in detail (adv)	amănunţit	[amənun'tsit]
hint, clue	indiciu (n)	[in'ditʃiu]
to give a hint	a şopti	[a ʃop'ti]
look (glance)	privire (f)	[pri'vire]
to have a look	a privi	[a pri'vi]
fixed (look)	fix	[fiks]
to blink (vi)	a clipi	[a kli'pi]
to wink (vi)	a clipi	[a kli'pi]
to nod (in assent)	a da din cap	[a da din 'kap]
sigh	oftat (n)	[of'tat]
to sigh (vi)	a ofta	[a of'ta]
to shudder (vi)	a tresări	[a tresə'ri]
gesture	gest (n)	[dʒest]
to touch (one's arm, etc.)	a se atinge	[a se a'tindʒe]
to seize (e.g., ~ by the arm)	a apuca	[a apu'ka]
to tap (on the shoulder)	a bate	[a 'bate]
Look out!	Atenţie!	[a'tentsie]
Really?	Oare?	[o'are]
Are you sure?	Eşti sigur?	[eʃti 'sigur]
Good luck!	Succes!	[suk'tʃes]
I see!	Clar!	[klar]
What a pity!	Ce păcat!	[tʃe pə'kat]

68. Agreement. Refusal

consent	consimţământ (n)	[konsimtsə'mint]
to consent (vi)	a fi de acord cu …	[a fi de a'kord ku]
approval	aprobare (f)	[apro'bare]
to approve (vt)	a aproba	[a apro'ba]
refusal	refuz (n)	[re'fuz]
to refuse (vi, vt)	a refuza	[a refu'za]
Great!	Perfect!	[per'fekt]
All right!	Bine!	['bine]

Okay! (I agree)	**De acord!**	[de a'kord]
forbidden (adj)	**interzis**	[inter'zis]
it's forbidden	**nu se poate**	[nu se po'ate]
it's impossible	**imposibil**	[impo'sibil]
incorrect (adj)	**incorect**	[inko'rekt]
to reject (~ a demand)	**a respinge**	[a res'pindʒe]
to support (cause, idea)	**a susține**	[a sus'tsine]
to accept (~ an apology)	**a accepta**	[a aktʃep'ta]
to confirm (vt)	**a confirma**	[a konfir'ma]
confirmation	**confirmare** (f)	[konfir'mare]
permission	**permisiune** (f)	[permisi'une]
to permit (vt)	**a permite**	[a per'mite]
decision	**hotărâre** (f)	[hotə'rire]
to say nothing (hold one's tongue)	**a tăcea**	[a tə'tʃa]
condition (term)	**condiție** (f)	[kon'ditsie]
excuse (pretext)	**pretext** (n)	[pre'tekst]
praise (compliments)	**laudă** (f)	['laudə]
to praise (vt)	**a lăuda**	[a ləu'da]

69. Success. Good luck. Failure

success	**reușită** (f)	[reu'ʃitə]
successfully (adv)	**reușit**	[reu'ʃit]
successful (adj)	**reușit**	[reu'ʃit]
luck (good luck)	**succes** (n)	[suk'tʃes]
Good luck!	**Succes!**	[suk'tʃes]
lucky (e.g. ~ day)	**norocos**	[noro'kos]
lucky (fortunate)	**norocos**	[noro'kos]
failure	**eșec** (n)	[e'ʃək]
misfortune	**ghinion** (n)	[gini'on]
bad luck	**ghinion** (n)	[gini'on]
unsuccessful (adj)	**nereușit**	[nereu'ʃit]
catastrophe	**catastrofă** (f)	[katas'trofə]
pride	**mândrie** (f)	[min'drie]
proud (adj)	**mândru**	['mindru]
to be proud	**a se mândri**	[a se min'dri]
winner	**învingător** (m)	[invingə'tor]
to win (vi)	**a învinge**	[a in'vindʒe]
to lose (not win)	**a pierde**	[a 'pjerde]
try	**încercare** (f)	[intʃer'kare]
to try (vi)	**a se strădui**	[a se strədu'i]
chance (opportunity)	**șansă** (f)	['ʃansə]

70. Quarrels. Negative emotions

shout (scream)	strigăt (n)	['strigət]
to shout (vi)	a striga	[a stri'ga]
to start to cry out	a striga	[a stri'ga]
quarrel	ceartă (f)	['tʃartə]
to quarrel (vi)	a se certa	[a se tʃer'ta]
fight (squabble)	scandal (n)	[skan'dal]
to make a scene	a face scandal	[a 'fatʃe skan'dal]
conflict	conflict (n)	[kon'flikt]
misunderstanding	neînțelegere (f)	[neintse'ledʒere]
insult	insultă (f)	[in'sultə]
to insult (vt)	a insulta	[a insul'ta]
insulted (adj)	ofensat	[ofen'sat]
resentment	jignire (f)	[ʒig'nire]
to offend (vt)	a jigni	[a ʒig'ni]
to take offence	a se supăra	[a se supə'ra]
indignation	indignare (f)	[indig'nare]
to be indignant	a se indigna	[a se indig'na]
complaint	plângere (f)	['plindʒere]
to complain (vi, vt)	a se plânge	[a se 'plindʒe]
apology	scuză (f)	['skuzə]
to apologize (vi)	a cere scuze	[a 'tʃere 'skuze]
to beg pardon	a cere iertare	[a 'tʃere er'tare]
criticism	critică (f)	['kritikə]
to criticize (vt)	a critica	[a kriti'ka]
accusation (charge)	învinuire (f)	[invinu'ire]
to accuse (vt)	a învinui	[a invinu'i]
revenge	răzbunare (f)	[rəzbu'nare]
to avenge (get revenge)	a răzbuna	[a rəzbu'na]
to pay back	a se revanşa	[a se revan'ʃa]
disdain	dispreț (n)	[dis'prets]
to despise (vt)	a disprețui	[a dispretsu'i]
hatred, hate	ură (f)	['urə]
to hate (vt)	a urî	[a u'ri]
nervous (adj)	nervos	[ner'vos]
to be nervous	a se enerva	[a se ener'va]
angry (mad)	supărat	[supə'rat]
to make angry	a supăra	[a supə'ra]
humiliation	umilire (f)	[umi'lire]
to humiliate (vt)	a umili	[a umi'li]
to humiliate oneself	a se umili	[a se umi'li]
shock	şoc (n)	[ʃok]
to shock (vt)	a şoca	[a ʃo'ka]
trouble (e.g. serious ~)	neplăcere (f)	[neplə'tʃere]

unpleasant (adj)	neplăcut	[neplə'kut]
fear (dread)	frică (f)	['frikə]
terrible (storm, heat)	năprasnic	[nə'prasnik]
scary (e.g. ~ story)	de groază	[de gro'azə]
horror	groază (f)	[gro'azə]
awful (crime, news)	înspăimântător	[inspəjmintə'tor]

to cry (weep)	a plânge	[a 'plindʒe]
to start crying	a plânge	[a 'plindʒe]
tear	lacrimă (f)	['lakrimə]

fault	greşeală (f)	[gre'ʃalə]
guilt (feeling)	vină (f)	['vinə]
dishonor (disgrace)	ruşine (f)	[ru'ʃine]
protest	protest (n)	[pro'test]
stress	stres (n)	[stres]

to disturb (vt)	a deranja	[a deran'ʒa]
to be furious	a se supăra	[a se supə'ra]
angry (adj)	supărat	[supə'rat]
to end (~ a relationship)	a pune capăt	[a 'pune 'kapət]
to swear (at sb)	a se sfădi	[a se sfə'di]

to scare (become afraid)	a se speria	[a se speri'ja]
to hit (strike with hand)	a lovi	[a lo'vi]
to fight (street fight, etc.)	a se bate	[a se 'bate]

to settle (a conflict)	a aplana	[a apla'na]
discontented (adj)	nemulţumit	[nemulʦu'mit]
furious (adj)	furios	[furi'os]

It's not good!	Nu e bine!	[nu e 'bine]
It's bad!	E rău!	[e rəu]

Medicine

71. Diseases

illness	boală (f)	[bo'alə]
to be ill	a fi bolnav	[a fi bol'nav]
health	sănătate (f)	[sənə'tate]
runny nose (coryza)	guturai (n)	[gutu'raj]
tonsillitis	anghină (f)	[a'nginə]
cold (illness)	răceală (f)	[rə'tʃalə]
to catch a cold	a răci	[a rə'tʃi]
bronchitis	bronşită (f)	[bron'ʃitə]
pneumonia	pneumonie (f)	[pneumo'nie]
flu, influenza	gripă (f)	['gripə]
shortsighted (adj)	miop	[mi'op]
longsighted (adj)	prezbit	[prez'bit]
strabismus (crossed eyes)	strabism (n)	[stra'bism]
squint-eyed (adj)	saşiu	[sa'ʃiu]
cataract	cataractă (f)	[kata'raktə]
glaucoma	glaucom (n)	[glau'kom]
stroke	congestie (f)	[kon'dʒestie]
heart attack	infarct (n)	[in'farkt]
myocardial infarction	infarct (n) miocardic	[in'farkt mio'kardik]
paralysis	paralizie (f)	[parali'zie]
to paralyse (vt)	a paraliza	[a parali'za]
allergy	alergie (f)	[aler'dʒie]
asthma	astmă (f)	['astmə]
diabetes	diabet (n)	[dia'bet]
toothache	durere (f) de dinţi	[du'rere de dinʦ]
caries	carie (f)	['karie]
diarrhoea	diaree (f)	[dia'ree]
constipation	constipaţie (f)	[konsti'paʦie]
stomach upset	deranjament (n) la stomac	[deranʒa'ment la sto'mak]
food poisoning	intoxicare (f)	[intoksi'kare]
to get food poisoning	a se intoxica	[a se intoksi'ka]
arthritis	artrită (f)	[ar'tritə]
rickets	rahitism (n)	[rahi'tism]
rheumatism	reumatism (n)	[reuma'tism]
atherosclerosis	ateroscleroză (f)	[arterioskle'rozə]
gastritis	gastrită (f)	[gas'tritə]
appendicitis	apendicită (f)	[apendi'tʃitə]

cholecystitis	colecistită (f)	[koletʃis'titə]
ulcer	ulcer (n)	[ul'tʃer]
measles	pojar	[po'ʒar]
rubella (German measles)	rubeolă (f)	[ruʒe'olə]
jaundice	icter (n)	['ikter]
hepatitis	hepatită (f)	[hepa'titə]
schizophrenia	schizofrenie (f)	[skizofre'nie]
rabies (hydrophobia)	turbare (f)	[tur'bare]
neurosis	nevroză (f)	[ne'vrozə]
concussion	comoție (f) cerebrală	[ko'motsie tʃerə'bralə]
cancer	cancer (n)	['kantʃer]
sclerosis	scleroză (f)	[skle'rozə]
multiple sclerosis	scleroză multiplă (f)	[skle'rozə mul'tiplə]
alcoholism	alcoolism (n)	[alkoo'lizm]
alcoholic (n)	alcoolic (m)	[alko'olik]
syphilis	sifilis (n)	['sifilis]
AIDS	SIDA (f)	['sida]
tumour	tumoare (f)	[tumo'are]
malignant (adj)	malignă	[ma'lignə]
benign (adj)	benignă	[be'nignə]
fever	friguri (n pl)	['friguri]
malaria	malarie (f)	[mala'rie]
gangrene	cangrenă (f)	[kan'grenə]
seasickness	rău (n) de mare	[rəu de 'mare]
epilepsy	epilepsie (f)	[epilep'sie]
epidemic	epidemie (f)	[epide'mie]
typhus	tifos (n)	['tifos]
tuberculosis	tuberculoză (f)	[tuberku'lozə]
cholera	holeră (f)	['holerə]
plague (bubonic ~)	ciumă (f)	['tʃiumə]

72. Symptoms. Treatments. Part 1

symptom	simptom (n)	[simp'tom]
temperature	temperatură (f)	[tempera'turə]
high temperature (fever)	febră (f)	['febrə]
pulse (heartbeat)	puls (n)	[puls]
dizziness (vertigo)	amețeală (f)	[ame'tsialə]
hot (adj)	fierbinte	[fier'binte]
shivering	frisoane (n pl)	[friso'ane]
pale (e.g. ~ face)	palid	['palid]
cough	tuse (f)	['tuse]
to cough (vi)	a tuşi	[a tu'ʃi]
to sneeze (vi)	a strănuta	[a strənu'ta]
faint	leşin (n)	[le'ʃin]

to faint (vi)	a leşina	[a leʃi'na]
bruise (hématome)	vânătaie (f)	[vinə'tae]
bump (lump)	cucui (n)	[ku'kuj]
to bang (bump)	a se lovi	[a se lo'vi]
contusion (bruise)	contuzie (f)	[kon'tuzie]
to get a bruise	a se lovi	[a se lo'vi]
to limp (vi)	a şchiopăta	[a ʃkiopə'ta]
dislocation	luxaţie (f)	[luk'satsie]
to dislocate (vt)	a luxa	[a luk'sa]
fracture	fractură (f)	[frak'turə]
to have a fracture	a fractura	[a fraktu'ra]
cut (e.g. paper ~)	tăietură (f)	[təe'turə]
to cut oneself	a se tăia	[a se tə'ja]
bleeding	sângerare (f)	[sindʒe'rare]
burn (injury)	arsură (f)	[ar'surə]
to get burned	a se frige	[a se 'fridʒe]
to prick (vt)	a înţepa	[a intse'pa]
to prick oneself	a se înţepa	[a s intse'pa]
to injure (vt)	a se răni	[a se rə'ni]
injury	vătămare (f)	[vətə'mare]
wound	rană (f)	['ranə]
trauma	traumă (f)	['traumə]
to be delirious	a delira	[a deli'ra]
to stutter (vi)	a se bâlbâi	[a se bilbi'i]
sunstroke	insolaţie (f)	[inso'latsie]

73. Symptoms. Treatments. Part 2

pain, ache	durere (f)	[du'rere]
splinter (in foot, etc.)	ghimpe (m)	['gimpe]
sweat (perspiration)	transpiraţie (f)	[transpi'ratsie]
to sweat (perspire)	a transpira	[a transpi'ra]
vomiting	vomă (f)	['vomə]
convulsions	convulsii (f pl)	[kon'vulsij]
pregnant (adj)	gravidă (f)	[gra'vidə]
to be born	a se naşte	[a se 'naʃte]
delivery, labour	naştere (f)	['naʃtere]
to deliver (~ a baby)	a naşte	[a 'naʃte]
abortion	avort (n)	[a'vort]
breathing, respiration	respiraţie (f)	[respi'ratsie]
in-breath (inhalation)	inspiraţie (f)	[inspi'ratsie]
out-breath (exhalation)	expiraţie (f)	[ekspi'ratsie]
to exhale (breathe out)	a expira	[a ekspi'ra]
to inhale (vi)	a inspira	[a inspi'ra]
disabled person	invalid (m)	[inva'lid]
cripple	infirm (m)	[in'firm]

drug addict	narcoman (m)	[narko'man]
deaf (adj)	surd	[surd]
mute (adj)	mut	[mut]
deaf mute (adj)	surdo-mut	[surdo'mut]

mad, insane (adj)	nebun	[ne'bun]
madman	nebun (m)	[ne'bun]
(demented person)		
madwoman	nebună (f)	[ne'bunə]
to go insane	a înnebuni	[a înnebu'ni]

gene	genă (f)	['dʒenə]
immunity	imunitate (f)	[imuni'tate]
hereditary (adj)	ereditar	[eredi'tar]
congenital (adj)	congenital	[kondʒeni'tal]

virus	virus (m)	['virus]
microbe	microb (m)	[mi'krob]
bacterium	bacterie (f)	[bak'terie]
infection	infecţie (f)	[in'fektsie]

74. Symptoms. Treatments. Part 3

| hospital | spital (n) | [spi'tal] |
| patient | pacient (m) | [patʃi'ent] |

diagnosis	diagnostic (n)	[diag'nostik]
cure	tratament (n)	[trata'ment]
to get treatment	a urma tratament	[a ur'ma trata'ment]
to treat (~ a patient)	a trata	[a tra'ta]
to nurse (look after)	a îngriji	[a îngri'ʒi]
care (nursing ~)	îngrijire (f)	[ingri'ʒire]

operation, surgery	operaţie (f)	[ope'ratsie]
to bandage (head, limb)	a pansa	[a pan'sa]
bandaging	pansare (f)	[pan'sare]

vaccination	vaccin (n)	[vak'tʃin]
to vaccinate (vt)	a vaccina	[a vaktʃi'na]
injection	injecţie (f)	[in'ʒektsie]
to give an injection	a face injecţie	[a 'fatʃe in'ʒektsie]

amputation	amputare (f)	[ampu'tare]
to amputate (vt)	a amputa	[a ampu'ta]
coma	comă (f)	['komə]
to be in a coma	a fi în comă	[a fi in 'komə]
intensive care	reanimare (f)	[reani'mare]

to recover (· from flu)	a se vindeca	[a se vinde'ka]
condition (patient's ~)	stare (f)	['stare]
consciousness	conştiinţă (f)	[konʃti'intsə]
memory (faculty)	memorie (f)	[me'morie]
to pull out (tooth)	a extrage	[a eks'tradʒe]
filling	plombă (f)	['plombə]

to fill (a tooth)	a plomba	[a plom'ba]
hypnosis	hipnoză (f)	[hip'nozə]
to hypnotize (vt)	a hipnotiza	[a hipnoti'za]

75. Doctors

doctor	medic (m)	['medik]
nurse	asistentă (f) medicală	[asis'tentə medi'kalə]
personal doctor	medic (m) personal	['medik perso'nal]

dentist	stomatolog (m)	[stomato'log]
optician	oculist (m)	[oku'list]
general practitioner	terapeut (m)	[terape'ut]
surgeon	chirurg (m)	[ki'rurg]

psychiatrist	psihiatru (m)	[psihi'atru]
paediatrician	pediatru (m)	[pedi'atru]
psychologist	psiholog (m)	[psiho'log]
gynaecologist	ginecolog (m)	[dʒineko'log]
cardiologist	cardiolog (m)	[kardio'log]

76. Medicine. Drugs. Accessories

medicine, drug	medicament (n)	[medika'ment]
remedy	remediu (n)	[re'medju]
prescription	rețetă (f)	[re'tsetə]

tablet, pill	pastilă (f)	[pas'tilə]
ointment	unguent (n)	[ungu'ent]
ampoule	fiolă (f)	[fi'olə]
mixture, solution	mixtură (f)	[miks'turə]
syrup	sirop (n)	[si'rop]
capsule	pilulă (f)	[pi'lulə]
powder	praf (n)	[praf]

gauze bandage	bandaj (n)	[ban'daʒ]
cotton wool	vată (f)	['vatə]
iodine	iod (n)	[jod]

plaster	leucoplast (n)	[leuko'plast]
eyedropper	pipetă (f)	[pi'petə]
thermometer	termometru (n)	[termo'metru]
syringe	seringă (f)	[se'ringə]

| wheelchair | cărucior (n) pentru invalizi | [kəru'tʃior 'pentru inva'lizi] |
| crutches | cârje (f pl) | ['kirʒe] |

painkiller	anestezic (n)	[anes'tezik]
laxative	laxativ (n)	[laksa'tiv]
spirits (ethanol)	spirt (n)	[spirt]
medicinal herbs	plante (f pl) medicinale	['plante meditʃi'nale]
herbal (~ tea)	din plante medicinale	[din 'plante meditʃi'nale]

77. Smoking. Tobacco products

tobacco	tutun (n)	[tu'tun]
cigarette	ţigară (f)	[tsi'garə]
cigar	ţigară (f) de foi	[tsi'garə de foj]
pipe	pipă (f)	['pipə]
packet (of cigarettes)	pachet (n)	[pa'ket]
matches	chibrituri (n pl)	[ki'briturʲ]
matchbox	cutie (f) de chibrituri	[ku'tie de ki'briturʲ]
lighter	brichetă (f)	[bri'ketə]
ashtray	scrumieră (f)	[skru'mjerə]
cigarette case	tabacheră (n)	[taba'kerə]
cigarette holder	muştiuc (n)	[muʃ'tjuk]
filter (cigarette tip)	filtru (n)	['filtru]
to smoke (vi, vt)	a fuma	[a fu'ma]
to light a cigarette	a începe să fumeze	[a in'tʃepe sə fu'meze]
smoking	fumat (n)	[fu'mat]
smoker	fumător (m)	[fumə'tor]
cigarette end	muc (n) de ţigară	[muk de tsi'garə]
smoke, fumes	fum (n)	[fum]
ash	scrum (n)	[skrum]

HUMAN HABITAT

City

city, town	**oraş** (n)	[o'raʃ]
capital city	**capitală** (f)	[kapi'talə]
village	**sat** (n)	[sat]
city map	**planul** (n) **oraşului**	['planul o'raʃuluj]
city centre	**centrul** (n) **oraşului**	['tʃentrul o'raʃuluj]
suburb	**suburbie** (f)	[subur'bie]
suburban (adj)	**din suburbie**	[din subur'bie]
outskirts	**margine** (f)	['mardʒine]
environs (suburbs)	**împrejurimi** (f pl)	[impreʒu'rimʲ]
city block	**cartier** (n)	[kar'tjer]
residential block (area)	**cartier** (n) **locativ**	[ka'rtjer loka'tiv]
traffic	**circulaţie** (f)	[tʃirku'latsie]
traffic lights	**semafor** (n)	[sema'for]
public transport	**transport** (n) **urban**	[trans'port ur'ban]
crossroads	**intersecţie** (f)	[inter'sektsie]
zebra crossing	**trecere** (f)	['tretʃere]
pedestrian subway	**trecere** (f) **subterană**	['tretʃere subte'ranə]
to cross (~ the street)	**a traversa**	[a traver'sa]
pedestrian	**pieton** (m)	[pie'ton]
pavement	**trotuar** (n)	[trotu'ar]
bridge	**pod** (n)	[pod]
embankment (river walk)	**faleză** (f)	[fa'lezə]
fountain	**havuz** (n)	[ha'vuz]
allée (garden walkway)	**alee** (f)	[a'lee]
park	**parc** (n)	[park]
boulevard	**bulevard** (n)	[bule'vard]
square	**piaţă** (f)	['pjatsə]
avenue (wide street)	**prospect** (n)	[pros'pekt]
street	**stradă** (f)	['stradə]
side street	**stradelă** (f)	[stra'delə]
dead end	**fundătură** (f)	[fundə'turə]
house	**casă** (f)	['kasə]
building	**clădire** (f)	[klə'dire]
skyscraper	**zgârie-nori** (m)	['zgirie norʲ]
facade	**faţadă** (f)	[fa'tsadə]
roof	**acoperiş** (n)	[akope'riʃ]

window	fereastră (f)	[fe'riastrə]
arch	arc (n)	[ark]
column	coloană (f)	[kolo'anə]
corner	colţ (n)	[kolʦ]

shop window	vitrină (f)	[vi'trinə]
signboard (store sign, etc.)	firmă (f)	['firmə]
poster (e.g., playbill)	afiş (n)	[a'fiʃ]
advertising poster	afişaj (n)	[afi'ʃaʒ]
hoarding	panou (n) publicitar	[pa'nu publitʃi'tar]

rubbish	gunoi (n)	[gu'noj]
rubbish bin	coş (n) de gunoi	[koʃ de gu'noj]
to litter (vi)	a face murdărie	[a 'fatʃe murdə'rie]
rubbish dump	groapă (f) de gunoi	[gro'apə de gu'noj]

telephone box	cabină (f) telefonică	[ka'binə tele'fonikə]
lamppost	stâlp (m) de felinar	[stilp de feli'nar]
bench (park ~)	bancă (f)	['bankə]

police officer	poliţist (m)	[poli'ʦist]
police	poliţie (f)	[po'liʦie]
beggar	cerşetor (m)	[ʧerʃə'tor]
homeless (n)	vagabond (m)	[vaga'bond]

79. Urban institutions

shop	magazin (n)	[maga'zin]
chemist, pharmacy	farmacie (f)	[farma'ʦie]
optician (spectacles shop)	optică (f)	['optikə]
shopping centre	centru (n) comercial	['ʧentru komerʦi'al]
supermarket	supermarket (n)	[super'market]

bakery	brutărie (f)	[brutə'rie]
baker	brutar (m)	[bru'tar]
cake shop	cofetărie (f)	[kofetə'rie]
grocery shop	băcănie (f)	[bəkə'nie]
butcher shop	halā (f) de carne	['halə de 'karne]

| greengrocer | magazin (m) de legume | [maga'zin de le'gume] |
| market | piaţă (f) | ['pjaʦə] |

coffee bar	cafenea (f)	[kafe'nia]
restaurant	restaurant (n)	[restau'rant]
pub, bar	berărie (f)	[berə'rie]
pizzeria	pizzerie (f)	[piʦe'rie]

hairdresser	frizerie (f)	[frize'rie]
post office	poştă (f)	['puʃtə]
dry cleaners	curăţătorie (f) chimică	[kurəʦəto'rie 'kimikə]
photo studio	atelier (n) foto	[ate'ljer 'foto]

| shoe shop | magazin (n) de încălţăminte | [maga'zin de inkəlʦə'minte] |
| bookshop | librărie (f) | [librə'rie] |

sports shop	**magazin** (n) **sportiv**	[maga'zin spor'tiv]
clothes repair shop	**croitorie** (f)	[kroito'rie]
formal wear hire	**închiriere** (f) **de haine**	[inki'rjere de 'hajne]
video rental shop	**închiriere** (f) **de filme**	[inki'rjere de 'filme]
circus	**circ** (n)	[tʃirk]
zoo	**grădină** (f) **zoologică**	[grə'dinə zoo'lodʒikə]
cinema	**cinematograf** (n)	[tʃinemato'graf]
museum	**muzeu** (n)	[mu'zeu]
library	**bibliotecă** (f)	[biblio'tekə]
theatre	**teatru** (n)	[te'atru]
opera (opera house)	**operă** (f)	['operə]
nightclub	**club** (n) **de noapte**	['klub de no'apte]
casino	**cazinou** (n)	[kazi'nou]
mosque	**moschee** (f)	[mos'kee]
synagogue	**sinagogă** (f)	[sina'gogə]
cathedral	**catedrală** (f)	[kate'dralə]
temple	**templu** (n)	['templu]
church	**biserică** (f)	[bi'serikə]
college	**institut** (n)	[insti'tut]
university	**universitate** (f)	[universi'tate]
school	**şcoală** (f)	[ʃko'alə]
prefecture	**prefectură** (f)	[prefek'turə]
town hall	**primărie** (f)	[primə'rie]
hotel	**hotel** (n)	[ho'tel]
bank	**bancă** (f)	['bankə]
embassy	**ambasadă** (f)	[amba'sadə]
travel agency	**agenţie** (f) **de turism**	[adʒen'tsie de tu'rism]
information office	**birou** (n) **de informaţii**	[bi'rou de infor'matsij]
currency exchange	**schimb** (n) **valutar**	[skimb valu'tar]
underground, tube	**metrou** (n)	[me'trou]
hospital	**spital** (n)	[spi'tal]
petrol station	**benzinărie** (f)	[benzinə'rie]
car park	**parcare** (f)	[par'kare]

80. Signs

signboard (store sign, etc.)	**firmă** (f)	['firmə]
notice (door sign, etc.)	**inscripţie** (f)	[in'skriptsie]
poster	**afiş** (n)	[a'fiʃ]
direction sign	**semn** (n)	[semn]
arrow (sign)	**indicator** (n)	[indika'tor]
caution	**avertisment** (n)	[avertis'ment]
warning sign	**avertisment** (n)	[avertis'ment]
to warn (vt)	**a avertiza**	[a averti'za]
rest day (weekly ~)	**zi** (f) **de odihnă**	[zi de o'dihnə]

| timetable (schedule) | orar (n) | [o'rar] |
| opening hours | ore (f pl) de lucru | ['ore de 'lukru] |

WELCOME!	BINE AȚI VENIT!	['bine 'atsʲ ve'nit]
ENTRANCE	INTRARE	[in'trare]
WAY OUT	IEȘIRE	[je'ʃire]

PUSH	ÎMPINGE	[im'pindʒe]
PULL	TRAGE	['tradʒe]
OPEN	DESCHIS	[des'kis]
CLOSED	ÎNCHIS	[in'kis]

| WOMEN | PENTRU FEMEI | ['pentru fe'mej] |
| MEN | PENTRU BĂRBAȚI | ['pentru bər'batsʲ] |

DISCOUNTS	REDUCERI	[re'dutʃerʲ]
SALE	LICHIDARE DE STOC	[liki'dare de stok]
NEW!	NOU	['nou]
FREE	GRATUIT	[gratu'it]

ATTENTION!	ATENȚIE!	[a'tentsie]
NO VACANCIES	NU SUNT LOCURI	[nu 'sunt 'lokurʲ]
RESERVED	REZERVAT	[rezer'vat]

| ADMINISTRATION | ADMINISTRAȚIE | [adminis'tratsie] |
| STAFF ONLY | NUMAI PENTRU ANGAJAȚI | ['numaj 'pentru anga'ʒats] |

BEWARE OF THE DOG!	CÂINE RĂU	['kine 'rəu]
NO SMOKING	NU FUMAȚI!	[nu fu'mats]
DO NOT TOUCH!	NU ATINGEȚI!	[nu a'tindʒets]

DANGEROUS	PERICULOS	[periku'los]
DANGER	PERICOL	[pe'rikol]
HIGH VOLTAGE	TENSIUNE ÎNALTĂ	[tensi'une i'naltə]
NO SWIMMING!	SCĂLDATUL INTERZIS!	[skəl'datul inter'zis]
OUT OF ORDER	NU FUNCȚIONEAZĂ	[nu funktsio'nʲazə]

FLAMMABLE	INFLAMABIL	[infla'mabil]
FORBIDDEN	INTERZIS	[inter'zis]
NO TRESPASSING!	TRECEREA INTERZISĂ	['tretʃerʲa inter'zisə]
WET PAINT	PROASPĂT VOPSIT	[pro'aspət vop'sit]

81. Urban transport

bus, coach	autobuz (n)	[auto'buz]
tram	tramvai (n)	[tram'vaj]
trolleybus	troleibuz (n)	[trolej'buz]
route (bus ~)	rută (f)	['rutə]
number (e.g. bus ~)	număr (n)	['numər]

to go by ...	a merge cu ...	[a 'merdʒe ku]
to get on (~ the bus)	a se urca	[a se ur'ka]
to get off ...	a coborî	[a kobo'ri]
stop (e.g. bus ~)	stație (f)	['statsie]

next stop	**staţia** (f) **următoare**	['staʦija urməto'are]
terminus	**ultima staţie** (f)	['ultima 'staʦie]
timetable	**orar** (n)	[o'rar]
to wait (vt)	**a aştepta**	[a aʃtep'ta]
ticket	**bilet** (n)	[bi'let]
fare	**costul** (n) **biletului**	['kostul bi'letuluj]
cashier (ticket seller)	**casier** (m)	[ka'sjer]
ticket inspection	**control** (n)	[kon'trol]
ticket inspector	**controlor** (m)	[kontro'lor]
to be late (for …)	**a întârzia**	[a intir'zija]
to miss (~ the train, etc.)	**a pierde …**	[a 'pjerdə]
to be in a hurry	**a se grăbi**	[a se grə'bi]
taxi, cab	**taxi** (n)	[ta'ksi]
taxi driver	**taximetrist** (m)	[taksime'trist]
by taxi	**cu taxiul**	[ku ta'ksjul]
taxi rank	**staţie** (f) **de taxiuri**	['staʦie de ta'ksjurⁱ]
to call a taxi	**a chema un taxi**	[a ke'ma un ta'ksi]
to take a taxi	**a lua un taxi**	[a lu'a un ta'ksi]
traffic	**circulaţie** (f) **pe stradă**	[ʧirku'laʦie pe 'stradə]
traffic jam	**ambuteiaj** (n)	[ambute'jaʒ]
rush hour	**oră** (f) **de vârf**	[orə de virf]
to park (vi)	**a se parca**	[a se par'ka]
to park (vt)	**a parca**	[a par'ka]
car park	**parcare** (f)	[par'kare]
underground, tube	**metrou** (n)	[me'trou]
station	**staţie** (f)	['staʦie]
to take the tube	**a merge cu metroul**	[a 'merdʒe ku me'troul]
train	**tren** (n)	[tren]
train station	**gară** (f)	['garə]

82. Sightseeing

monument	**monument** (n)	[monu'ment]
fortress	**cetate** (f)	[ʧe'tate]
palace	**palat** (n)	[pa'lat]
castle	**castel** (n)	[kas'tel]
tower	**turn** (n)	[turn]
mausoleum	**mausoleu** (n)	[mawzo'leu]
architecture	**arhitectură** (f)	[arhitek'turə]
medieval (adj)	**medieval**	[medie'val]
ancient (adj)	**vechi**	[vekⁱ]
national (adj)	**naţional**	[naʦio'nal]
famous (monument, etc.)	**cunoscut**	[kunos'kut]
tourist	**turist** (m)	[tu'rist]
guide (person)	**ghid** (m)	[gid]
excursion, sightseeing tour	**excursie** (f)	[eks'kursie]

| to show (vt) | a arăta | [a arǝ'ta] |
| to tell (vt) | a povesti | [a poves'ti] |

to find (vt)	a găsi	[a gǝ'si]
to get lost (lose one's way)	a se pierde	[a se 'pjerde]
map (e.g. underground ~)	schemă (f)	['skemǝ]
map (e.g. city ~)	plan (m)	[plan]

souvenir, gift	suvenir (n)	[suve'nir]
gift shop	magazin (n) de suveniruri	[maga'zin de suve'nirurʲ]
to take pictures	a fotografia	[a fotografi'ja]
to have one's picture taken	a se fotografia	[a se fotografi'ja]

83. Shopping

to buy (purchase)	a cumpăra	[a kumpǝ'ra]
shopping	cumpărătură (f)	[kumpǝrǝ'turǝ]
to go shopping	a face cumpărături	[a 'fatʃe kumpǝrǝ'turʲ]
shopping	shopping (n)	['ʃoping]

| to be open (ab. shop) | a fi deschis | [a fi des'kis] |
| to be closed | a se închide | [a se in'kide] |

footwear, shoes	încălțăminte (f)	[inkǝltsǝ'minte]
clothes, clothing	haine (f pl)	['hajne]
cosmetics	cosmetică (f)	[kos'metikǝ]
food products	produse (n pl)	[pro'duse]
gift, present	cadou (n)	[ka'dou]

| shop assistant (masc.) | vânzător (m) | [vinzǝ'tor] |
| shop assistant (fem.) | vânzătoare (f) | [vinzǝto'are] |

cash desk	casă (f)	['kasǝ]
mirror	oglindă (f)	[og'lindǝ]
counter (shop ~)	tejghea (f)	[teʒ'gʲa]
fitting room	cabină (f) de probă	[ka'binǝ de 'probǝ]

to try on	a proba	[a pro'ba]
to fit (ab. dress, etc.)	a veni	[a ve'ni]
to fancy (vt)	a plăcea	[a plǝ'tʃa]

price	preț (n)	[prets]
price tag	indicator (n) de prețuri	[indika'tor de 'pretsurʲ]
to cost (vt)	a costa	[a kos'ta]
How much?	Cât?	[kit]
discount	reducere (f)	[re'dutʃere]

inexpensive (adj)	ieftin	['jeftin]
cheap (adj)	ieftin	['jeftin]
expensive (adj)	scump	[skump]
It's expensive	E scump	[e skump]

| hire (n) | închiriere (f) | [inkiri'ere] |
| to hire (~ a dinner jacket) | a lua în chirie | [a lu'a in ki'rie] |

| credit (trade credit) | credit (n) | ['kredit] |
| on credit (adv) | în credit | [in 'kredit] |

84. Money

money	bani (m pl)	[ban']
currency exchange	schimb (n)	[skimb]
exchange rate	curs (n)	[kurs]
cashpoint	bancomat (n)	[banko'mat]
coin	monedă (f)	[mo'nedə]

| dollar | dolar (m) | [do'lar] |
| euro | euro (m) | ['euro] |

lira	liră (f)	['lirə]
Deutschmark	marcă (f)	['markə]
franc	franc (m)	[frank]
pound sterling	liră (f) sterlină	['lirə ster'linə]
yen	yen (f)	['jen]

debt	datorie (f)	[dato'rie]
debtor	datornic (m)	[da'tornik]
to lend (money)	a da cu împrumut	[a da ku impru'mut]
to borrow (vi, vt)	a lua cu împrumut	[a lu'a ku impru'mut]

bank	bancă (f)	['bankə]
account	cont (n)	[kont]
to deposit into the account	a pune în cont	[a 'pune in 'kont]
to withdraw (vt)	a scoate din cont	[a sko'ate din kont]

credit card	carte (f) de credit	['karte de 'kredit]
cash	numerar (n)	[nume'rar]
cheque	cec (n)	[tʃek]
to write a cheque	a scrie un cec	[a 'skrie un tʃek]
chequebook	carte (f) de cecuri	['karte de 'tʃekur']

wallet	portvizit (n)	[portvi'zit]
purse	portofel (n)	[porto'fel]
safe	seif (n)	['sejf]

heir	moştenitor (m)	[moʃteni'tor]
inheritance	moştenire (f)	[moʃte'nire]
fortune (wealth)	avere (f)	[a'vere]

lease	arendă (f)	[a'rendə]
rent (money)	chirie (f)	[ki'rie]
to rent (sth from sb)	a închiria	[a inkiri'ja]

price	preţ (n)	[prets]
cost	valoare (f)	[valo'are]
sum	sumă (f)	['sumə]

| to spend (vt) | a cheltui | [a keltu'i] |
| expenses | cheltuieli (f pl) | [keltu'el'] |

to economize (vi, vt)	a economisi	[a ekonomi'si]
economical	econom	[eko'nom]

to pay (vi, vt)	a plăti	[a plə'ti]
payment	plată (f)	['platə]
change (give the ~)	rest (n)	[rest]

tax	impozit (n)	[im'pozit]
fine	amendă (f)	[a'mendə]
to fine (vt)	a amenda	[a amen'da]

85. Post. Postal service

post office	poştă (f)	['poʃtə]
post (letters, etc.)	corespondenţă (f)	[korespon'dentsə]
postman	poştaş (m)	[poʃ'taʃ]
opening hours	ore (f pl) de lucru	['ore de 'lukru]

letter	scrisoare (f)	[skriso'are]
registered letter	scrisoare (f) recomandată	[skriso'are rekoman'datə]
postcard	carte (f) poştală	['karte poʃ'talə]
telegram	telegramă (f)	[tele'gramə]
parcel	colet (n)	[ko'let]
money transfer	mandat (n) poştal	[man'dat poʃ'tal]

to receive (vt)	a primi	[a pri'mi]
to send (vt)	a expedia	[a ekspedi'ja]
sending	expediere (f)	[ekspe'djere]

address	adresă (f)	[a'dresə]
postcode	cod (n) poştal	[kod poʃ'tal]
sender	expeditor (m)	[ekspedi'tor]
receiver	destinatar (m)	[destina'tar]

name (first name)	prenume (n)	[pre'nume]
surname (last name)	nume (n)	['nume]

postage rate	tarif (n)	[ta'rif]
standard (adj)	normal	[nor'mal]
economical (adj)	econom	[eko'nom]

weight	greutate (f)	[greu'tate]
to weigh (~ letters)	a cântări	[a kıntə'ri]
envelope	plic (n)	[plik]
postage stamp	timbru (n)	['timbru]
to stamp an envelope	a lipi timbrul	[a li'pi 'timbrul]

Dwelling. House. Home

86. House. Dwelling

house	**casă** (f)	['kasə]
at home (adv)	**acasă**	[a'kasə]
yard	**curte** (f)	['kurte]
fence (iron ~)	**gard** (n)	[gard]
brick (n)	**cărămidă** (f)	[kərə'midə]
brick (as adj)	**de, din cărămidă**	[de, din kərə'midə]
stone (n)	**piatră** (f)	['pjatrə]
stone (as adj)	**de, din piatră**	[de, din 'pjatrə]
concrete (n)	**beton** (n)	[be'ton]
concrete (as adj)	**de, din beton**	[de, din be'ton]
new (new-built)	**nou**	['nou]
old (adj)	**vechi**	[vekʲ]
decrepit (house)	**vechi**	[vekʲ]
modern (adj)	**contemporan**	[kontempo'ran]
multistorey (adj)	**cu multe etaje**	[ku 'multe e'taʒe]
tall (~ building)	**înalt**	[i'nalt]
floor, storey	**etaj** (n)	[e'taʒ]
single-storey (adj)	**cu un singur etaj**	[ku un 'singur e'taʒ]
ground floor	**etajul** (n) **de jos**	[e'taʒul de ʒos]
top floor	**etajul** (n) **de sus**	[e'taʒul de sus]
roof	**acoperiş** (n)	[akope'riʃ]
chimney	**tub** (n)	[tub]
roof tiles	**ţiglă** (f)	['tsiglə]
tiled (adj)	**de, din ţiglă**	[de, din 'tsiglə]
loft (attic)	**mansardă** (f)	[man'sardə]
window	**fereastră** (f)	[fe'rʲastrə]
glass	**sticlă** (f)	['stiklə]
window ledge	**pervaz** (n)	[per'vaz]
shutters	**oblon** (n) **la fereastră**	[o'blon la fe'rʲastrə]
wall	**perete** (m)	[pe'rete]
balcony	**balcon** (n)	[bal'kon]
downpipe	**burlan** (n)	[bur'lan]
upstairs (to be ~)	**deasupra**	[dʲa'supra]
to go upstairs	**a urca**	[a ur'ka]
to come down (the stairs)	**a coborî**	[a kobo'ri]
to move (to new premises)	**a se muta**	[a se mu'ta]

87. House. Entrance. Lift

entrance	intrare (f)	[in'trare]
stairs (stairway)	scară (f)	['skarə]
steps	trepte (f pl)	['trepte]
banisters	balustradă (f)	[balu'stradə]
lobby (hotel ~)	hol (n)	[hol]

postbox	cutie (f) poştală	[ku'tie poʃ'talə]
waste bin	ladă (f) de gunoi	['ladə de gu'noj]
refuse chute	conductă (f) de gunoi	[kon'duktə de gu'noj]

lift	lift (n)	[lift]
goods lift	ascensor (n) de marfă	[astʃen'sor de 'marfə]
lift cage	cabină (f)	[ka'binə]
to take the lift	a merge cu liftul	[a 'merdʒe ku 'liftul]

flat	apartament (n)	[aparta'ment]
residents (~ of a building)	locatari (m pl)	[loka'tari]
neighbour (masc.)	vecin (m)	[ve'tʃin]
neighbour (fem.)	vecină (f)	[ve'tʃinə]
neighbours	vecini (m pl)	[ve'tʃini]

88. House. Electricity

electricity	electricitate (f)	[elektritʃi'tate]
light bulb	bec (n)	[bek]
switch	întrerupător (n)	[întrerupə'tor]
fuse (plug fuse)	siguranţă (f)	[sigu'rantsə]

cable, wire (electric ~)	cablu (n)	['kablu]
wiring	instalaţie (f) electrică	[insta'latsie e'lektrikə]
electricity meter	contor (n)	[kon'tor]
readings	indicaţie (f)	[indi'katsie]

89. House. Doors. Locks

door	uşă (f)	['uʃə]
gate (vehicle ~)	poartă (f)	[po'artə]
handle, doorknob	clanţă (f)	['klantsə]
to unlock (unbolt)	a descuia	[a desku'ja]
to open (vt)	a deschide	[a des'kide]
to close (vt)	a închide	[a i'nkide]

key	cheie (f)	['kee]
bunch (of keys)	legătură (f) de chei	[ləgə'turə de 'kej]
to creak (door, etc.)	a scârţâi	[a skirtsi'i]
creak	scârţâit (n)	[skirtsi'it]
hinge (door ~)	balama (f)	[bala'ma]
doormat	covoraş (n)	[kovo'raʃ]
door lock	încuietoare (f)	[inkueto'are]

83

keyhole	gaura (f) cheii	['gaura 'keij]
crossbar (sliding bar)	zăvor (n)	[zə'vor]
door latch	zăvor (n)	[zə'vor]
padlock	lacăt (n)	['lakət]

to ring (~ the door bell)	a suna	[a su'na]
ringing (sound)	sunet (n)	['sunet]
doorbell	sonerie (f)	[sone'rie]
doorbell button	buton (n)	[bu'ton]
knock (at the door)	bătaie (f)	[bə'tae]
to knock (vi)	a bate	[a 'bate]

code	cod (n)	[kod]
combination lock	lacăt (n) cu cod	['lakət ku kod]
intercom	interfon (n)	[inter'fon]
number (on the door)	număr (n)	['numər]
doorplate	placă (f)	['plakə]
peephole	vizor (f)	[vi'zor]

90. Country house

village	sat (n)	[sat]
vegetable garden	grădină (f) de zarzavat	[grə'dinə de zarza'vat]
fence	gard (n)	[gard]
picket fence	îngrăditură (f)	[ingrədi'turə]
wicket gate	portiță (f)	[por'titsə]

granary	hambar (n)	[ham'bar]
cellar	beci (n)	[betʃi]
shed (garden ~)	magazie (f)	[maga'zie]
water well	fântână (f)	[fin'tinə]

stove (wood-fired ~)	sobă (f)	['sobə]
to stoke the stove	a face focul	[a 'fatʃe 'fokul]
firewood	lemne (n pl)	['lemne]
log (firewood)	bucată (f) de lemn	[bu'katə de lemn]

veranda	verandă (f)	[ve'randə]
deck (terrace)	terasă (f)	[te'rasə]
stoop (front steps)	verandă (f)	[ve'randə]
swing (hanging seat)	scrânciob (n)	['skrintʃiob]

91. Villa. Mansion

country house	casă (f) în afara localității	['kasə in a'fara lokali'tətsij]
country-villa	vilă (f)	['vilə]
wing (~ of a building)	aripă (f)	[a'ripə]

garden	grădină (f)	[grə'dinə]
park	parc (n)	[park]
conservatory (greenhouse)	seră (f)	['serə]
to look after (garden, etc.)	a îngriji	[a ingri'ʒi]

swimming pool	**bazin** (n)	[ba'zin]
gym (home gym)	**sală** (f) **de sport**	['salə de sport]
tennis court	**teren** (n) **de tenis**	[te'ren de 'tenis]
home theater (room)	**cinematograf** (n)	[tʃinemato'graf]
garage	**garaj** (n)	[ga'raʒ]
private property	**proprietate** (f) **privată**	[proprie'tate pri'vatə]
private land	**proprietate** (f) **privată**	[proprie'tate pri'vatə]
warning (caution)	**avertizare** (f)	[averti'zare]
warning sign	**avertisment** (n)	[avertis'ment]
security	**pază** (f)	['pazə]
security guard	**paznic** (m)	['paznik]
burglar alarm	**alarmă** (f)	[a'larmə]

92. Castle. Palace

castle	**castel** (n)	[kas'tel]
palace	**palat** (n)	[pa'lat]
fortress	**cetate** (f)	[tʃe'tate]
wall (round castle)	**zid** (n)	[zid]
tower	**turn** (n)	[turn]
keep, donjon	**turnul** (n) **principal**	['turnul printʃi'pal]
portcullis	**porți** (f pl) **rulante**	['portsi ru'lante]
subterranean passage	**subsol** (n)	[sub'sol]
moat	**şanț** (n)	[ʃants]
chain	**lanț** (n)	[lants]
arrow loop	**meterez** (n)	[mete'rez]
magnificent (adj)	**măreț**	[mə'rets]
majestic (adj)	**maiestuos**	[maestu'os]
impregnable (adj)	**de necucerit**	[de nekutʃe'rit]
medieval (adj)	**medieval**	[medie'val]

93. Flat

flat	**apartament** (n)	[aparta'ment]
room	**cameră** (f)	['kamerə]
bedroom	**dormitor** (n)	[dormi'tor]
dining room	**sufragerie** (f)	[sufradʒe'rie]
living room	**salon** (n)	[sa'lon]
study (home office)	**cabinet** (n)	[kabi'net]
entry room	**antreu** (n)	[an'treu]
bathroom	**baie** (f)	['bae]
water closet	**toaletă** (f)	[toa'letə]
ceiling	**pod** (n)	[pod]
floor	**podea** (f)	[po'dʲa]
corner	**colț** (n)	[kolts]

94. Flat. Cleaning

to clean (vi, vt)	a face ordine	[a 'fatʃe 'ordine]
to put away (to stow)	a strânge	[a 'strindʒe]
dust	praf (n)	[praf]
dusty (adj)	prăfuit	[prəfu'it]
to dust (vt)	a şterge praful	[a 'ʃterdʒe 'praful]
vacuum cleaner	aspirator (n)	[aspira'tor]
to vacuum (vt)	a da cu aspiratorul	[a da ku aspira'torul]

to sweep (vi, vt)	a mătura	[a mətu'ra]
sweepings	gunoi (n)	[gu'noj]
order	ordine (f)	['ordine]
disorder, mess	dezordine (f)	[de'zordine]

mop	teu (n)	['teu]
duster	cârpă (f)	['kirpə]
short broom	mătură (f)	['məturə]
dustpan	făraş (n)	[fə'raʃ]

95. Furniture. Interior

furniture	mobilă (f)	['mobilə]
table	masă (f)	['masə]
chair	scaun (n)	['skaun]
bed	pat (n)	[pat]
sofa, settee	divan (n)	[di'van]
armchair	fotoliu (n)	[fo'tolju]

bookcase	dulap (n) de cărţi	[du'lap de kərts]
shelf	raft (n)	[raft]

wardrobe	dulap (n) de haine	[du'lap de 'hajne]
coat rack (wall-mounted ~)	cuier (n) perete	[ku'jer pe'rete]
coat stand	cuier (n) pom	[ku'jer pom]

chest of drawers	comodă (f)	[ko'modə]
coffee table	măsuţă (f)	[mə'sutsə]

mirror	oglindă (f)	[og'lində]
carpet	covor (n)	[ko'vor]
small carpet	carpetă (f)	[kar'petə]

fireplace	şemineu (n)	[ʃəmi'neu]
candle	lumânare (f)	[lumi'nare]
candlestick	sfeşnic (n)	['sfeʃnik]

drapes	draperii (f pl)	[drape'rij]
wallpaper	tapet (n)	[ta'pet]
blinds (jalousie)	jaluzele (f pl)	[ʒalu'zele]

table lamp	lampă (f) de birou	['lampə de bi'rou]
wall lamp (sconce)	lampă (f)	['lampə]

standard lamp	lampă (f) cu picior	['lampə ku pi'tʃior]
chandelier	lustră (f)	['lustrə]

leg (of a chair, table)	picior (n)	[pi'tʃior]
armrest	braţ (n) la fotoliu	['braʦ la fo'tolju]
back (backrest)	spătar (n)	[spə'tar]
drawer	sertar (n)	[ser'tar]

96. Bedding

bedclothes	lenjerie (f)	[lenʒe'rie]
pillow	pernă (f)	['pernə]
pillowslip	faţă (f) de pernă	['faʦə de 'pernə]
duvet	plapumă (f)	['plapumə]
sheet	cearşaf (n)	[tʃar'ʃaf]
bedspread	pătură (f)	[pəturə]

97. Kitchen

kitchen	bucătărie (f)	[bukətə'rie]
gas	gaz (n)	[gaz]
gas cooker	aragaz (n)	[ara'gaz]
electric cooker	plită (f) electrică	['plitə e'lektrikə]
oven	cuptor (n)	[kup'tor]
microwave oven	cuptor (n) cu microunde	[kup'tor ku mikro'unde]

refrigerator	frigider (n)	[fridʒi'der]
freezer	congelator (n)	[kondʒela'tor]
dishwasher	maşină (f) de spălat vase	[ma'ʃinə de spə'lat 'vase]

mincer	maşină (f) de tocat carne	[ma'ʃinə de to'kat 'karne]
juicer	storcător (n)	[storkə'tor]
toaster	prăjitor (n) de pâine	[prəʒi'tor de 'pine]
mixer	mixer (n)	['mikser]

coffee machine	fierbător (n) de cafea	[fierbə'tor de ka'fʲa]
coffee pot	ibric (n)	[i'brik]
coffee grinder	râşniţă (f) de cafea	['riʃniʦə de ka'fʲa]

kettle	ceainic (n)	['tʃajnik]
teapot	ceainic (n)	['tʃajnik]
lid	capac (n)	[ka'pak]
tea strainer	strecurătoare (f)	[strekurəto'are]

spoon	lingură (f)	['lingurə]
teaspoon	linguriţă (f) de ceai	[lingu'riʦə de tʃaj]
soup spoon	lingură (f)	['lingurə]
fork	furculiţă (f)	[furku'liʦə]
knife	cuţit (n)	[ku'ʦit]

tableware (dishes)	vase (n pl)	['vase]
plate (dinner ~)	farfurie (f)	[farfu'rie]

saucer	**farfurioară** (f)	[farfurio'arə]
shot glass	**păhărel** (n)	[pəhə'rel]
glass (tumbler)	**pahar** (n)	[pa'har]
cup	**ceaşcă** (f)	['tʃaʃkə]

sugar bowl	**zaharniţă** (f)	[za'harnitsə]
salt cellar	**solniţă** (f)	['solnitsə]
pepper pot	**piperniţă** (f)	[pi'pernitsə]
butter dish	**untieră** (f)	[un'tjerə]

stock pot (soup pot)	**cratiţă** (f)	['kratitsə]
frying pan (skillet)	**tigaie** (f)	[ti'gae]
ladle	**polonic** (n)	[polo'nik]
colander	**strecurătoare** (f)	[strekurəto'are]
tray (serving ~)	**tavă** (f)	['tavə]

bottle	**sticlă** (f)	['stiklə]
jar (glass)	**borcan** (n)	[bor'kan]
tin (can)	**cutie** (f)	[ku'tie]

bottle opener	**deschizător** (n) **de sticle**	[deskizə'tor de 'stikle]
tin opener	**deschizător** (n) **de conserve**	[deskizə'tor de kon'serve]
corkscrew	**tirbuşon** (n)	[tirbu'ʃon]
filter	**filtru** (n)	['filtru]
to filter (vt)	**a filtra**	[a fil'tra]

waste (food ~, etc.)	**gunoi** (n)	[gu'noj]
waste bin (kitchen ~)	**coş** (n) **de gunoi**	[koʃ de gu'noj]

98. Bathroom

bathroom	**baie** (f)	['bae]
water	**apă** (f)	['apə]
tap	**robinet** (n)	[robi'net]
hot water	**apă** (f) **fierbinte**	['apə fjer'binte]
cold water	**apă** (f) **rece**	['apə 'retʃe]

toothpaste	**pastă** (f) **de dinţi**	['pastə de dintsʲ]
to clean one's teeth	**a se spăla pe dinţi**	[a se spə'la pe dintsʲ]

to shave (vi)	**a se bărbieri**	[a se bərbie'ri]
shaving foam	**spumă** (f) **de ras**	['spumə de 'ras]
razor	**brici** (n)	['britʃi]

to wash (one's hands, etc.)	**a spăla**	[a spə'la]
to have a bath	**a se spăla**	[a se spə'la]
shower	**duş** (n)	[duʃ]
to have a shower	**a face duş**	[a 'fatʃe duʃ]

bath	**cadă** (f)	['kadə]
toilet (toilet bowl)	**closet** (n)	[klo'set]
sink (washbasin)	**chiuvetă** (f)	[kju'vetə]
soap	**săpun** (n)	[sə'pun]
soap dish	**săpunieră** (f)	[səpu'njerə]

sponge	burete (n)	[bu'rete]
shampoo	şampon (n)	[ʃam'pon]
towel	prosop (n)	[pro'sop]
bathrobe	halat (n)	[ha'lat]

laundry (laundering)	spălat (n)	[spə'lat]
washing machine	maşină (f) de spălat	[ma'ʃinə de spə'lat]
to do the laundry	a spăla haine	[a spə'la 'hajne]
washing powder	detergent (n)	[deter'dʒent]

99. Household appliances

TV, telly	televizor (n)	[televi'zor]
tape recorder	casetofon (n)	[kaseto'fon]
video	videomagnetofon (n)	[videomagneto'fon]
radio	aparat (n) de radio	[apa'rat de 'radio]
player (CD, MP3, etc.)	CD player (n)	[si'di 'pleer]

video projector	proiector (n) video	[proek'tor 'video]
home cinema	sistem (n) home cinema	[sis'tem 'houm 'sinema]
DVD player	DVD-player (n)	[divi'di 'pleer]
amplifier	amplificator (n)	[amplifi'kator]
video game console	consolă (f) de jocuri	[kon'solə de 'ʒokurʲ]

video camera	cameră (f) video	['kamerə 'video]
camera (photo)	aparat (n) foto	[apa'rat 'foto]
digital camera	aparat (n) foto digital	[apa'rat 'foto didʒi'tal]

vacuum cleaner	aspirator (n)	[aspira'tor]
iron (e.g. steam ~)	fier (n) de călcat	[fier de kəl'kat]
ironing board	masă (f) de călcat	['masə de kəl'kat]

telephone	telefon (n)	[tele'fon]
mobile phone	telefon (n) mobil	[tele'fon mo'bil]
typewriter	maşină (f) de scris	[ma'ʃinə de skris]
sewing machine	maşină (f) de cusut	[ma'ʃine de ku'sut]

microphone	microfon (n)	[mikro'fon]
headphones	căşti (f pl)	[kəʃtʲ]
remote control (TV)	telecomandă (f)	[teleko'mandə]

CD, compact disc	CD (n)	[si'di]
cassette, tape	casetă (f)	[ka'setə]
vinyl record	placă (f)	['plakə]

100. Repairs. Renovation

renovations	reparaţie (f)	[repa'ratsie]
to renovate (vt)	a face reparaţie	[a 'fatʃe repa'ratsie]
to repair, to fix (vt)	a repara	[a repa'ra]
to put in order	a pune în ordine	[a 'pune in 'ordine]
to redo (do again)	a reface	[a re'fatʃe]

paint	vopsea (f)	[vop'sʲa]
to paint (~ a wall)	a vopsi	[a vop'si]
house painter	zugrav (m)	[zu'grav]
paintbrush	pensulă (f)	['pensulə]

| whitewash | var (n) | [var] |
| to whitewash (vt) | a vărui | [a vəru'i] |

wallpaper	tapet (n)	[ta'pet]
to wallpaper (vt)	a tapeta	[a tape'ta]
varnish	lac (n)	[lak]
to varnish (vt)	a lăcui	[a ləku'i]

101. Plumbing

water	apă (f)	['apə]
hot water	apă (f) fierbinte	['apə fjer'binte]
cold water	apă (f) rece	['apə 'retʃe]
tap	robinet (n)	[robi'net]

drop (of water)	picătură (f)	[pikə'turə]
to drip (vi)	a picura	[a piku'ra]
to leak (ab. pipe)	a curge	[a 'kurdʒe]
leak (pipe ~)	scurgere (f)	['skurdʒere]
puddle	baltă (f)	['baltə]

pipe	ţeavă (f)	['tsʲavə]
valve (e.g., ball ~)	ventil (n)	[ven'til]
to be clogged up	a se înfunda	[a se infun'da]

tools	instrumente (n pl)	[instru'mente]
adjustable spanner	cheie (f) reglabilă	['kee re'glabilə]
to unscrew (lid, filter, etc.)	a deşuruba	[a deʃuru'ba]
to screw (tighten)	a înşuruba	[a inʃuru'ba]

to unclog (vt)	a curăţa	[a kurə'tsa]
plumber	instalator (m)	[instala'tor]
basement	subsol (n)	[sub'sol]
sewerage (system)	canalizare (f)	[kanali'zare]

102. Fire. Conflagration

fire (accident)	foc (n)	[fok]
flame	flacără (f)	['flakərə]
spark	scânteie (f)	[skin'tee]
smoke (from fire)	fum (n)	[fum]
torch (flaming stick)	făclie (f)	[fək'lie]
campfire	foc (n)	[fok]

petrol	benzină (f)	[ben'zinə]
paraffin	petrol (n)	[pe'trol]
flammable (adj)	inflamabil	[infla'mabil]

explosive (adj)	**explozibil**	[eksplo'zibil]
NO SMOKING	**NU FUMAŢI!**	[nu fu'mats]
safety	**siguranţă** (f)	[sigu'rantsə]
danger	**pericol** (n)	[pe'rikol]
dangerous (adj)	**periculos**	[periku'los]
to catch fire	**a lua foc**	[a lu'a 'fok]
explosion	**explozie** (f)	[eks'plozie]
to set fire	**a incendia**	[a intʃendi'a]
arsonist	**incendiator** (m)	[intʃendia'tor]
arson	**incendiere** (f)	[intʃen'djere]
to blaze (vi)	**a arde cu flăcări mari**	[a 'arde ku fləkə'ri 'mari]
to burn (be on fire)	**a arde**	[a 'arde]
to burn down	**a arde din temelie**	[a 'arde din teme'lie]
firefighter, fireman	**pompier** (m)	[pom'pjer]
fire engine	**maşină** (f) **de pompieri**	[ma'ʃinə de pom'pjeri]
fire brigade	**echipă** (f) **de pompieri**	[ekipə de pom'pjeri]
fire engine ladder	**scară** (f) **de incendiu**	['skarə de in'tʃendju]
fire hose	**furtun** (n)	[fur'tun]
fire extinguisher	**stingător** (n)	[stingə'tor]
helmet	**cască** (f)	['kaskə]
siren	**sirenă** (f)	[si'renə]
to cry (for help)	**a striga**	[a stri'ga]
to call for help	**a chema în ajutor**	[a ke'ma in aʒu'tor]
rescuer	**salvator** (m)	[salva'tor]
to rescue (vt)	**a salva**	[a sal'va]
to arrive (vi)	**a veni**	[a ve'ni]
to extinguish (vt)	**a stinge**	[a 'stindʒe]
water	**apă** (f)	['apə]
sand	**nisip** (n)	[ni'sip]
ruins (destruction)	**ruine** (f pl)	[ru'ine]
to collapse (building, etc.)	**a se prăbuşi**	[a se prəbu'ʃi]
to fall down (vi)	**a se dărâma**	[a se dəri'ma]
to cave in (ceiling, floor)	**a se surpa**	[a se sur'pa]
piece of debris	**dărâmătură** (f)	[dərəmə'turə]
ash	**scrum** (n)	[skrum]
to suffocate (die)	**a se sufoca**	[a se sufo'ka]
to be killed (perish)	**a deceda**	[a detʃe'da]

HUMAN ACTIVITIES

Job. Business. Part 1

103. Office. Working in the office

office (company ~)	**oficiu** (n)	[o'fitʃiu]
office (director's ~)	**cabinet** (n)	[kabi'net]
reception desk	**recepţie** (f)	[re'tʃeptsie]
secretary	**secretar** (m)	[sekre'tar]
director	**director** (m)	[di'rektor]
manager	**manager** (m)	['menedʒə]
accountant	**contabil** (f)	[kon'tabil]
employee	**colaborator** (m)	[kolabora'tor]
furniture	**mobilă** (f)	['mobilə]
desk	**masă** (f)	['masə]
desk chair	**fotoliu** (n)	[fo'tolju]
drawer unit	**noptieră** (f)	[nop'tjerə]
coat stand	**cuier** (n) **pom**	[ku'jer pom]
computer	**calculator** (n)	[kalkula'tor]
printer	**imprimantă** (f)	[impri'mantə]
fax machine	**fax** (n)	[faks]
photocopier	**copiator** (n)	[kopia'tor]
paper	**hârtie** (f)	[hir'tie]
office supplies	**rechizite** (n pl) **de birou**	[reki'zite de bi'rou]
mouse mat	**pad** (n)	[pad], [pəd]
sheet of paper	**foaie** (f)	[fo'ae]
binder	**mapă** (f)	['mapə]
catalogue	**catalog** (n)	[kata'log]
phone directory	**îndrumar** (n)	[indru'mar]
documentation	**documentaţie** (f)	[dokumen'tatsie]
brochure (e.g. 12 pages ~)	**broşură** (f)	[bro'ʃurə]
leaflet (promotional ~)	**foaie** (f)	[fo'ae]
sample	**model** (n)	[mo'del]
training meeting	**trening** (n)	['trening]
meeting (of managers)	**şedinţă** (f)	[ʃe'dintsə]
lunch time	**pauză** (f) **de prânz**	['pauze de 'prinz]
to make a copy	**a face copie**	[a 'fatʃe 'kopie]
to make multiple copies	**a multiplica**	[a multipli'ka]
to receive a fax	**a primi fax**	[a pri'mi 'faks]
to send a fax	**a trimite fax**	[a tri'mite 'faks]
to call (by phone)	**a suna**	[a su'na]

| to answer (vt) | a răspunde | [a rəs'punde] |
| to put through | a face legătura | [a 'faʧe legə'tura] |

to arrange, to set up	a stabili	[a stabi'li]
to demonstrate (vt)	a demonstra	[a demonst'ra]
to be absent	a lipsi	[a lip'si]
absence	lipsă (f)	['lipsə]

104. Business processes. Part 1

occupation	ocupație (f)	[oku'patsie]
firm	firmă (f)	['firmə]
company	companie (f)	[kompa'nie]
corporation	corporație (f)	[korpo'ratsie]
enterprise	întreprindere (f)	[intre'prindere]
agency	agenție (f)	[adʒen'tsie]

agreement (contract)	acord (n)	[a'kord]
contract	contract (n)	[kon'trakt]
deal	afacere (f)	[a'faʧere]
order (to place an ~)	comandă (f)	[ko'mandə]
terms (of the contract)	condiție (f)	[kon'ditsie]

wholesale (adv)	en-gros	[an'gro]
wholesale (adj)	en-gros	[an'gro]
wholesale (n)	vânzare (f) en-gros	[vin'zare an'gro]
retail (adj)	cu bucata	[ku bu'kata]
retail (n)	vânzare (f) cu bucata	[vin'zare ku bu'kata]

competitor	concurent (m)	[konku'rent]
competition	concurență (f)	[konku'rentsə]
to compete (vi)	a concura	[a konku'ra]

| partner (associate) | partener (m) | [parte'ner] |
| partnership | parteneriat (n) | [parteneri'at] |

crisis	criză (f)	['krizə]
bankruptcy	faliment (n)	[fali'ment]
to go bankrupt	a da faliment	[a da fali'ment]
difficulty	dificultate (f)	[difikul'tate]
problem	problemă (f)	[pro'blemə]
catastrophe	catastrofă (f)	[katas'trofə]

economy	economie (f)	[ekono'mie]
economic (~ growth)	economic	[eko'nomik]
economic recession	scădere (f) economică	[skə'dere eko'nomikə]

| goal (aim) | scop (n) | [skop] |
| task | obiectiv (n) | [objek'tiv] |

to trade (vi)	a face comerț	[a 'faʧe ko'merts]
network (distribution ~)	rețea (f)	[re'tsia]
inventory (stock)	depozit (n)	[de'pozit]
range (assortment)	sortiment (n)	[sorti'ment]

leader (leading company)	**lider** (m)	['lider]
large (~ company)	**mare**	['mare]
monopoly	**monopol** (n)	[mono'pol]

theory	**teorie** (f)	[teo'rie]
practice	**practică** (f)	['praktikə]
experience (in my ~)	**experiență** (f)	[ekspe'rjentsə]
trend (tendency)	**tendință** (f)	[ten'dintsə]
development	**dezvoltare** (f)	[dezvol'tare]

105. Business processes. Part 2

profit (foregone ~)	**profit** (n)	[pro'fit]
profitable (~ deal)	**profitabil**	[profi'tabil]

delegation (group)	**delegație** (f)	[dele'gatsie]
salary	**salariu** (n)	[sa'larju]
to correct (an error)	**a corecta**	[a korek'ta]
business trip	**deplasare** (f)	[depla'sare]
commission	**comisie** (f)	[ko'misie]

to control (vt)	**a controla**	[a kontro'la]
conference	**conferință** (f)	[konfe'rintsə]
licence	**licență** (f)	[li'tʃentsə]
reliable (~ partner)	**de încredere**	[de in'kredere]

initiative (undertaking)	**început** (n)	[intʃe'put]
norm (standard)	**normă** (f)	['normə]
circumstance	**circumstanță** (f)	[tʃirkum'stantsə]
duty (of an employee)	**obligație** (f)	[obli'gatsie]

organization (company)	**organizație** (f)	[organi'zatsie]
organization (process)	**organizare** (f)	[organi'zare]
organized (adj)	**organizat**	[organi'zat]
cancellation	**contramandare** (f)	[kontraman'dare]
to cancel (call off)	**a anula**	[a anu'la]
report (official ~)	**raport** (n)	[ra'port]

patent	**brevet** (f)	[bre'vet]
to patent (obtain patent)	**a breveta**	[a breve'ta]
to plan (vt)	**a planifica**	[a planifi'ka]

bonus (money)	**primă** (f)	['primə]
professional (adj)	**profesional**	[profesio'nal]
procedure	**procedură** (f)	[protʃe'durə]

to examine (contract, etc.)	**a examina**	[a ekzami'na]
calculation	**calcul** (n)	['kalkul]
reputation	**reputație** (f)	[repu'tatsie]
risk	**risc** (n)	[risk]

to manage, to run	**a conduce**	[a kon'dutʃe]
information (report)	**informații** (f pl)	[infor'matsij]
property	**proprietate** (f)	[proprie'tate]

union	alianță (f)	[ali'antsə]
life insurance	asigurare (f) de viață	[asigu'rare de 'vjatsə]
to insure (vt)	a asigura	[a asigu'ra]
insurance	asigurare (f)	[asigu'rare]

auction (~ sale)	licitație (f)	[litʃi'tatsie]
to notify (inform)	a înștiința	[a inʃtiin'tsa]
management (process)	conducere (f)	[kon'dutʃere]
service (~ industry)	serviciu (n)	[ser'vitʃiu]

forum	for (n)	[for]
to function (vi)	a funcționa	[a funktsio'na]
stage (phase)	etapă (f)	[e'tapə]
legal (~ services)	juridic	[ʒu'ridik]
lawyer (legal advisor)	jurist (m)	[ʒu'rist]

106. Production. Works

plant	uzină (f)	[u'zinə]
factory	fabrică (f)	['fabrikə]
workshop	atelier (n)	[ate'ljer]
works, production site	fabricație (f)	[fabri'katsie]

industry (manufacturing)	industrie (f)	[in'dustrie]
industrial (adj)	industrial	[industri'al]
heavy industry	industrie (f) grea	[in'dustrie grʲa]
light industry	industrie (f) ușoară	[in'dustrie uʃo'arə]

products	producție (f)	[pro'duktsie]
to produce (vt)	a produce	[a pro'dutʃe]
raw materials	materie (f) primă	[ma'terie 'primə]

foreman (construction ~)	șef (m) de brigadă	[ʃef de bri'gadə]
workers team (crew)	brigadă (f)	[bri'gadə]
worker	muncitor (m)	[muntʃi'tor]

working day	zi (f) lucrătoare	['zi lukrəto'are]
pause (rest break)	pauză (f)	['pauzə]
meeting	adunare (f)	[adu'nare]
to discuss (vt)	a discuta	[a disku'ta]

plan	plan (n)	[plan]
to fulfil the plan	a îndeplini planul	[a indepli'ni 'planul]
rate of output	normă (f)	['normə]
quality	calitate (f)	[kali'tate]
control (checking)	control (n)	[kon'trol]
quality control	controlul (n) calității	[kon'trolul kali'tətsij]

workplace safety	protecția (f) muncii	[pro'tektsija 'muntʃij]
discipline	disciplină (f)	[distʃi'plinə]
violation (of safety rules, etc.)	încălcare (f)	[inkəl'kare]
to violate (rules)	a încălca	[a inkəl'ka]
strike	grevă (f)	['grevə]
striker	grevist (m)	[gre'vist]

to be on strike	a face grevă	[a 'fatʃe 'grevə]
trade union	sindicat (n)	[sindi'kat]

to invent (machine, etc.)	a inventa	[a inven'ta]
invention	invenție (f)	[in'ventsie]
research	cercetare (f)	[tʃertʃe'tare]
to improve (make better)	a îmbunătăți	[a imbunətə'tsi]
technology	tehnologie (f)	[tehnolo'dʒie]
technical drawing	plan (n)	[plan]

load, cargo	încărcătură (f)	[inkərkə'turə]
loader (person)	hamal (m)	[ha'mal]
to load (vehicle, etc.)	a încărca	[a inkər'ka]
loading (process)	încărcătură (f)	[inkərkə'turə]
to unload (vi, vt)	a descărca	[a deskər'ka]
unloading	descărcare (f)	[deskər'kare]

transport	transport (n)	[trans'port]
transport company	companie (f) de transport	[kompa'nie de trans'port]
to transport (vt)	a transporta	[a transpor'ta]

wagon	vagon (n) marfar	[va'gon mar'far]
tank (e.g., oil ~)	cisternă (f)	[tʃis'ternə]
lorry	autocamion (n)	[autoka'mjon]

machine tool	maşină-unealtă (f)	[ma'ʃinə u'nʲaltə]
mechanism	mecanism (n)	[meka'nizm]

industrial waste	deşeuri (n pl)	[de'ʃeurʲ]
packing (process)	ambalare (f)	[amba'lare]
to pack (vt)	a ambala	[a amba'la]

107. Contract. Agreement

contract	contract (n)	[kon'trakt]
agreement	contract (f)	[kon'trakt]
addendum	anexă (f)	[a'neksə]

to sign a contract	a încheia un contract	[a inke'ja un kon'trakt]
signature	semnătură (f)	[semnə'turə]
to sign (vt)	a semna	[a sem'na]
seal (stamp)	ştampilă (f)	[ʃtam'pilə]

subject of the contract	obiectul (n) contractului	[o'bjektul kon'traktuluj]
clause	paragraf (n)	[para'graf]
parties (in contract)	părți (f pl)	[pərtsʲ]
legal address	adresă (f) juridică	[a'dresə ʒu'ridikə]

to violate the contract	a încălca contractul	[a inkəl'ka kon'traktul]
commitment (obligation)	obligație (f)	[obli'gatsie]
responsibility	răspundere (f)	[rəs'pundere]
force majeure	forțe (f pl) majore	['fortse ma'ʒore]
dispute	dispută (f)	[dis'putə]
penalties	sancțiuni (f pl)	[sanktsi'unʲ]

108. Import & Export

import	**import** (n)	[im'port]
importer	**importator** (m)	[importa'tor]
to import (vt)	**a importa**	[a impor'ta]
import (as adj.)	**din import**	[din im'port]
exporter	**exportator** (m)	[eksporta'tor]
to export (vt)	**a exporta**	[a ekspor'ta]
goods (merchandise)	**marfă** (f)	['marfə]
consignment, lot	**lot** (n)	[lot]
weight	**greutate** (f)	[greu'tate]
volume	**volum** (n)	[vo'lum]
cubic metre	**metru** (m) **cub**	['metru 'kub]
manufacturer	**producător** (m)	[produkə'tor]
transport company	**companie** (f) **de transport**	[kompa'nie de trans'port]
container	**container** (m)	[kon'tajner]
border	**graniţă** (f)	['granitsə]
customs	**vamă** (f)	['vamə]
customs duty	**taxă** (f) **vamală**	['taksə va'malə]
customs officer	**vameş** (m)	['vameʃ]
smuggling	**contrabandă** (f)	[kontra'bandə]
contraband (smuggled goods)	**contrabandă** (f)	[kontra'bandə]

109. Finances

share, stock	**acţiune** (f)	[aktsi'une]
bond (certificate)	**obligaţie** (f)	[obli'gatsie]
promissory note	**poliţă** (f)	['politsə]
stock exchange	**bursă** (f)	['bursə]
stock price	**cursul** (n) **acţiunii**	['kursul aktsi'unij]
to go down (become cheaper)	**a se ieftini**	[a se efti'ni]
to go up (become more expensive)	**a se scumpi**	[a se skum'pi]
controlling interest	**pachet** (n) **de control**	[pa'ket de kon'trol]
investment	**investiţii** (f pl)	[inves'titsij]
to invest (vt)	**a investi**	[a inves'ti]
percent	**procent** (n)	[pro'tʃent]
interest (on investment)	**dobândă** (f)	[do'bɨndə]
profit	**profit** (n)	[pro'fit]
profitable (adj)	**profitabil**	[profi'tabil]
tax	**impozit** (n)	[im'pozit]
currency (foreign ~)	**valută** (f)	[va'lutə]

| national (adj) | naţional | [natsio'nal] |
| exchange (currency ~) | schimb (n) | [skimb] |

| accountant | contabil (m) | [kon'tabil] |
| accounting | contabilitate (f) | [kontabili'tate] |

bankruptcy	faliment (n)	[fali'ment]
collapse, ruin	faliment (n)	[fali'ment]
ruin	faliment (n)	[fali'ment]
to be ruined (financially)	a falimenta	[a falimen'ta]
inflation	inflaţie (f)	[in'flatsie]
devaluation	devalorizare (f)	[devalori'zare]

capital	capital (n)	[kapi'tal]
income	venit (n)	[ve'nit]
turnover	rotaţie (f)	[ro'tatsie]
resources	resurse (f pl)	[re'surse]
monetary resources	mijloace (n pl) băneşti	[miʒlo'atʃe bə'neʃtʲ]
to reduce (expenses)	a reduce	[a re'dutʃe]

110. Marketing

marketing	marketing (n)	['marketing]
market	piaţă (f)	['pjatsə]
market segment	segment (n) de piaţă	[seg'ment de 'pjatsə]
product	produs (n)	[pro'dus]
goods (merchandise)	marfă (f)	['marfə]

brand	marcă (f)	['markə]
trademark	marcă (f) comercială	['markə komertʃi'alə]
logotype	logotip (n)	[logo'tip]
logo	logo (m)	['logo]

demand	cerere (f)	['tʃerere]
supply	ofertă (f)	[o'fertə]
need	necesitate (f)	[netʃesi'tate]
consumer	consumator (m)	[konsu'mator]

analysis	analiză (f)	[ana'lizə]
to analyse (vt)	a analiza	[a anali'za]
positioning	poziţionare (f)	[pozitsio'nare]
to position (vt)	a poziţiona	[a pozitsio'na]

price	preţ (n)	[prets]
pricing policy	politica (f) preţurilor	[po'litika 'pretsurilor]
price formation	stabilirea (f) preţurilor	[stabi'lirʲa 'pretsurilor]

111. Advertising

advertising	reclamă (f)	[re'klamə]
to advertise (vt)	a face reclamă	[a 'fatʃe re'klamə]
budget	buget (n)	[bu'dʒet]

ad, advertisement	**reclamă** (f)	[re'klamə]
TV advertising	**publicitate** (f) **TV**	[publitʃi'tate te've]
radio advertising	**publicitate** (f) **radio**	[publitʃi'tate 'radio]
outdoor advertising	**reclamă** (f) **exterioară**	[re'klamə eksterio'arə]
mass medias	**mass-media** (f)	['mas 'media]
periodical (n)	**ediţie** (f) **periodică**	[e'ditsie peri'odikə]
image (public appearance)	**imagine** (f)	[i'madʒine]
slogan	**lozincă** (f)	[lo'zinkə]
motto (maxim)	**deviză** (f)	[de'vizə]
campaign	**campanie** (f)	[kam'panie]
advertising campaign	**campanie** (f) **publicitară**	[kam'panie publitʃi'tarə]
target group	**grup** (n) **ţintă**	[grup 'tsintə]
business card	**carte** (f) **de vizită**	['karte de 'vizitə]
leaflet (promotional ~)	**foaie** (f)	[fo'ae]
brochure (e.g. 12 pages ~)	**broşură** (f)	[bro'ʃurə]
pamphlet	**pliant** (n)	[pli'ant]
newsletter	**buletin** (n)	[bule'tin]
signboard (store sign, etc.)	**firmă** (f)	['firmə]
poster	**afiş** (n)	[a'fiʃ]
hoarding	**panou** (n)	[pa'nou]

112. Banking

bank	**bancă** (f)	['bankə]
branch (of a bank)	**sucursală** (f)	[sukur'salə]
consultant	**consultant** (m)	[konsul'tant]
manager (director)	**director** (m)	[di'rektor]
bank account	**cont** (n)	[kont]
account number	**numărul** (n) **contului**	['numərul 'kontuluj]
current account	**cont** (n) **curent**	[kont ku'rent]
deposit account	**cont** (n) **de acumulare**	[kont de akumu'lare]
to open an account	**a deschide un cont**	[a des'kide un kont]
to close the account	**a închide contul**	[a i'nkide 'kontul]
to deposit into the account	**a pune în cont**	[a 'pune in 'kont]
to withdraw (vt)	**a extrage din cont**	[a eks'tradʒe din kont]
deposit	**depozit** (n)	[de'pozit]
to make a deposit	**a depune**	[a de'pune]
wire transfer	**transfer** (n)	[trans'fer]
to wire, to transfer	**a transfera**	[a transfe'ra]
sum	**sumă** (f)	['sumə]
How much?	**Cât?**	[kit]
signature	**semnătură** (f)	[semnə'turə]
to sign (vt)	**a semna**	[a sem'na]

credit card	carte (f) de credit	['karte de 'kredit]
code (PIN code)	cod (n)	[kod]
credit card number	numărul (n) cărții de credit	['numərul kərtsij de 'kredit]
cashpoint	bancomat (n)	[banko'mat]

cheque	cec (n)	[tʃek]
to write a cheque	a scrie un cec	[a 'skrie un tʃek]
chequebook	carte (f) de cecuri	['karte de 'tʃekurɪ]

loan (bank ~)	credit (n)	['kredit]
to apply for a loan	a solicita un credit	[a solitʃi'ta pe 'kredit]
to get a loan	a lua pe credit	[a lu'a pe 'kredit]
to give a loan	a acorda credit	[a akor'da 'kredit]
guarantee	garanție (f)	[garan'tsie]

113. Telephone. Phone conversation

telephone	telefon (n)	[tele'fon]
mobile phone	telefon (n) mobil	[tele'fon mo'bil]
answerphone	răspuns (n) automat	[rəs'puns auto'mat]

| to call (by phone) | a suna, a telefona | [a su'na], [a tele'fona] |
| call, ring | apel (n), convorbire (f) | [a'pel], [konvor'bire] |

to dial a number	a forma un număr	[a for'ma un 'numər]
Hello!	Alo!	[a'lo]
to ask (vt)	a întreba	[a intre'ba]
to answer (vi, vt)	a răspunde	[a rəs'punde]

to hear (vt)	a auzi	[a au'zi]
well (adv)	bine	['bine]
not well (adv)	rău	['rəu]
noises (interference)	bruiaj (n)	[bru'jaʒ]
receiver	receptor (n)	[retʃep'tor]
to pick up (~ the phone)	a lua receptorul	[a lu'a retʃep'torul]
to hang up (~ the phone)	a pune receptorul	[a 'pune retʃep'torul]

busy (engaged)	ocupat	[oku'pat]
to ring (ab. phone)	a suna	[a su'na]
telephone book	carte (f) de telefon	['karte de tele'fon]

local (adj)	local	[lo'kal]
local call	apel (n) local	[a'pel lo'kal]
trunk (e.g. ~ call)	interurban	[interur'ban]
trunk call	apel (n) interurban	[a'pel interur'ban]
international (adj)	internațional	[internatsio'nal]
international call	apel (n) interna ional	[a'pel internatsio'nal]

114. Mobile telephone

| mobile phone | telefon (n) mobil | [tele'fon mo'bil] |
| display | ecran (n) | [e'kran] |

| button | **buton** (n) | [bu'ton] |
| SIM card | **cartelă** (f) **SIM** | [kar'telə 'sim] |

battery	**baterie** (f)	[bate'rie]
to be flat (battery)	**a se descărca**	[a se deskər'ka]
charger	**încărcător** (m)	[inkərkə'tor]

menu	**meniu** (n)	[me'nju]
settings	**setări** (f)	[se'tərʲ]
tune (melody)	**melodie** (f)	[melo'die]
to select (vt)	**a selecta**	[a selek'ta]

calculator	**calculator** (n)	[kalkula'tor]
voice mail	**răspuns** (n) **automat**	[rəs'puns auto'mat]
alarm clock	**ceas** (n) **deşteptător**	[tʃas deʃteptə'tor]
contacts	**carte** (f) **de telefoane**	['karte de telefo'ane]

| SMS (text message) | **SMS** (n) | [ese'mes] |
| subscriber | **abonat** (m) | [abo'nat] |

115. Stationery

| ballpoint pen | **stilou** (n) | [sti'lou] |
| fountain pen | **condei** (n) | [kon'dej] |

pencil	**creion** (n)	[kre'jon]
highlighter	**marcher** (n)	['marker]
felt-tip pen	**cariocă** (f)	[kari'okə]

| notepad | **carneţel** (n) | [karnə'tsəl] |
| diary | **agendă** (f) | [a'dʒendə] |

ruler	**riglă** (f)	['riglə]
calculator	**calculator** (f)	[kalkula'tor]
rubber	**radieră** (f)	[radi'erə]
drawing pin	**piuneză** (f)	[pju'nezə]
paper clip	**clamă** (f)	['klamə]

glue	**lipici** (n)	[li'pitʃi]
stapler	**capsator** (n)	[kapsa'tor]
hole punch	**perforator** (n)	[perfo'rator]
pencil sharpener	**ascuţitoare** (f)	[askutsito'are]

116. Various kinds of documents

account (report)	**raport** (n)	[ra'port]
agreement	**contract** (f)	[kon'trakt]
application form	**cerere** (f)	['tʃerere]
authentic (adj)	**autentic**	[au'tentik]
badge (identity tag)	**ecuson** (n)	[eku'son]
business card	**carte** (f) **de vizită**	['karte de 'vizitə]
certificate (~ of quality)	**certificat** (n)	[tʃertifi'kat]

cheque (e.g. draw a ~)	cec (n)	[tʃek]
bill (in restaurant)	notă (f) de plată	['notə de 'platə]
constitution	constituţie (f)	[konsti'tutsie]
contract (agreement)	acord (n)	[a'kord]
copy	copie (f)	['kopie]
copy (of a contract, etc.)	exemplar (n)	[egzem'plar]
customs declaration	declaraţie (f)	[dekla'ratsie]
document	act (n)	[akt]
driving licence	permis (n) de conducere	[per'mis de kon'dutʃere]
addendum	anexă (f)	[a'neksə]
form	anchetă (f)	[an'ketə]
ID card (e.g., warrant card)	legalizare (f)	[legali'zare]
inquiry (request)	solicitare (f)	[solitʃi'tare]
invitation card	invitaţie (f)	[invi'tatsie]
invoice	factură (f)	[fak'turə]
law	lege (f)	['ledʒe]
letter (mail)	scrisoare (f)	[skriso'are]
letterhead	formular (n)	[formu'lar]
list (of names, etc.)	listă (f)	['listə]
manuscript	manuscris (n)	[manu'skris]
newsletter	buletin (n)	[bule'tin]
note (short letter)	notă (f)	['notə]
pass (for worker, visitor)	autorizaţie (f)	[autori'zatsie]
passport	paşaport (n)	[paʃa'port]
permit	permis (n)	[per'mis]
curriculum vitae, CV	CV (n)	[si'vi]
debt note, IOU	recipisă (f)	[retʃi'pisə]
receipt (for purchase)	chitanţă (f)	[ki'tantsə]
till receipt	cec (n)	[tʃek]
report (mil.)	raport (n)	[ra'port]
to show (ID, etc.)	a prezenta	[a prezen'ta]
to sign (vt)	a semna	[a sem'na]
signature	semnătură (f)	[semnə'turə]
seal (stamp)	ştampilă (f)	[ʃtam'pilə]
text	text (n)	[tekst]
ticket (for entry)	bilet (n)	[bi'let]
to cross out	a tăia	[a tə'ja]
to fill in (~ a form)	a completa	[a komple'ta]
waybill (shipping invoice)	foaie (f) de însoţire	[fo'ae de inso'tsire]
will (testament)	testament (n)	[testa'ment]

117. Kinds of business

accounting services	servicii (n pl) de contabilitate	[ser'vitʃij de kontabili'tate]
advertising	reclamă (f)	[re'klamə]
advertising agency	agenţie (f) de reclamă	[adʒen'tsie de re'klamə]

| air-conditioners | ventilator (n) | [ventila'tor] |
| airline | companie (f) aeriană | [kompa'nie aeri'anə] |

alcoholic beverages	băuturi (f pl) alcoolice	[bəu'turi alko'olitʃe]
antiques (antique dealers)	anticariat (n)	[antikari'at]
art gallery (contemporary ~)	galerie (f)	[gale'rie]
audit services	servicii (n pl) de audit	[ser'vitʃij de au'dit]

banking industry	afacere (f) bancară	[a'fatʃere ba'nkarə]
beauty salon	salon (n) de frumusețe	[sa'lon de frumu'setse]
bookshop	librărie (f)	[librə'rie]
brewery	fabricarea (f) berii	[fabri'karia 'berij]
business centre	centru (n) de afaceri	['tʃentru de a'fatʃeri]
business school	şcoală (f) de afaceri	[ʃko'alə de a'fatʃeri]

casino	cazinou (n)	[kazi'nou]
chemist, pharmacy	farmacie (f)	[farma'tʃie]
cinema	cinematograf (n)	[tʃinemato'graf]
construction	construcție (f)	[kon'struktsie]
consulting	consulting (n)	[kon'salting]

dental clinic	stomatologie (f)	[stomatolo'dʒie]
design	design (n)	[di'zajn]
dry cleaners	curăţătorie (f) chimică	[kurəʦəto'rie 'kimikə]

employment agency	agenție (f) de cadre	[adʒen'tsie de 'kadre]
financial services	servicii (n pl) financiare	[ser'vitʃij finantʃi'are]
food products	produse (n pl) alimentare	[pro'duse alimen'tare]
furniture (e.g. house ~)	mobilă (f)	['mobilə]
clothing, garment	haine (f pl)	['hajne]
hotel	hotel (n)	[ho'tel]

ice-cream	îngheţată (f)	[inge'tsatə]
industry (manufacturing)	industrie (f)	[in'dustrie]
insurance	asigurare (f) medicală	[asigu'rare medi'kalə]
Internet	internet (n)	[inter'net]
investments (finance)	investiţii (f pl)	[inves'titsij]
jeweller	bijutier (m)	[biʒu'tjer]
jewellery	bijuterii (f pl)	[biʒute'rij]

laundry (shop)	spălătorie (f)	[spələto'rie]
legal adviser	servicii (n pl) juridice	[ser'vitʃij ʒu'riditʃe]
light industry	industrie (f) uşoară	[in'dustrie uʃo'arə]

magazine	revistă (f)	[re'vistə]
mail order selling	vânzare (f) după catalog	[vin'zare 'dupə kata'log]
medicine	medicină (f)	[medi'tʃinə]
museum	muzeu (n)	[mu'zeu]

news agency	birou (n) de informaţii	[bi'rou de infor'matsij]
newspaper	ziar (n)	[zjar]
nightclub	club (n) de noapte	['klub de no'apte]

oil (petroleum)	petrol (n)	[pe'trol]
courier services	curierat (n)	[kurie'rat]
pharmaceutics	farmaceutică (f)	[farmatʃe'utikə]

printing (industry)	**poligrafie** (f)	[poligra'fie]
pub	**bar** (n)	[bar]
publishing house	**editură** (f)	[edi'turə]
radio (~ station)	**radio** (n)	['radio]
real estate	**bunuri** (n pl) **imobiliare**	['bunurʲ imobili'are]
restaurant	**restaurant** (n)	[restau'rant]
security company	**agenție** (f) **de pază**	[aʤen'ʦie de 'pazə]
shop	**magazin** (n)	[maga'zin]
sport	**sport** (n)	[sport]
stock exchange	**bursă** (f)	['bursə]
supermarket	**supermarket** (n)	[super'market]
swimming pool (public ~)	**bazin** (n)	[ba'zin]
tailor shop	**atelier** (n)	[ate'ljer]
television	**televiziune** (f)	[televizi'une]
theatre	**teatru** (n)	[te'atru]
trade (commerce)	**comerț** (n)	[ko'merʦ]
transport companies	**transporturi** (n)	[trans'porturʲ]
travel	**turism** (n)	[tu'rism]
undertakers	**pompe** (f pl) **funebre**	['pompe fu'nebre]
veterinary surgeon	**veterinar** (m)	[veteri'nar]
warehouse	**depozit** (n)	[de'pozit]
waste collection	**transportarea** (f) **deşeurilor**	[transpor'tarʲa de'ʃeurilor]

Job. Business. Part 2

118. Show. Exhibition

exhibition, show	expoziție (f)	[ekspo'zitsie]
trade show	expoziție (f) de comerț	[ekspo'zitsie de ko'merts]
participation	participare (f)	[partitʃi'pare]
to participate (vi)	a participa	[a partitʃi'pa]
participant (exhibitor)	participant (m)	[partitʃi'pant]
director	director (m)	[di'rektor]
organizers' office	direcție (f)	[di'rektsie]
organizer	organizator (m)	[organiza'tor]
to organize (vt)	a organiza	[a organi'za]
participation form	cerere (f) de participare	['tʃerere de partitʃi'pare]
to fill in (vt)	a completa	[a komple'ta]
details	detalii (n pl)	[de'talij]
information	informație (f)	[infor'matsie]
price (cost, rate)	preț (n)	[prets]
including	inclusiv	[inklu'siv]
to include (vt)	a include	[a in'klude]
to pay (vi, vt)	a plăti	[a plə'ti]
registration fee	tarif (n) de înregistrare	[tarif de inredʒis'trare]
entrance	intrare (f)	[in'trare]
pavilion, hall	pavilion (n)	[pavili'on]
to register (vt)	a înscrie	[a in'skrie]
badge (identity tag)	ecuson (n)	[eku'son]
stand	stand (n)	[stand]
to reserve, to book	a rezerva	[a rezer'va]
display case	vitrină (f)	[vi'trinə]
spotlight	corp (n) de iluminat	['korp de ilumi'nat]
design	design (n)	[di'zajn]
to place (put, set)	a instala	[a insta'la]
distributor	distribuitor (m)	[distribui'tor]
supplier	furnizor (m)	[furni'zor]
country	țară (f)	['tsarə]
foreign (adj)	străin	[strə'in]
product	produs (n)	[pro'dus]
association	asociație (f)	[asotʃi'atsie]
conference hall	sală (f) de conferințe	['salə de konfe'rintse]
congress	congres (n)	[kon'gres]

contest (competition)	concurs (n)	[ko'nkurs]
visitor (attendee)	vizitator (m)	[vizita'tor]
to visit (attend)	a vizita	[a vizi'ta]
customer	client (m)	[kli'ent]

119. Mass Media

newspaper	ziar (n)	[zjar]
magazine	revistă (f)	[re'vistə]
press (printed media)	presă (f)	['presə]
radio	radio (n)	['radio]
radio station	post (n) de radio	[post de 'radio]
television	televiziune (f)	[televizi'une]

presenter, host	prezentator (m)	[prezenta'tor]
newsreader	prezentator (m)	[prezenta'tor]
commentator	comentator (m)	[komenta'tor]

journalist	jurnalist (m)	[ʒurna'list]
correspondent (reporter)	corespondent (m)	[korespon'dent]
press photographer	foto-reporter (m)	['foto re'porter]
reporter	reporter (m)	[re'porter]

editor	redactor (m)	[re'daktor]
editor-in-chief	redactor-şef (m)	[re'daktor 'ʃef]
to subscribe (to …)	a se abona	[a se abo'na]
subscription	abonare (f)	[abo'nare]
subscriber	abonat (m)	[abo'nat]
to read (vi, vt)	a citi	[a tʃi'ti]
reader	cititor (m)	[tʃiti'tor]

circulation (of a newspaper)	tiraj (n)	[ti'raʒ]
monthly (adj)	lunar	[lu'nar]
weekly (adj)	săptămânal	[səptəmi'nal]
issue (edition)	număr (n)	['numər]
new (~ issue)	nou	['nou]

headline	titlu (n)	['titlu]
short article	notă (f)	['notə]
column (regular article)	rubrică (f)	['rubrikə]
article	articol (n)	[ar'tikol]
page	pagină (f)	['padʒinə]

reportage, report	reportaj (n)	[repor'taʒ]
event (happening)	eveniment (n)	[eveni'ment]
sensation (news)	senzaţie (f)	[sen'zatsie]
scandal	scandal (n)	[skan'dal]
scandalous (adj)	scandalos	[skanda'los]
great (~ scandal)	zgomotos	[zgomo'tos]

programme (e.g. cooking ~)	emisiune (f)	[emisi'une]
interview	interviu (n)	[inter'vju]
live broadcast	în direct (m)	[in di'rekt]
channel	post (n)	[post]

120. Agriculture

agriculture	agricultură (f)	[agrikul'turə]
peasant (masc.)	ţăran (m)	[tsə'ran]
peasant (fem.)	ţărancă (f)	[tsə'rankə]
farmer	fermier (m)	[fer'mjer]
tractor	tractor (n)	[trak'tor]
combine, harvester	combină (f)	[kom'binə]
plough	plug (n)	[plug]
to plough (vi, vt)	a ara	[a a'ra]
ploughland	ogor (n)	[o'gor]
furrow (in field)	brazdă (f)	['brazdə]
to sow (vi, vt)	a semăna	[a semə'na]
seeder	semănătoare (f)	[semənəto'are]
sowing (process)	semănare (f)	[semə'nare]
scythe	coasă (f)	[ko'asə]
to mow, to scythe	a cosi	[a ko'si]
spade (tool)	hârleţ (n)	[hir'lets]
to till (vt)	a săpa	[a sə'pa]
hoe	sapă (f)	['sapə]
to hoe, to weed	a plivi	[a pli'vi]
weed (plant)	buruiană (f)	[buru'janə]
watering can	stropitoare (f)	[stropito'are]
to water (plants)	a uda	[a u'da]
watering (act)	irigare (f)	[iri'gare]
pitchfork	furcă (f)	['furkə]
rake	greblă (f)	['greblə]
fertiliser	îngrăşământ (n)	[ingrəʃə'mint]
to fertilise (vt)	a îngrăşa	[a ingrə'ʃa]
manure (fertiliser)	gunoi (n) de grajd	[gu'noj de graʒd]
field	câmp (n)	[kimp]
meadow	luncă (f)	['lunkə]
vegetable garden	grădină (f) de zarzavat	[grə'dinə de zarza'vat]
orchard (e.g. apple ~)	grădină (f)	[grə'dinə]
to graze (vt)	a paşte	[a 'paʃte]
herdsman	păstor (m)	[pəs'tor]
pasture	păşune (f)	[pə'ʃune]
cattle breeding	zootehnie (f)	[zooteh'nie]
sheep farming	ovicultură (f)	[ovikul'turə]
plantation	plantaţie (f)	[plan'tatsie]
row (garden bed ~s)	strat (n)	[strat]
hothouse	răsadniţă (f)	[rə'sadnitsə]

| drought (lack of rain) | secetă (f) | ['setʃetə] |
| dry (~ summer) | secetos | [setʃe'tos] |

| cereal crops | cereale (f pl) | [tʃere'ale] |
| to harvest, to gather | a strânge | [a 'strindʒe] |

miller (person)	morar (m)	[mo'rar]
mill (e.g. gristmill)	moară (f)	[mo'arə]
to grind (grain)	a măcina grăunțe	[a mətʃi'na grə'untse]
flour	făină (f)	[fə'inə]
straw	paie (n pl)	['pae]

121. Building. Building process

building site	şantier (n)	[ʃan'tjer]
to build (vt)	a construi	[a konstru'i]
building worker	constructor (m)	[kon'struktor]

project	proiect (n)	[pro'ekt]
architect	arhitect (m)	[arhi'tekt]
worker	muncitor (m)	[muntʃi'tor]

foundations (of a building)	fundament (n)	[funda'ment]
roof	acoperiş (n)	[akope'riʃ]
foundation pile	pilon (m)	[pi'lon]
wall	perete (m)	[pe'rete]

| reinforcing bars | armătură (f) | [armə'turə] |
| scaffolding | schele (f) | ['skele] |

concrete	beton (n)	[be'ton]
granite	granit (n)	[gra'nit]
stone	piatră (f)	['pjatrə]
brick	cărămidă (f)	[kərə'midə]

| sand | nisip (n) | [ni'sip] |
| cement | ciment (n) | [tʃi'ment] |

| plaster (for walls) | tencuială (f) | [tenku'jalə] |
| to plaster (vt) | a tencui | [a tenku'i] |

paint	vopsea (f)	[vop'sʲa]
to paint (~ a wall)	a vopsi	[a vop'si]
barrel	butoi (n)	[bu'toj]

crane	macara (f)	[maka'ra]
to lift, to hoist (vt)	a ridica	[a ridi'ka]
to lower (vt)	a coborî	[a kobo'ri]

bulldozer	buldozer (n)	[bul'dozer]
excavator	excavator (n)	[ekskava'tor]
scoop, bucket	căuş (n)	[kə'uʃ]
to dig (excavate)	a săpa	[a sə'pa]
hard hat	cască (f)	['kaskə]

122. Science. Research. Scientists

science	ştiinţă (f)	[ʃti'intsə]
scientific (adj)	ştiinţific	[ʃtiin'tsifik]
scientist	savant (m)	[sa'vant]
theory	teorie (f)	[teo'rie]
axiom	axiomă (f)	[aksi'omə]
analysis	analiză (f)	[ana'lizə]
to analyse (vt)	a analiza	[a anali'za]
argument (strong ~)	argument (n)	[argu'ment]
substance (matter)	substanţă (f)	[sub'stantsə]
hypothesis	ipoteză (f)	[ipo'tezə]
dilemma	dilemă (f)	[di'lemə]
dissertation	disertaţie (f)	[diser'tatsie]
dogma	dogmă (f)	['dogmə]
doctrine	doctrină (f)	[dok'trinə]
research	cercetare (f)	[tʃertʃe'tare]
to research (vt)	a cerceta	[a tʃertʃe'ta]
tests (laboratory ~)	verificare (f)	[verifi'kare]
laboratory	laborator (n)	[labora'tor]
method	metodă (f)	[me'todə]
molecule	moleculă (f)	[mole'kulə]
monitoring	monitorizare (n)	[monitori'zare]
discovery (act, event)	descoperire (f)	[deskope'rire]
postulate	postulat (n)	[postu'lat]
principle	principiu (n)	[prin'tʃipju]
forecast	prognoză (f)	[prog'nozə]
to forecast (vt)	a prognoza	[a progno'za]
synthesis	sinteză (f)	[sin'tezə]
trend (tendency)	tendinţă (f)	[ten'dintsə]
theorem	teoremă (f)	[teo'remə]
teachings	învăţătură (f)	[invətsə'turə]
fact	fapt (n)	[fapt]
expedition	expediţie (f)	[ekspe'ditsie]
experiment	experiment (n)	[eksperi'ment]
academician	academician (m)	[akdemi'tʃian]
bachelor (e.g. ~ of Arts)	bacalaureat (n)	[bakalaure'at]
doctor (PhD)	doctor (m)	['doktor]
Associate Professor	docent (m)	[do'tʃent]
Master (e.g. ~ of Arts)	magistru (m)	[ma'dʒistru]
professor	profesor (m)	[pro'fesor]

Professions and occupations

job	**serviciu** (n)	[ser'vitʃiu]
staff (work force)	**cadre** (n pl)	['kadre]
career	**carieră** (f)	[ka'rjerə]
prospects (chances)	**perspectivă** (f)	[perspek'tivə]
skills (mastery)	**îndemânare** (f)	[indemi'nare]
selection (screening)	**alegere** (f)	[a'ledʒere]
employment agency	**agenţie** (f) **de cadre**	[adʒen'tsie de 'kadre]
curriculum vitae, CV	**CV** (n)	[si'vi]
job interview	**interviu** (n)	[inter'vju]
vacancy	**post** (n) **vacant**	['post va'kant]
salary, pay	**salariu** (n)	[sa'larju]
fixed salary	**salariu** (n)	[sa'larju]
pay, compensation	**plată** (f)	['platə]
position (job)	**funcţie** (f)	['funktsie]
duty (of an employee)	**obligaţie** (f)	[obli'gatsie]
range of duties	**domeniu** (n)	[do'menju]
busy (I'm ~)	**ocupat**	[oku'pat]
to fire (dismiss)	**a concedia**	[a kontʃedi'a]
dismissal	**concediere** (f)	[kontʃe'djere]
unemployment	**şomaj** (n)	[ʃo'maʒ]
unemployed (n)	**şomer** (m)	[ʃo'mer]
retirement	**pensie** (f)	['pensie]
to retire (from job)	**a se pensiona**	[a se pensio'na]

director	**director** (m)	[di'rektor]
manager (director)	**administrator** (m)	[adminis'trator]
boss	**conducător** (m)	[kondukə'tor]
superior	**şef** (m)	[ʃef]
superiors	**conducere** (f)	[kon'dutʃere]
president	**preşedinte** (m)	[preʃə'dinte]
chairman	**preşedinte** (m)	[preʃə'dinte]
deputy (substitute)	**adjunct** (m)	[a'dʒunkt]
assistant	**asistent** (m)	[asis'tent]
secretary	**secretar** (m)	[sekre'tar]

personal assistant	secretar (m) personal	[sekre'tar perso'nal]
businessman	om (m) de afaceri	[om de a'fatʃerɪ]
entrepreneur	întreprinzător (m)	[intreprinzə'tor]
founder	fondator (m)	[fonda'tor]
to found (vt)	a fonda	[a fon'da]

founding member	fondator (m)	[fonda'tor]
partner	partener (m)	[parte'ner]
shareholder	acționar (m)	[aktsio'nar]

millionaire	milionar (m)	[milio'nar]
billionaire	miliardar (n)	[miliar'dar]
owner, proprietor	proprietar (m)	[proprie'tar]
landowner	proprietar (m) funciar	[proprie'tar funtʃi'ar]

client	client (m)	[kli'ent]
regular client	client (m) fidel	[kli'ent fi'del]
buyer (customer)	cumpărător (m)	[kumpərə'tor]
visitor	vizitator (m)	[vizita'tor]

professional (n)	profesionist (m)	[profesio'nist]
expert	expert (m)	[eks'pert]
specialist	specialist (m)	[spetʃia'list]

| banker | bancher (m) | [ban'ker] |
| broker | broker (m) | ['broker] |

cashier	casier (m)	[ka'sjer]
accountant	contabil (f)	[kon'tabil]
security guard	paznic (m)	['paznik]

investor	investitor (m)	[investi'tor]
debtor	datornic (m)	[da'tornik]
creditor	creditor (m)	[kredi'tor]
borrower	datornic (m)	[da'tornik]

| importer | importator (m) | [importa'tor] |
| exporter | exportator (m) | [eksporta'tor] |

manufacturer	producător (m)	[produkə'tor]
distributor	distribuitor (m)	[distribui'tor]
middleman	intermediar (m)	[intermedi'ar]

consultant	consultant (m)	[konsul'tant]
sales representative	reprezentant (m)	[reprezen'tant]
agent	agent (m)	[a'dʒent]
insurance agent	agent (m) de asigurare	[a'dʒent de asigu'rare]

125. Service professions

cook	bucătar (m)	[bukə'tar]
chef (kitchen chef)	bucătar-şef (m)	[bukə'tar 'ʃəf]
baker	brutar (m)	[bru'tar]
barman	barman (m)	['barman]

waiter	**chelner** (m)	['kelner]
waitress	**chelneriță** (f)	[kelne'ritsə]
lawyer, barrister	**avocat** (m)	[avo'kat]
lawyer (legal expert)	**jurist** (m)	[ʒu'rist]
notary public	**notar** (m)	[no'tar]
electrician	**electrician** (m)	[elektritʃi'an]
plumber	**instalator** (m)	[instala'tor]
carpenter	**dulgher** (m)	[dul'ger]
masseur	**masor** (m)	[ma'sor]
masseuse	**masezā** (f)	[ma'sezə]
doctor	**medic** (m)	['medik]
taxi driver	**taximetrist** (m)	[taksime'trist]
driver	**şofer** (m)	[ʃo'fer]
delivery man	**curier** (m)	[ku'rjer]
chambermaid	**femeie** (f) **de serviciu**	[fe'mee de ser'vitʃiu]
security guard	**paznic** (m)	['paznik]
flight attendant (fem.)	**stewardesă** (f)	[stjuar'desə]
schoolteacher	**profesor** (m)	[pro'fesor]
librarian	**bibliotecar** (m)	[bibliote'kar]
translator	**traducător** (m)	[tradukə'tor]
interpreter	**interpret** (m)	[inter'pret]
guide	**ghid** (m)	[gid]
hairdresser	**frizer** (m)	[fri'zer]
postman	**poştaş** (m)	[poʃ'taʃ]
salesman (store staff)	**vânzător** (m)	[vinzə'tor]
gardener	**grădinar** (m)	[grədi'nar]
domestic servant	**servitor** (m)	[servi'tor]
maid (female servant)	**servitoare** (f)	[servito'are]
cleaner (cleaning lady)	**femeie** (f) **de serviciu**	[fe'mee de ser'vitʃiu]

126. Military professions and ranks

private	**soldat** (m)	[sol'dat]
sergeant	**sergent** (m)	[ser'dʒent]
lieutenant	**locotenent** (m)	[lokote'nent]
captain	**căpitan** (m)	[kəpi'tan]
major	**maior** (m)	[ma'jor]
colonel	**colonel** (m)	[kolo'nel]
general	**general** (m)	[dʒene'ral]
marshal	**mareşal** (m)	[mare'ʃal]
admiral	**amiral** (m)	[ami'ral]
military (n)	**militar** (m)	[mili'tar]
soldier	**soldat** (m)	[sol'dat]
officer	**ofițer** (m)	[ofi'tser]

commander	comandant (m)	[koman'dant]
border guard	grănicer (m)	[grəni'tʃer]
radio operator	radist (m)	[ra'dist]
scout (searcher)	cercetaş (m)	[tʃertʃe'taʃ]
pioneer (sapper)	genist (m)	[dʒe'nist]
marksman	trăgător (m)	[trəgə'tor]
navigator	navigator (m)	[naviga'tor]

127. Officials. Priests

| king | rege (m) | ['redʒe] |
| queen | regină (f) | [re'dʒinə] |

| prince | prinţ (m) | [prints] |
| princess | prinţesă (f) | [prin'tsesə] |

| czar | ţar (m) | [tsar] |
| czarina | ţarină (f) | [tsa'rinə] |

president	preşedinte (m)	[preʃə'dinte]
Secretary (minister)	ministru (m)	[mi'nistru]
prime minister	prim-ministru (m)	['prim mi'nistru]
senator	senator (m)	[sena'tor]

diplomat	diplomat (m)	[diplo'mat]
consul	consul (m)	['konsul]
ambassador	ambasador (m)	[ambasa'dor]
counselor (diplomatic officer)	consilier (m)	[konsi'ljer]

official, functionary (civil servant)	funcţionar (m)	[funktsio'nar]
prefect	prefect (m)	[pre'fekt]
mayor	primar (m)	[pri'mar]

| judge | judecător (m) | [ʒudekə'tor] |
| prosecutor | procuror (m) | [proku'ror] |

missionary	misionar (m)	[misio'nar]
monk	călugăr (m)	[kə'lugər]
abbot	abate (m)	[a'bate]
rabbi	rabin (m)	[ra'bin]

vizier	vizir (m)	[vi'zir]
shah	şah (m)	[ʃah]
sheikh	şeic (m)	['ʃejk]

128. Agricultural professions

beekeeper	apicultor (m)	[apikul'tor]
shepherd	păstor (m)	[pəs'tor]
agronomist	agronom (m)	[agro'nom]
cattle breeder	zootehnician (m)	[zootehnitʃi'an]

veterinary surgeon	**veterinar** (m)	[veteri'nar]
farmer	**fermier** (m)	[fer'mjer]
winemaker	**vinificator** (m)	[vinifika'tor]
zoologist	**zoolog** (m)	[zoo'log]
cowboy	**cowboy** (m)	['kauboj]

129. Art professions

actor	**actor** (m)	[ak'tor]
actress	**actriță** (f)	[ak'tritsə]
singer (masc.)	**cântăreț** (m)	[kintə'rets]
singer (fem.)	**cântăreață** (f)	[kintə'rɪatsə]
dancer (masc.)	**dansator** (m)	[dansa'tor]
dancer (fem.)	**dansatoare** (f)	[dansato'are]
performer (masc.)	**artist** (m)	[ar'tist]
performer (fem.)	**artistă** (f)	[ar'tistə]
musician	**muzician** (m)	[muzitʃi'an]
pianist	**pianist** (m)	[pia'nist]
guitar player	**chitarist** (m)	[kita'rist]
conductor (orchestra ~)	**dirijor** (m)	[diri'ʒor]
composer	**compozitor** (m)	[kompo'zitor]
impresario	**impresar** (m)	[impre'sar]
film director	**regizor** (m)	[re'dʒizor]
producer	**producător** (m)	[produkə'tor]
scriptwriter	**scenarist** (m)	[stʃena'rist]
critic	**critic** (m)	['kritik]
writer	**scriitor** (m)	[skrii'tor]
poet	**poet** (m)	[po'et]
sculptor	**sculptor** (m)	['skulptor]
artist (painter)	**pictor** (m)	['piktor]
juggler	**jongler** (m)	[ʒon'gler]
clown	**clovn** (m)	[klovn]
acrobat	**acrobat** (m)	[akro'bat]
magician	**magician** (m)	[madʒitʃi'an]

130. Various professions

doctor	**medic** (m)	['medik]
nurse	**asistentă** (f) **medicală**	[asis'tentə medi'kalə]
psychiatrist	**psihiatru** (m)	[psihi'atru]
dentist	**stomatolog** (m)	[stomato'log]
surgeon	**chirurg** (m)	[ki'rurg]
astronaut	**astronaut** (m)	[astrona'ut]
astronomer	**astronom** (m)	[astro'nom]

pilot	**pilot** (m)	[pi'lot]
driver (of a taxi, etc.)	**şofer** (m)	[ʃo'fer]
train driver	**maşinist** (m)	[maʃi'nist]
mechanic	**mecanic** (m)	[me'kanik]

miner	**miner** (m)	[mi'ner]
worker	**muncitor** (m)	[muntʃi'tor]
locksmith	**lăcătuş** (m)	[ləkə'tuʃ]
joiner (carpenter)	**tâmplar** (m)	[tim'plar]
turner (lathe operator)	**strungar** (m)	[strun'gar]
building worker	**constructor** (m)	[kon'struktor]
welder	**sudor** (m)	[su'dor]

professor (title)	**profesor** (m)	[pro'fesor]
architect	**arhitect** (m)	[arhi'tekt]
historian	**istoric** (m)	[is'torik]
scientist	**savant** (m)	[sa'vant]
physicist	**fizician** (m)	[fizitʃi'an]
chemist (scientist)	**chimist** (m)	[ki'mist]

archaeologist	**arheolog** (m)	[arheo'log]
geologist	**geolog** (m)	[dʒeo'log]
researcher (scientist)	**cercetător** (m)	[tʃertʃetə'tor]

babysitter	**dădacă** (f)	[də'dakə]
teacher, educator	**pedagog** (m)	[peda'gog]

editor	**redactor** (m)	[re'daktor]
editor-in-chief	**redactor-şef** (m)	[re'daktor 'ʃef]
correspondent	**corespondent** (m)	[korespon'dent]
typist (fem.)	**dactilografă** (f)	[daktilo'grafə]

designer	**designer** (m)	[di'zajner]
computer expert	**operator** (m)	[opera'tor]
programmer	**programator** (m)	[programa'tor]
engineer (designer)	**inginer** (m)	[indʒi'ner]

sailor	**marinar** (m)	[mari'nar]
seaman	**marinar** (m)	[mari'nar]
rescuer	**salvator** (m)	[salva'tor]

firefighter	**pompier** (m)	[pom'pjer]
police officer	**poliţist** (m)	[poli'tsist]
watchman	**paznic** (m)	['paznik]
detective	**detectiv** (m)	[detek'tiv]

customs officer	**vameş** (m)	['vameʃ]
bodyguard	**gardă** (f) **de corp**	['gardə de 'korp]
prison officer	**supraveghetor** (m)	[supravege'tor]
inspector	**inspector** (m)	[in'spektor]

sportsman	**sportiv** (m)	[spor'tiv]
trainer, coach	**antrenor** (m)	[antre'nor]
butcher	**măcelar** (m)	[mətʃe'lar]
cobbler (shoe repairer)	**cizmar** (m)	[tʃiz'mar]
merchant	**comerciant** (m)	[komertʃi'ant]

loader (person)	hamal (m)	[ha'mal]
fashion designer	modelier (n)	[mode'ljer]
model (fem.)	model (n)	[mo'del]

131. Occupations. Social status

| schoolboy | elev (m) | [e'lev] |
| student (college ~) | student (m) | [stu'dent] |

philosopher	filozof (m)	[filo'zof]
economist	economist (m)	[ekono'mist]
inventor	inventator (m)	[inventa'tor]

unemployed (n)	şomer (m)	[ʃo'mer]
retiree, pensioner	pensionar (m)	[pensio'nar]
spy, secret agent	spion (m)	[spi'on]

prisoner	arestat (m)	[ares'tat]
striker	grevist (m)	[gre'vist]
bureaucrat	birocrat (m)	[biro'krat]
traveller (globetrotter)	călător (m)	[kələ'tor]

| gay, homosexual (n) | homosexual (m) | [homoseksu'al] |
| hacker | hacker (m) | ['haker] |

bandit	bandit (m)	[ban'dit]
hit man, killer	asasin (m) plătit	[asa'sin plə'tit]
drug addict	narcoman (m)	[narko'man]
drug dealer	vânzător (m) de droguri	[vinzə'tor de 'drogurʲ]
prostitute (fem.)	prostituată (f)	[prostitu'atə]
pimp	proxenet (m)	[prokse'net]

sorcerer	vrăjitor (m)	[vrəʒi'tor]
sorceress (evil ~)	vrăjitoare (f)	[vrəʒito'are]
pirate	pirat (m)	[pi'rat]
slave	rob (m)	[rob]
samurai	samurai (m)	[samu'raj]
savage (primitive)	sălbatic (m)	[səl'batik]

Sports

132. Kinds of sports. Sportspersons

sportsman	**sportiv** (m)	[spor'tiv]
kind of sport	**gen** (n) **de sport**	['dʒen de 'sport]
basketball	**baschet** (n)	['basket]
basketball player	**baschetbalist** (m)	[basketba'list]
baseball	**base-ball** (n)	['bejsbol]
baseball player	**jucător** (m) **de base-ball**	[ʒukə'tor de 'bejsbol]
football	**fotbal** (n)	['fotbal]
football player	**fotbalist** (m)	[fotba'list]
goalkeeper	**portar** (m)	[por'tar]
ice hockey	**hochei** (n)	['hokej]
ice hockey player	**hocheist** (m)	[hoke'ist]
volleyball	**volei** (n)	['volej]
volleyball player	**voleibalist** (m)	[volejba'list]
boxing	**box** (n)	[boks]
boxer	**boxer** (m)	[bok'ser]
wrestling	**luptă** (f)	['luptə]
wrestler	**luptător** (m)	[luptə'tor]
karate	**carate** (n)	[ka'rate]
karate fighter	**karatist** (m)	[kara'tist]
judo	**judo** (n)	['dʒudo]
judo athlete	**judocan** (m)	[dʒudo'kan]
tennis	**tenis** (n)	['tenis]
tennis player	**tenisman** (m)	[tenis'man]
swimming	**înot** (n)	[i'not]
swimmer	**înotător** (m)	[inotə'tor]
fencing	**scrimă** (f)	['skrimə]
fencer	**jucător** (m) **de scrimă**	[ʒukə'tor de 'skrimə]
chess	**şah** (n)	[ʃah]
chess player	**şahist** (m)	[ʃa'hist]
alpinism	**alpinism** (n)	[alpi'nizm]
alpinist	**alpinist** (m)	[alpi'nist]
running	**alergare** (f)	[aler'gare]

runner	alergător (m)	[alergə'tor]
athletics	atletism (n)	[atle'tizm]
athlete	atlet (m)	[at'let]

horse riding	hipism (n)	[hi'pism]
horse rider	călăreț (m)	[kələ'reʦ]

figure skating	patinaj (n) artistic	[pati'naʒ ar'tistik]
figure skater (masc.)	patinator (m) artistic	[patina'tor ar'tistik]
figure skater (fem.)	patinatore (f) artistică	[patinato'are ar'tistikə]

powerlifting	atletică (f) grea	[at'letikə grʲa]
powerlifter	halterofil (m)	[haltero'fil]

car racing	raliu (n)	[ra'liu]
racer (driver)	pilot (m) de curse	[pi'lot de 'kurse]

cycling	ciclism (n)	[ʧi'klizm]
cyclist	ciclist (m)	[ʧi'klist]

long jump	sărituri (f pl) în lungime	[səri'turʲ in lun'ʤime]
pole vaulting	săritură (f) cu prăjina	[səri'turə ku prə'ʒina]
jumper	săritor (m)	[səri'tor]

133. Kinds of sports. Miscellaneous

American football	fotbal (n) american	['fotbal ameri'kan]
badminton	badminton (n)	[bedmin'ton]
biathlon	biatlon (n)	[biat'lon]
billiards	biliard (n)	[bi'ljard]

bobsleigh	bob (n)	[bob]
bodybuilding	culturism (n)	[kultu'rism]
water polo	polo (n) pe apă	['polo pe 'apə]
handball	handbal (n)	['handbal]
golf	golf (n)	[golf]

rowing	canotaj (n)	[kano'taʒ]
scuba diving	scufundare (f)	[skufun'dare]
cross-country skiing	concurs (n) de schi	[ko'nkurs de 'ski]
table tennis (ping-pong)	tenis (n) de masă	['tenis de 'masə]

sailing	iahting (n)	['jahting]
rally	raliu (n)	[ra'liu]
rugby	rugby (n)	['regbi]
snowboarding	snowboard (n)	[snou'bord]
archery	tragere (f) cu arcul	['traʤere 'ku 'arkul]

134. Gym

barbell	halteră (f)	[hal'terə]
dumbbells	haltere (f pl)	['haltere]

training machine	dispozitiv (n) pentru antrenament	[dispozi'tiv 'pentru antrena'ment]
exercise bicycle	bicicletă (f)	[bitʃi'kletə]
treadmill	pistă (f) de alergare	['pistə de aler'gare]

horizontal bar	bară (f)	['barə]
parallel bars	bare (f pl)	['bare]
vault (vaulting horse)	cal (m) de gimnastică	['kal de dʒim'nastikə]
mat (exercise ~)	saltea (f)	[sal'tʲa]

| aerobics | aerobică (f) | [ae'robikə] |
| yoga | yoga (f) | ['joga] |

135. Ice hockey

ice hockey	hochei (n)	['hokej]
ice hockey player	hocheist (m)	[hoke'ist]
to play ice hockey	a juca hochei	[a ʒu'ka 'hokej]
ice	gheață (f)	['gʲaʦə]

puck	puc (n)	[puk]
ice hockey stick	crosă (f)	['krosə]
ice skates	patine (f pl)	[pa'tine]

| board (ice hockey rink ~) | bandă (f) | ['bandə] |
| shot | lovitură (f) | [lovi'turə] |

goaltender	portar (m)	[por'tar]
goal (score)	gol (n)	[gol]
to score a goal	a marca un gol	[a mar'ka un gol]

| period | repriză (f) | [re'prizə] |
| substitutes bench | bancă (f) de rezervă | ['bankə de re'zervə] |

136. Football

football	fotbal (n)	['fotbal]
football player	fotbalist (m)	[fotba'list]
to play football	a juca fotbal	[a ʒu'ka 'fotbal]

major league	ligă (f) superioară	['ligə superio'arə]
football club	club (n) de fotbal	['klub de 'fotbal]
coach	antrenor (m)	[antre'nor]
owner, proprietor	proprietar (m)	[proprie'tar]

team	echipă (f)	[e'kipə]
team captain	căpitanul (m) echipei	[kəpi'tanul e'kipej]
player	jucător (m)	[ʒukə'tor]
substitute	jucător (m) de rezervă	[ʒukə'tor de re'zervə]

| forward | atacant (m) | [ata'kant] |
| centre forward | atacant (m) la centru | [ata'kant la 'ʧentru] |

scorer	golgheter (m)	[gol'geter]
defender, back	apărător (m)	[apərə'tor]
midfielder, halfback	mijlocaş (m)	[miʒlo'kaʃ]

match	meci (n)	['metʃi]
to meet (vi, vt)	a se întâlni	[a se intil'ni]
final	finală (f)	[fi'nalə]
semi-final	semifinală (f)	[semifi'nalə]
championship	campionat (n)	[kampio'nat]

period, half	repriză (f)	[re'prizə]
first period	prima repriză (f)	['prima re'prizə]
half-time	pauză (f)	['pauzə]

goal	poartă (f)	[po'artə]
goalkeeper	portar (m)	[por'tar]
goalpost	bară (f)	['barə]
crossbar	bară (f) transversală	['barə transver'salə]
net	plasă (f)	['plasə]
to concede a goal	a rata gol	[a rə'ta gol]

ball	minge (f)	['mindʒe]
pass	pasă (f)	['pasə]
kick	lovitură (f)	[lovi'turə]
to kick (~ the ball)	a da o lovitură	[a da o lovi'turə]
free kick (direct ~)	lovitură (f) de pedeapsă	[lovi'turə de pe'dʲapsə]
corner kick	lovitură (f) de colţ	[lovi'turə de 'kolts]

attack	atac (n)	[a'tak]
counterattack	contraatac (n)	[kontraa'tak]
combination	combinaţie (f)	[kombi'natsie]

referee	arbitru (m)	[ar'bitru]
to blow the whistle	a fluiera	[a flue'ra]
whistle (sound)	fluier (n)	['flujer]
foul, misconduct	încălcare (f)	[inkəl'kare]
to commit a foul	a încălca	[a inkəl'ka]
to send off	a elimina de pe teren	[a elimi'na de pe te'ren]

yellow card	cartonaş (n) galben	[karto'naʃ 'galben]
red card	cartonaş (n) roşu	[karto'naʃ 'roʃu]
disqualification	descalificare (f)	[deskalifi'kare]
to disqualify (vt)	a descalifica	[a deskalifi'ka]

penalty kick	penalti (n)	[pe'nalti]
wall	perete (m)	[pe'rete]
to score (vi, vt)	a marca	[a mar'ka]
goal (score)	gol (n)	[gol]
to score a goal	a marca un gol	[a mar'ka un gol]

substitution	înlocuire (f)	[inloku'ire]
to replace (a player)	a înlocui	[a inloku'i]
rules	reguli (f pl)	['regulʲ]
tactics	tactică (f)	['taktikə]
stadium	stadion (n)	[stadi'on]
terrace	tribună (f)	[tri'bunə]

| fan, supporter | suporter (m) | [su'porter] |
| to shout (vi) | a striga | [a stri'ga] |

| scoreboard | tablă (f) | ['tablə] |
| score | scor (n) | [skor] |

| defeat | înfrângere (f) | [in'frindʒere] |
| to lose (not win) | a pierde | [a 'pjerde] |

| draw | egalitate (f) | [egali'tate] |
| to draw (vi) | a juca la egalitate | [a ʒu'ka la egali'tate] |

victory	victorie (f)	[vik'torie]
to win (vi, vt)	a învinge	[a in'vindʒe]
champion	campion (m)	[kampi'on]
best (adj)	cel mai bun	[tʃel maj bun]
to congratulate (vt)	a felicita	[a felitʃi'ta]

commentator	comentator (m)	[komenta'tor]
to commentate (vt)	a comenta	[a komen'ta]
broadcast	transmisiune (f)	[trans'misjune]

137. Alpine skiing

skis	schiuri (n)	['skjurɪ]
to ski (vi)	a schia	[a ski'a]
mountain-ski resort	stațiune (f) de schi montan	[statsi'une de ski mon'tan]
ski lift	ascensor (m)	[astʃen'sor]

ski poles	bețe (n pl)	['betse]
slope	pantă (f)	['pantə]
slalom	slalom (n)	['slalom]

138. Tennis. Golf

golf	golf (n)	[golf]
golf club	club (n) de golf	['klub de 'golf]
golfer	jucător (m) de golf	[ʒukə'tor de 'golf]

hole	gaură (f)	['gaurə]
club	crosă (f)	['krosə]
golf trolley	cărucior (n) pentru crose	[kəru'tʃior 'pentru 'krose]

| tennis | tenis (n) | ['tenis] |
| tennis court | teren (n) de tenis | [te'ren de 'tenis] |

| serve | serviciu (n) | [ser'vitʃiu] |
| to serve (vt) | a servi | [a ser'vi] |

racket	paletă (f)	[pa'letə]
net	plasă (f)	['plasə]
ball	minge (f)	['mindʒe]

139. Chess

chess	şah (n)	[ʃah]
chessmen	piese (f pl)	['pjese]
chess player	şahist (m)	[ʃa'hist]
chessboard	tablă (f) de şah	['tablə de ʃah]
chessman	piesă (f)	['pjesə]
White (white pieces)	piese (f pl) albe	['pjese 'albe]
Black (black pieces)	piese (f pl) negre	['pjese 'negre]
pawn	pion (m)	[pi'on]
bishop	nebun (m)	[ne'bun]
knight	cal (m)	[kal]
rook	turn (n)	[turn]
queen	regină (f)	[re'dʒinə]
king	rege (m)	['redʒe]
move	mutare (f)	[mu'tare]
to move (vi, vt)	a muta	[a mu'ta]
to sacrifice (vt)	a sacrifica	[a sakrifi'ka]
castling	rocadă (f)	[ro'kadə]
check	şah (n)	[ʃah]
checkmate	mat (n)	[mat]
chess tournament	turneu (n) de şah	[tur'neu de ʃah]
Grand Master	mare maestru (m)	['mare ma'estru]
combination	combinaţie (f)	[kombi'natsie]
game (in chess)	partidă (f)	[par'tidə]
draughts	joc (n) de dame	[ʒok de 'dame]

140. Boxing

boxing	box (n)	[boks]
fight (bout)	luptă (f)	['luptə]
boxing match	duel (n)	[du'el]
round (in boxing)	rundă (f)	['rundə]
ring	ring (n)	[ring]
gong	gong (n)	[gong]
punch	lovitură (f)	[lovi'turə]
knockdown	cnocdaun (n)	['knokdaun]
knockout	cnocaut (n)	['knokaut]
to knock out	a face cnocaut	[a 'fatʃe 'knokaut]
boxing glove	mănuşă (f) de box	[mə'nuʃə de 'boks]
referee	arbitru (m)	[ar'bitru]
lightweight	categorie (f) uşoară	[katego'rie uʃo'arə]
middleweight	categorie (f) mijlocie	[katego'rie miʒlo'tʃie]
heavyweight	categorie (f) grea	[katego'rie gr'a]

141. Sports. Miscellaneous

Olympic Games	**Jocuri** (n pl) **Olimpice**	['ʒokurʲ o'limpitʃe]
winner	**învingător** (m)	[invingə'tor]
to be winning	**a învinge**	[a in'vindʒe]
to win (vi)	**a câştiga**	[a kiʃti'ga]
leader	**lider** (m)	['lider]
to lead (vi)	**a fi în fruntea**	[a fi in 'fruntʲa]
first place	**primul loc** (n)	['primul lok]
second place	**al doilea loc** (n)	[al 'dojlʲa lok]
third place	**al treilea loc** (n)	[al 'trejlʲa lok]
medal	**medalie** (f)	[me'dalie]
trophy	**trofeu** (n)	[tro'feu]
prize cup (trophy)	**cupă** (f)	['kupə]
prize (in game)	**premiu** (n)	['premju]
main prize	**premiul** (n) **principal**	['premjul printʃi'pal]
record	**record** (n)	[re'kord]
to set a record	**a bate recordul**	[a 'bate re'kordul]
final	**finală** (f)	[fi'nalə]
final (adj)	**final**	[fi'nal]
champion	**campion** (m)	[kampi'on]
championship	**campionat** (n)	[kampio'nat]
stadium	**stadion** (n)	[stadi'on]
terrace	**tribună** (f)	[tri'bunə]
fan, supporter	**suporter** (m)	[su'porter]
opponent, rival	**adversar** (m)	[adver'sar]
start (start line)	**start** (n)	[start]
finish line	**finiş** (n)	['finiʃ]
defeat	**înfrângere** (f)	[in'frindʒere]
to lose (not win)	**a pierde**	[a 'pjerde]
referee	**arbitru** (m)	[ar'bitru]
jury (judges)	**juriu** (n)	['ʒurju]
score	**scor** (n)	[skor]
draw	**egalitate** (f)	[egali'tate]
to draw (vi)	**a juca la egalitate**	[a ʒu'ka la egali'tate]
point	**punct** (n)	[punkt]
result (final score)	**rezultat** (n)	[rezul'tat]
half-time	**pauză** (f)	['pauzə]
doping	**dopaj** (n)	[do'paʒ]
to penalise (vt)	**a penaliza**	[a penali'za]
to disqualify (vt)	**a descalifica**	[a deskalifi'ka]
apparatus	**aparat** (n)	[apa'rat]
javelin	**suliță** (f)	['sulitsə]

shot (metal ball)	**greutate** (f)	[greu'tate]
ball (snooker, etc.)	**bilă** (f)	['bilə]
aim (target)	**țintă** (f)	['tsintə]
target	**țintă** (f)	['tsintə]
to shoot (vi)	**a trage**	[a 'tradʒə]
accurate (~ shot)	**exact**	[e'gzakt]
trainer, coach	**antrenor** (m)	[antre'nor]
to train (sb)	**a antrena**	[a antre'na]
to train (vi)	**a se antrena**	[a se antre'na]
training	**antrenament** (n)	[antrena'ment]
gym	**sală** (f) **de sport**	['salə de sport]
exercise (physical)	**exercițiu** (n)	[egzer'tʃitsju]
warm-up (athlete ~)	**încălzire** (f)	[inkəl'zire]

Education

| school | şcoală (f) | [ʃko'alə] |
| headmaster | director (m) | [di'rektor] |

student (m)	elev (m)	[e'lev]
student (f)	elevă (f)	[e'levə]
schoolboy	elev (m)	[e'lev]
schoolgirl	elevă (f)	[e'levə]

to teach (sb)	a învăţa	[a invə'tsa]
to learn (language, etc.)	a învăţa	[a invə'tsa]
to learn by heart	a învăţa pe de rost	[a invə'tsa pe de rost]

to learn (~ to count, etc.)	a învăţa	[a invə'tsa]
to be at school	a merge la şcoală	[a 'merdʒe la ʃko'alə]
to go to school	a merge la şcoală	[a 'merdʒe la ʃko'alə]

| alphabet | alfabet (n) | [alfa'bet] |
| subject (at school) | disciplină (f) | [distʃi'plinə] |

classroom	clasă (f)	['klasə]
lesson	lecţie (f)	['lektsie]
playtime, break	recreaţie (f)	[rekre'atsie]
school bell	sunet (n)	['sunet]
school desk	bancă (f)	['bankə]
blackboard	tablă (f)	['tablə]

mark	notă (f)	['notə]
good mark	notă (f) bună	['notə 'bunə]
bad mark	notă (f) rea	['notə rʲa]
to give a mark	a pune notă	[a 'pune 'notə]

mistake, error	greşeală (f)	[gre'ʃalə]
to make mistakes	a greşi	[a gre'ʃi]
to correct (an error)	a corecta	[a korek'ta]
crib	fiţuică (f)	[fi'tsujkə]

| homework | temă (f) pentru acasă | ['temə 'pentru a'kasə] |
| exercise (in education) | exerciţiu (n) | [egzer'tʃitsju] |

| to be present | a fi prezent | [a fi pre'zent] |
| to be absent | a lipsi | [a lip'si] |

to punish (vt)	a pedepsi	[a pedep'si]
punishment	pedeapsă (f)	[pe'dʲapsə]
conduct (behaviour)	comportament (n)	[komporta'ment]
school report	agendă (f)	[a'dʒendə]

pencil	creion (n)	[kre'jon]
rubber	radieră (f)	[radi'erə]
chalk	cretă (f)	['kretə]
pencil case	penar (n)	[pe'nar]

schoolbag	ghiozdan (n)	[goz'dan]
pen	pix (n)	[piks]
exercise book	caiet (n)	[ka'et]
textbook	manual (n)	[manu'al]
compasses	compas (n)	[kom'pas]

| to make technical drawings | a schiţa | [a ski'tsa] |
| technical drawing | plan (n) | [plan] |

poem	poezie (f)	[poe'zie]
by heart (adv)	pe de rost	[pe de rost]
to learn by heart	a învăţa pe de rost	[a invə'tsa pe de rost]

| school holidays | vacanţă (f) | [va'kantsə] |
| to be on holiday | a fi în vacanţă | [a fi in va'kantsə] |

test (at school)	lucrare (f) de control	[lu'krare de kon'trol]
essay (composition)	compunere (f)	[kom'punere]
dictation	dictare (f)	[dik'tare]

exam (examination)	examen (n)	[e'gzamen]
to do an exam	a da examene	[a da e'gzamene]
experiment (e.g., chemistry ~)	experiment (f)	[eksperi'ment]

143. College. University

academy	academie (f)	[akade'mie]
university	universitate (f)	[universi'tate]
faculty (e.g., ~ of Medicine)	facultate (f)	[fakul'tate]

student (masc.)	student (m)	[stu'dent]
student (fem.)	studentă (f)	[stu'dentə]
lecturer (teacher)	profesor (m)	[pro'fesor]

| lecture hall, room | aulă (f) | [a'ulə] |
| graduate | absolvent (m) | [absol'vent] |

| diploma | diplomă (f) | ['diplomə] |
| dissertation | disertaţie (f) | [diser'tatsie] |

| study (report) | cercetare (f) | [tʃertʃe'tare] |
| laboratory | laborator (n) | [labora'tor] |

| lecture | prelegere (f) | [pre'ledʒere] |
| coursemate | coleg (m) de an | [ko'leg de an] |

| scholarship, bursary | bursă (f) | ['bursə] |
| academic degree | titlu (n) ştiinţific | ['titlu ʃtiin'tsifik] |

144. Sciences. Disciplines

mathematics	**matematică** (f)	[mate'matikə]
algebra	**algebră** (f)	[al'dʒebrə]
geometry	**geometrie** (f)	[dʒeome'trie]
astronomy	**astronomie** (f)	[astrono'mie]
biology	**biologie** (f)	[biolo'dʒie]
geography	**geografie** (f)	[dʒeogra'fie]
geology	**geologie** (f)	[dʒeolo'dʒie]
history	**istorie** (f)	[is'torie]
medicine	**medicină** (f)	[medi'tʃinə]
pedagogy	**pedagogie** (f)	[pedago'dʒie]
law	**drept** (n)	[drept]
physics	**fizică** (f)	['fizikə]
chemistry	**chimie** (f)	[ki'mie]
philosophy	**filozofie** (f)	[filozo'fie]
psychology	**psihologie** (f)	[psiholo'dʒie]

145. Writing system. Orthography

grammar	**gramatică** (f)	[gra'matikə]
vocabulary	**lexic** (n)	['leksik]
phonetics	**fonetică** (f)	[fo'netikə]
noun	**substantiv** (n)	[substan'tiv]
adjective	**adjectiv** (n)	[adʒek'tiv]
verb	**verb** (n)	[verb]
adverb	**adverb** (n)	[ad'verb]
pronoun	**pronume** (n)	[pro'nume]
interjection	**interjecție** (f)	[inter'ʒektsie]
preposition	**prepoziție** (f)	[prepo'zitsie]
root	**rădăcina** (f) **cuvântului**	[rədə'tʃina ku'vintuluj]
ending	**terminație** (f)	[termi'natsie]
prefix	**prefix** (n)	[pre'fiks]
syllable	**silabă** (f)	[si'labə]
suffix	**sufix** (n)	[su'fiks]
stress mark	**accent** (n)	[ak'tʃent]
apostrophe	**apostrof** (n)	[apo'strof]
full stop	**punct** (n)	[punkt]
comma	**virgulă** (f)	['virgulə]
semicolon	**punct** (n) **şi virgulă**	[punkt ʃi 'virgulə]
colon	**două puncte** (n pl)	['dowə 'punkte]
ellipsis	**puncte-puncte** (n pl)	['punkte 'punkte]
question mark	**semn** (n) **de întrebare**	[semn de intre'bare]
exclamation mark	**semn** (n) **de exclamare**	[semn de ekskla'mare]

inverted commas	ghilimele (f pl)	[gili'mele]
in inverted commas	în ghilimele	[in gili'mele]
parenthesis	paranteze (f pl)	[paran'teze]
in parenthesis	în paranteze	[in paran'teze]

hyphen	cratimă (f)	['kratimə]
dash	cratimă (f)	['kratimə]
space (between words)	spaţiu (n) liber	['spatsju 'liber]

| letter | literă (f) | ['literə] |
| capital letter | majusculă (f) | [ma'ʒuskulʲa] |

| vowel (n) | vocală (f) | [vo'kalə] |
| consonant (n) | consoană (f) | [konso'anə] |

sentence	prepoziţie (f)	[prepo'zitsie]
subject	subiect (n)	[su'bjekt]
predicate	predicat (n)	[predi'kat]

line	rând (n)	[rind]
on a new line	alineat	[aline'at]
paragraph	paragraf (n)	[para'graf]

word	cuvânt (n)	[ku'vint]
group of words	îmbinare (f) de cuvinte	[imbi'nare de ku'vinte]
expression	expresie (f)	[eks'presie]
synonym	sinonim (n)	[sino'nim]
antonym	antonim (n)	[anto'nim]

rule	regulă (f)	['regulə]
exception	excepţie (f)	[eks'tfeptsie]
correct (adj)	corect	[ko'rekt]

conjugation	conjugare (f)	[konʒu'gare]
declension	declinare (f)	[dekli'nare]
nominal case	caz (n)	[kaz]
question	întrebare (f)	[intre'bare]
to underline (vt)	a sublinia	[a siblini'a]
dotted line	linie (f) punctată	['linie punk'tatə]

146. Foreign languages

language	limbă (f)	['limbə]
foreign (adj)	străin	[strə'in]
to study (vt)	a studia	[a studi'a]
to learn (language, etc.)	a învăţa	[a invə'tsa]

to read (vi, vt)	a citi	[a tʃi'ti]
to speak (vi, vt)	a vorbi	[a vor'bi]
to understand (vt)	a înţelege	[a intse'ledʒe]
to write (vt)	a scrie	[a 'skrie]

| fast (adv) | repede | ['repede] |
| slowly (adv) | încet | [in'tʃet] |

fluently (adv)	**liber**	['liber]
rules	**reguli** (f pl)	['regulʲ]
grammar	**gramatică** (f)	[gra'matikə]
vocabulary	**lexic** (n)	['leksik]
phonetics	**fonetică** (f)	[fo'netikə]

textbook	**manual** (n)	[manu'al]
dictionary	**dicţionar** (n)	[diktsio'nar]
teach-yourself book	**manual** (n) **autodidactic**	[manu'al autodi'daktik]
phrasebook	**ghid** (n) **de conversaţie**	[gid de konver'satsie]

cassette, tape	**casetă** (f)	[ka'setə]
videotape	**casetă** (f) **video**	[ka'setə 'video]
CD, compact disc	**CD** (n)	[si'di]
DVD	**DVD** (n)	[divi'di]

alphabet	**alfabet** (n)	[alfa'bet]
to spell (vt)	**a spune pe litere**	[a vor'bi pe 'litere]
pronunciation	**pronunţie** (f)	[pro'nuntsie]

accent	**accent** (n)	[ak'tʃent]
with an accent	**cu accent**	['ku ak'tʃent]
without an accent	**fără accent**	['fərə ak'tʃent]

word	**cuvânt** (n)	[ku'vint]
meaning	**sens** (n)	[sens]

course (e.g. a French ~)	**cursuri** (n)	['kursurʲ]
to sign up	**a se înscrie**	[a se in'skrie]
teacher	**profesor** (m)	[pro'fesor]

translation (process)	**traducere** (f)	[tra'dutʃere]
translation (text, etc.)	**traducere** (f)	[tra'dutʃere]
translator	**traducător** (m)	[tradukə'tor]
interpreter	**translator** (m)	[trans'lator]

polyglot	**poliglot** (m)	[poli'glot]
memory	**memorie** (f)	[me'morie]

147. Fairy tale characters

Father Christmas	**Santa Claus** (m)	['santa 'klaus]
mermaid	**sirenă** (f)	[si'renə]

magician, wizard	**vrăjitor** (m)	[vrəʒi'tor]
fairy	**vrăjitoare** (f)	[vrəʒito'are]
magic (adj)	**miraculos**	[miraku'los]
magic wand	**baghetă** (f) **magică**	[ba'getə 'madʒikə]

fairy tale	**poveste** (f)	[po'veste]
miracle	**minune** (f)	[mi'nune]
dwarf	**gnom** (m)	[gnom]
to turn into ...	**a se preface în ...**	[a se pre'fatʃe in]
ghost	**stafie** (f)	[sta'fie]

phantom	fantomă (f)	[fan'tomə]
monster	monstru (m)	['monstru]
dragon	dragon (m)	[dra'gon]
giant	uriaş (m)	[uri'aʃ]

148. Zodiac Signs

Aries	Berbec (m)	[ber'bek]
Taurus	Taur (m)	['taur]
Gemini	Gemeni (m pl)	['dʒemenʲ]
Cancer	Rac (m)	[rak]
Leo	Leu (m)	['leu]
Virgo	Fecioară (f)	[fetʃio'arə]

Libra	Balanţă (f)	[ba'lantsə]
Scorpio	Scorpion (m)	[skorpi'on]
Sagittarius	Săgetător (m)	[sədʒetə'tor]
Capricorn	Capricorn (m)	[kapri'korn]
Aquarius	Vărsător (m)	[vərsə'tor]
Pisces	Peşti (m pl)	[peʃtʲ]

character	caracter (m)	[karak'ter]
character traits	trăsături (f pl) de caracter	[trəsə'turʲ de karak'ter]
behaviour	comportament (n)	[komporta'ment]
to tell fortunes	a prezice	[a pre'zitʃe]
fortune-teller	prezicătoare (f)	[prezikəto'are]
horoscope	horoscop (n)	[horo'skop]

Arts

theatre	**teatru** (n)	[te'atru]
opera	**operă** (f)	['operə]
operetta	**operetă** (f)	[ope'retə]
ballet	**balet** (n)	[ba'let]

theatre poster	**afiş** (n)	[a'fiʃ]
theatre company	**trupă** (f)	['trupə]
tour	**turneu** (n)	[tur'neu]
to be on tour	**a juca în turneu**	[a ʒu'ka in tur'neu]
to rehearse (vi, vt)	**a repeta**	[a repe'ta]
rehearsal	**repetiţie** (f)	[repe'titsie]
repertoire	**repertoriu** (n)	[reper'torju]

performance	**reprezentaţie** (f)	[rəprəzən'tatje]
theatrical show	**spectacol** (n)	[spekta'kol]
play	**piesă** (f) **de teatru**	['pjesə de te'atru]

ticket	**bilet** (n)	[bi'let]
booking office	**casă** (f) **de bilete**	['kasə de bi'lete]
lobby, foyer	**hol** (n)	[hol]
coat check (cloakroom)	**garderobă** (f)	[garde'robə]
cloakroom ticket	**număr** (n)	['numər]
binoculars	**binoclu** (n)	[bi'noklu]
usher	**controlor** (m)	[kontro'lor]

stalls (orchestra seats)	**parter** (n)	[par'ter]
balcony	**balcon** (n)	[bal'kon]
dress circle	**mezanin** (n)	[meza'nin]
box	**lojă** (f)	['loʒə]
row	**rând** (n)	[rind]
seat	**loc** (n)	[lok]

audience	**public** (n)	['publik]
spectator	**spectator** (m)	[spekta'tor]
to clap (vi, vt)	**a aplauda**	[a aplau'da]
applause	**aplauze** (f pl)	[ap'lauze]
ovation	**ovaţii** (f pl)	[o'vatsij]

stage	**scenă** (f)	['stʃenə]
curtain	**cortină** (f)	[kor'tinə]
scenery	**decor** (n)	[de'kor]
backstage	**culise** (f)	[ku'lise]

scene (e.g. the last ~)	**scenă** (f)	['stʃenə]
act	**act** (n)	[akt]
interval	**antract** (n)	[an'trakt]

150. Cinema

| actor | actor (m) | [ak'tor] |
| actress | actriță (f) | [ak'tritsə] |

cinema (industry)	cinema (n)	[tʃine'ma]
film	film (n)	[film]
episode	serie (f)	['serie]

detective film	detectiv (n)	[detek'tiv]
action film	film (n) de acțiune	['film de aktsi'une]
adventure film	film (n) de aventură	['film de aven'turə]
science fiction film	film (n) fantastic	['film fan'tastik]
horror film	film (m) de groază	['film de gro'azə]

comedy film	comedie (f)	[kome'die]
melodrama	melodramă (f)	[melo'dramə]
drama	dramă (f)	['dramə]

fictional film	film (n) artistic	[film ar'tistik]
documentary	film (n) documentar	[film dokumen'tar]
cartoon	desene (n) animate	[de'sene ani'mate]
silent films	film (n) mut	[film mut]

role (part)	rol (n)	[rol]
leading role	rolul (n) principal	['rolul printʃi'pal]
to play (vi, vt)	a juca	[a ʒu'ka]

film star	stea (f) de cinema	[st'a de tʃine'ma]
well-known (adj)	cunoscut	[kunos'kut]
famous (adj)	vestit	[ves'tit]
popular (adj)	popular	[popu'lar]

script (screenplay)	scenariu (n)	[stʃe'narju]
scriptwriter	scenarist (m)	[stʃena'rist]
film director	regizor (m)	[re'dʒizor]
producer	producător (m)	[produkə'tor]
assistant	asistent (m)	[asis'tent]
cameraman	operator (m)	[opera'tor]
stuntman	cascador (m)	[kaska'dor]

to shoot a film	a turna un film	[a tur'na un film]
audition, screen test	probe (f pl)	['probe]
shooting	filmări (f pl)	[filmərʲ]
film crew	echipă (f) de filmare	[e'kipə de fil'mare]
film set	teren (n) de filmare	[te'ren de fil'mare]
camera	cameră (f) de luat vederi	['kamerə de lu'at ve'derʲ]

cinema	cinematograf (n)	[tʃinemato'graf]
screen (e.g. big ~)	ecran (n)	[e'kran]
to show a film	a prezenta un film	[a prezen'ta 'un 'film]

soundtrack	linie (f) sonoră	['linie so'norə]
special effects	efecte (n pl) speciale	[e'fekte spetʃi'ale]
subtitles	subtitluri (n pl)	[sub'titlurʲ]

| credits | **titrări** (f pl) | [tit'rərʲ] |
| translation | **traducere** (f) | [tra'dutʃere] |

151. Painting

art	**artă** (f)	['artə]
fine arts	**arte** (f pl) **frumoase**	['arte frumo'ase]
art gallery	**galerie** (f)	[gale'rie]
art exhibition	**expoziție** (f) **de tablouri**	[ekspo'zitsie de tab'lourʲ]

painting (art)	**pictură** (f)	[pik'turə]
graphic art	**grafică** (f)	['grafikə]
abstract art	**abstracționism** (n)	[abstraktsio'nism]
impressionism	**impresionism** (n)	[impresio'nism]

picture (painting)	**tablou** (n)	[tab'lou]
drawing	**desen** (n)	[de'sen]
poster	**afiş** (n)	[a'fiʃ]

illustration (picture)	**ilustraţie** (f)	[ilus'tratsie]
miniature	**miniatură** (f)	[minia'turə]
copy (of painting, etc.)	**copie** (f)	['kopie]
reproduction	**reproducere** (f)	[repro'dutʃere]

mosaic	**mozaic** (n)	[moza'ik]
stained glass window	**vitraliu** (n)	[vi'tralju]
fresco	**frescă** (f)	['freskə]
engraving	**gravură** (f)	[gra'vurə]

bust (sculpture)	**bust** (n)	[bust]
sculpture	**sculptură** (f)	[skulp'turə]
statue	**statuie** (f)	[sta'tue]
plaster of Paris	**ghips** (n)	[gips]
plaster (as adj)	**de, din ghips**	[de, din gips]

portrait	**portret** (n)	[por'tret]
self-portrait	**autoportret** (n)	[autopor'tret]
landscape painting	**peisaj** (n)	[pej'saʒ]
still life	**natură** (f) **moartă**	[na'turə mo'artə]
caricature	**caricatură** (f)	[karika'turə]

paint	**vopsea** (f)	[vop'sʲa]
watercolor paint	**acuarelă** (f)	[akua'relə]
oil (paint)	**ulei** (n)	[u'lej]
pencil	**creion** (n)	[kre'jon]
Indian ink	**tuş** (n)	[tuʃ]
charcoal	**cărbune** (m)	[kər'bune]

to draw (vi, vt)	**a schiţa**	[a ski'tsa]
to paint (vi, vt)	**a schiţa**	[a ski'tsa]
to pose (vi)	**a poza**	[a po'za]
artist's model (masc.)	**naturist** (m)	[natu'rist]
artist's model (fem.)	**naturistă** (f)	[natu'ristə]
artist (painter)	**pictor** (m)	['piktor]

work of art	operă (f)	['operə]
masterpiece	capodoperă (f)	[kapo'doperə]
studio (artist's workroom)	atelier (n)	[ate'ljer]

canvas (cloth)	pânză (f)	['pinzə]
easel	şevalet (n)	[ʃəva'let]
palette	paletă (f)	[pa'letə]

frame (picture ~, etc.)	ramă (f)	['ramə]
restoration	restaurare (f)	[restau'rare]
to restore (vt)	a restaura	[a restau'ra]

152. Literature & Poetry

literature	literatură (f)	[litera'turə]
author (writer)	autor (m)	[au'tor]
pseudonym	pseudonim (n)	[pseudo'nim]

book	carte (f)	['karte]
volume	volum (n)	[vo'lum]
table of contents	cuprins (n)	[ku'prins]
page	pagină (f)	['padʒinə]
main character	erou (m) principal	[e'rou printʃi'pal]
autograph	autograf (n)	[auto'graf]

short story	povestire (f)	[poves'tire]
story (novella)	nuvelă (f)	[nu'velə]
novel	roman (n)	[ro'man]
work (writing)	compunere (f)	[kom'punere]
fable	fabulă (f)	['fabulə]
detective novel	detectiv (m)	[detek'tiv]

poem (verse)	poezie (f)	[poe'zie]
poetry	poezie (f)	[poe'zie]
poem (epic, ballad)	poem (n)	[po'em]
poet	poet (m)	[po'et]

fiction	literatură (f) artistică	[litera'turə ar'tistikə]
science fiction	science fiction (n)	['saens 'fikʃn]
adventures	aventură (f)	[aven'turə]
educational literature	literatură (f) ştiinţifică	[litera'turə ʃtiin'tsifikə]
children's literature	literatură (f) pentru copii	[litera'turə 'pentru ko'pij]

153. Circus

circus	circ (n)	[tʃirk]
travelling circus	circ (n) pe roţi	[tʃirk pe 'rots]
programme	program (n)	[pro'gram]
performance	spectacol (n)	[spekta'kol]

| act (circus ~) | număr (n) | ['numər] |
| circus ring | arenă (f) | [a'renə] |

| pantomime (act) | pantomimă (f) | [panto'mimə] |
| clown | clovn (m) | [klovn] |

acrobat	acrobat (m)	[akro'bat]
acrobatics	acrobatică (f)	[akro'batikə]
gymnast	gimnast (m)	[dʒim'nast]
acrobatic gymnastics	gimnastică (f)	[dʒim'nastikə]
somersault	tumbă (f)	['tumbə]

strongman	atlet (m)	[at'let]
tamer (e.g., lion ~)	îmblânzitor (m)	[imblinzi'tor]
rider (circus horse ~)	călăreţ (m)	[kələ'rets]
assistant	asistent (m)	[asis'tent]

stunt	truc (n)	[truk]
magic trick	scamatorie (f)	[skama'torie]
conjurer, magician	scamator (m)	[skama'tor]

juggler	jongler (m)	[ʒon'gler]
to juggle (vi, vt)	a jongla	[a ʒon'gla]
animal trainer	dresor (m)	[dre'sor]
animal training	dresare (f)	[dre'sare]
to train (animals)	a dresa	[a dre'sa]

154. Music. Pop music

music	muzică (f)	['muzikə]
musician	muzician (m)	[muzitʃi'an]
musical instrument	instrument (n) muzical	[instru'ment muzi'kal]
to play …	a cânta la …	[a kin'ta 'la]

guitar	chitară (f)	[ki'tarə]
violin	vioară (f)	[vio'arə]
cello	violoncel (n)	[violon'tʃel]
double bass	contrabas (n)	[kontra'bas]
harp	harpă (f)	['harpə]

piano	pianină (f)	[pia'nino]
grand piano	pian (n) cu coadă	['pjan ku ku'ado]
organ	orgă (f)	['orgə]

wind instruments	instrumente (n pl) de suflat	[instru'mente de suf'lat]
oboe	oboi (m)	[o'boj]
saxophone	saxofon (n)	[sakso'fon]
clarinet	clarinet (n)	[klari'net]
flute	flaut (n)	['flaut]
trumpet	trompetă (f)	[trom'petə]

| accordion | acordeon (n) | [akorde'on] |
| drum | tobă (f) | ['tobə] |

duo	duet (n)	[du'et]
trio	trio (n)	['trio]
quartet	cvartet (n)	[kvar'tet]

choir	**cor** (n)	[kor]
orchestra	**orchestră** (f)	[orˈkestrə]
pop music	**muzică** (f) **pop**	[ˈmuzikə pop]
rock music	**muzică** (f) **rock**	[ˈmuzikə rok]
rock group	**formaţie** (n) **rock**	[forˈmatsie rok]
jazz	**jazz** (n)	[ʤaz]
idol	**idol** (m)	[ˈidol]
admirer, fan	**fan** (m)	[fan]
concert	**concert** (n)	[konˈʧert]
symphony	**simfonie** (f)	[simfoˈnie]
composition	**operă** (f)	[ˈoperə]
to compose (write)	**a compune**	[a komˈpune]
singing (n)	**cântare** (f)	[kinˈtare]
song	**cântec** (n)	[ˈkintek]
tune (melody)	**melodie** (f)	[meloˈdie]
rhythm	**ritm** (n)	[ritm]
blues	**blues** (n)	[bluz]
sheet music	**note** (f pl)	[ˈnote]
baton	**baghetă** (f)	[baˈgetə]
bow	**arcuş** (n)	[arˈkuʃ]
string	**coardă** (f)	[koˈardə]
case (e.g. guitar ~)	**husă** (f)	[ˈhusə]

Rest. Entertainment. Travel

155. Trip. Travel

tourism, travel	**turism** (n)	[tu'rism]
tourist	**turist** (m)	[tu'rist]
trip, voyage	**călătorie** (f)	[kələto'rie]
adventure	**aventură** (f)	[aven'turə]
trip, journey	**voiaj** (n)	[vo'jaʒ]
holiday	**concediu** (n)	[kon'ʧedju]
to be on holiday	**a fi în concediu**	[a fi in kon'ʧedju]
rest	**odihnă** (f)	[o'dihnə]
train	**tren** (n)	[tren]
by train	**cu trenul**	[ku 'trenul]
aeroplane	**avion** (n)	[a'vjon]
by aeroplane	**cu avionul**	[ku a'vjonul]
by car	**cu automobilul**	[ku automo'bilul]
by ship	**cu vaporul**	[ku va'porul]
luggage	**bagaj** (n)	[ba'gaʒ]
suitcase	**valiză** (f)	[va'lizə]
luggage trolley	**cărucior** (n) **pentru bagaj**	[kəru'ʧior 'pentru ba'gaʒ]
passport	**paşaport** (n)	[paʃa'port]
visa	**viză** (f)	['vizə]
ticket	**bilet** (n)	[bi'let]
air ticket	**bilet** (n) **de avion**	[bi'let de a'vjon]
guidebook	**ghid** (m)	[gid]
map (tourist ~)	**hartă** (f)	['hartə]
area (rural ~)	**localitate** (f)	[lokali'tate]
place, site	**loc** (n)	[lok]
exotica (n)	**exotism** (n)	[egzo'tism]
exotic (adj)	**exotic**	[e'gzotik]
amazing (adj)	**uimitor**	[ujmi'tor]
group	**grup** (n)	[grup]
excursion, sightseeing tour	**excursie** (f)	[eks'kursie]
guide (person)	**ghid** (m)	[gid]

156. Hotel

hotel	**hotel** (n)	[ho'tel]
motel	**motel** (n)	[mo'tel]
three-star (~ hotel)	**trei stele**	[trej 'stele]

five-star	**cinci stele**	[ʧinʧ 'stele]
to stay (in a hotel, etc.)	**a se opri**	[a se o'pri]
room	**cameră** (f)	['kamerə]
single room	**cameră pentru o persoană** (n)	['kamerə 'pentru o perso'anə]
double room	**cameră pentru două persoane** (n)	['kamerə 'pentru 'dowə perso'ane]
to book a room	**a rezerva o cameră**	[a rezer'va o 'kamerə]
half board	**demipensiune** (f)	[demipensi'une]
full board	**pensiune** (f)	[pensi'une]
with bath	**cu baie**	[ku 'bae]
with shower	**cu duş**	[ku duʃ]
satellite television	**televiziune** (f) **prin satelit**	[televizi'une 'prin sate'lit]
air-conditioner	**aer** (n) **condiţionat**	['aer konditsio'nat]
towel	**prosop** (n)	[pro'sop]
key	**cheie** (f)	['kee]
administrator	**administrator** (m)	[adminis'trator]
chambermaid	**femeie** (f) **de serviciu**	[fe'mee de ser'viʧiu]
porter	**hamal** (m)	[ha'mal]
doorman	**portar** (m)	[por'tar]
restaurant	**restaurant** (n)	[restau'rant]
pub, bar	**bar** (n)	[bar]
breakfast	**micul dejun** (n)	['mikul de'ʒun]
dinner	**cină** (f)	['ʧinə]
buffet	**masă suedeză** (f)	['masə sue'dezə]
lobby	**vestibul** (n)	[vesti'bul]
lift	**lift** (n)	[lift]
DO NOT DISTURB	**NU DERANJAŢI!**	[nu deran'ʒats]
NO SMOKING	**NU FUMAŢI!**	[nu fu'mats]

157. Books. Reading

book	**carte** (f)	['karte]
author	**autor** (m)	[au'tor]
writer	**scriitor** (m)	[skrii'tor]
to write (~ a book)	**a scrie**	[a 'skrie]
reader	**cititor** (m)	[ʧiti'tor]
to read (vi, vt)	**a citi**	[a ʧi'ti]
reading (activity)	**lectură** (f)	[lek'turə]
silently (to oneself)	**în gând**	[in gind]
aloud (adv)	**cu voce tare**	[ku 'voʧe 'tare]
to publish (vt)	**a publica**	[a publi'ka]
publishing (process)	**ediţie** (f)	[e'ditsie]
publisher	**editor** (m)	[edi'tor]

publishing house	**editură** (f)	[edi'turə]
to come out (be released)	**a apărea**	[a apə'rʲa]
release (of a book)	**publicare** (f)	[publi'kare]
print run	**tiraj** (n)	[ti'raʒ]
bookshop	**librărie** (f)	[librə'rie]
library	**bibliotecă** (f)	[biblio'tekə]
story (novella)	**nuvelă** (f)	[nu'velə]
short story	**povestire** (f)	[poves'tire]
novel	**roman** (n)	[ro'man]
detective novel	**detectiv** (n)	[detek'tiv]
memoirs	**memorii** (n pl)	[me'morij]
legend	**legendă** (f)	[le'dʒendə]
myth	**mit** (n)	[mit]
poetry, poems	**versuri** (n pl)	['versurʲ]
autobiography	**autobiografie** (f)	[autobiogra'fie]
selected works	**opere** (f pl) **alese**	['opere a'lese]
science fiction	**fantastică** (f)	[fan'tastikə]
title	**denumire** (f)	[denu'mire]
introduction	**prefață** (f)	[pre'faʦə]
title page	**foaie** (f) **de titlu**	[fo'ae de 'titlu]
chapter	**capitol** (n)	[ka'pitol]
extract	**fragment** (n)	[frag'ment]
episode	**episod** (n)	[epi'zod]
plot (storyline)	**subiect** (n)	[su'bjekt]
contents	**cuprins** (n)	[ku'prins]
table of contents	**cuprins** (n)	[ku'prins]
main character	**erou** (m) **principal**	[e'rou prinʧi'pal]
volume	**volum** (n)	[vo'lum]
cover	**copertă** (f)	[ko'pertə]
binding	**copertă** (f)	[ko'pertə]
bookmark	**semn** (n) **de carte**	[semn de 'karte]
page	**pagină** (f)	['padʒinə]
to page through	**a răsfoi**	[a rəsfo'i]
margins	**margine** (f)	['mardʒine]
annotation (marginal note, etc.)	**notă** (f) **marginală**	['notə mardʒi'nalə]
footnote	**însemnare** (f)	[insem'nare]
text	**text** (n)	[tekst]
type, fount	**caracter** (n)	[karak'ter]
misprint, typo	**greşeală** (f) **de tipar**	[gre'ʃalə de ti'par]
translation	**traducere** (f)	[tra'duʧere]
to translate (vt)	**a traduce**	[a tra'duʧe]
original (n)	**original** (n)	[oridʒi'nal]
famous (adj)	**vestit**	[ves'tit]
unknown (not famous)	**necunoscut**	[nekunos'kut]

| interesting (adj) | interesant | [intere'sant] |
| bestseller | best seller (n) | [best 'seler] |

dictionary	dicţionar (n)	[dikʦio'nar]
textbook	manual (n)	[manu'al]
encyclopedia	enciclopedie (f)	[entʃiklope'die]

158. Hunting. Fishing

hunting	vânătoare (f)	[vinəto'are]
to hunt (vi, vt)	a vâna	[a vi'na]
hunter	vânător (m)	[vinə'tor]

to shoot (vi)	a trage	[a 'tradʒə]
rifle	armă (f)	['armə]
bullet (shell)	cartuş (n)	[kar'tuʃ]
shot (lead balls)	alice (f)	[a'liʧe]

steel trap	capcană (f)	[kap'kanə]
snare (for birds, etc.)	cursă (f)	['kursə]
to lay a steel trap	a pune capcană	[a 'pune kap'kanə]

poacher	braconier (m)	[brako'njer]
game (in hunting)	vânat (n)	[vi'nat]
hound dog	câine (m) de vânătoare	['kine de vinəto'are]
safari	safari (n)	[sa'fari]
mounted animal	animal (n) împăiat	[ani'mal impə'jat]

fisherman	pescar (m)	[pes'kar]
fishing (angling)	pescuit (n)	[pesku'it]
to fish (vi)	a pescui	[a pesku'i]

fishing rod	undiţă (f)	['unditsə]
fishing line	sfoara (f) undiţei	[sfo'ara 'unditsej]
hook	cârlig (n)	[kir'lig]
float	plută (f)	['plutə]
bait	momeală (f)	[mo'mʲalə]

| to cast a line | a arunca undiţa | [a arun'ka 'unditsa] |
| to bite (ab. fish) | a trage la undiţă | [a 'tradʒe la 'unditsə] |

| catch (of fish) | pescuit (n) | [pesku'it] |
| ice-hole | copcă (f) | ['kopkə] |

fishing net	plasă (f)	['plasə]
boat	barcă (f)	['barkə]
to net (to fish with a net)	a prinde cu plasa	[a 'prinde 'ku 'plasa]

| to cast[throw] the net | a arunca plasa | [a arun'ka 'plasa] |
| to haul the net in | a scoate plasa | [a sko'ate 'plasa] |

whaler (person)	vânător (m) de balene	[vanə'tor də 'balenə]
whaleboat	balenieră (f)	[bale'njerə]
harpoon	harpon (n)	[har'pon]

159. Games. Billiards

billiards	biliard (n)	[bi'ljard]
billiard room, hall	sală (f) de biliard	['salə de bi'ljard]
ball (snooker, etc.)	bilă (f)	['bilə]
to pocket a ball	a băga bila	[a bə'ga 'bila]
cue	tac (n)	[tak]
pocket	gaură (f) de biliard	['gaurə de bi'ljard]

160. Games. Playing cards

diamonds	tobă (f)	['tobə]
spades	pică (f)	['pikə]
hearts	cupă (f)	['kupə]
clubs	treflă (f)	['treflə]
ace	as (m)	[as]
king	rege (m)	['redʒe]
queen	damă (f)	['damə]
jack, knave	valet (m)	[va'let]
playing card	carte (f) de joc	['karte de ʒok]
cards	cărţi (f pl) de joc	[kərts^j de ʒok]
trump	atu (n)	[a'tu]
pack of cards	pachet (n) de cărţi de joc	[pa'ket de kərts de ʒok]
to deal (vi, vt)	a împărţi	[a impər'tsi]
to shuffle (cards)	a amesteca	[a ameste'ka]
lead, turn (n)	rând (n)	[rind]
cardsharp	trişor (m)	[tri'ʃor]

161. Casino. Roulette

casino	cazinou (n)	[kazi'nou]
roulette (game)	ruletă (f)	[ru'letə]
bet	miză (f)	['mizə]
to place bets	a miza	[a mi'za]
red	roşu (m)	['roʃu]
black	negru (m)	['negru]
to bet on red	a miza pe roşu	[a mi'za pe 'roʃu]
to bet on black	a miza pe negru	[a mi'za pe 'negru]
croupier (dealer)	crupier (m)	[kru'pjer]
to spin the wheel	a învârti ruleta	[a invir'ti ru'leta]
rules (~ of the game)	reguli (f pl) de joc	['regul^j de ʒok]
chip	fisă (f)	['fisə]
to win (vi, vt)	a câştiga	[a kiʃti'ga]
win (winnings)	câştig (n)	[kiʃ'tig]

| to lose (~ 100 dollars) | a pierde | [a 'pjerde] |
| loss (losses) | pierdere (f) | ['perdere] |

player	jucător (m)	[ʒukə'tor]
blackjack (card game)	Black Jack (m)	[blək dʒek]
craps (dice game)	table (f pl)	['table]
fruit machine	joc (n) mecanic	[ʒok me'kanik]

162. Rest. Games. Miscellaneous

to stroll (vi, vt)	a se plimba	[a se plim'ba]
stroll (leisurely walk)	plimbare (f)	[plim'bare]
car ride	excursie (f)	[eks'kursie]
adventure	aventură (f)	[aven'turə]
picnic	picnic (n)	['piknik]

game (chess, etc.)	joc (n)	[ʒok]
player	jucător (m)	[ʒukə'tor]
game (one ~ of chess)	partidă (f)	[par'tidə]

collector (e.g. philatelist)	colecționar (m)	[kolektsio'nar]
to collect (stamps, etc.)	a colecționa	[a kolektsio'na]
collection	colecție (f)	[ko'lektsie]

crossword puzzle	rebus (n)	['rebus]
racecourse (hippodrome)	hipodrom (n)	[hipo'drom]
disco (discotheque)	discotecă (f)	[disko'tekə]

| sauna | saună (f) | ['saunə] |
| lottery | loterie (f) | [lote'rie] |

camping trip	camping (n)	['kemping]
camp	tabără (f)	['tabərə]
tent (for camping)	cort (n)	[kort]
compass	busolă (f)	[bu'solə]
camper	turist (m)	[tu'rist]

to watch (film, etc.)	a se uita	[a se uj'ta]
viewer	telespectator (m)	[telespekta'tor]
TV show (TV program)	emisiune (f) televizată	[emisi'une televi'zatə]

163. Photography

| camera (photo) | aparat (n) foto | [apa'rat 'foto] |
| photo, picture | fotografie (f) | [fotogra'fie] |

photographer	fotograf (m)	[foto'graf]
photo studio	studio (n) foto	[stu'djo 'foto]
photo album	album (n) foto	[al'bum 'foto]

| camera lens | obiectiv (n) | [objek'tiv] |
| telephoto lens | teleobiectiv (n) | [teleobjek'tiv] |

| filter | filtru (n) | ['filtru] |
| lens | lentilă (f) | [len'tilə] |

optics (high-quality ~)	optică (f)	['optikə]
diaphragm (aperture)	diafragmă (f)	[dia'fragmə]
exposure time (shutter speed)	timp (m) de expunere	['timp de eks'punere]
viewfinder	vizor (n)	[vi'zor]

digital camera	cameră (f) digitală	['kamerə didʒi'talə]
tripod	suport (n)	[su'port]
flash	blitz (n)	[bliʦ]

to photograph (vt)	a fotografia	[a fotografi'ja]
to take pictures	a fotografia	[a fotografi'ja]
to have one's picture taken	a se fotografia	[a se fotografi'ja]

focus	claritate (f)	[klari'tate]
to focus	a îndrepta	[a indrep'ta]
sharp, in focus (adj)	clar	[klar]
sharpness	claritatea (f) imaginii	[klari'tat'a i'madʒinij]

| contrast | contrast (n) | [kon'trast] |
| contrast (as adj) | de contrast | [de kon'trast] |

picture (photo)	fotografie (f)	[fotogra'fie]
negative (n)	negativ (n)	[nega'tiv]
film (a roll of ~)	film (n)	[film]
frame (still)	cadru (n)	['kadru]
to print (photos)	a tipări	[a tipə'ri]

164. Beach. Swimming

beach	plajă (f)	['plaʒə]
sand	nisip (n)	[ni'sip]
deserted (beach)	pustiu	[pus'tiu]

suntan	bronz (n)	[bronz]
to get a tan	a se bronza	[a se bron'za]
tanned (adj)	bronzat	[bron'zat]
sunscreen	cremă (f) pentru bronzat	['kremə 'pentru bron'zat]

bikini	bikini (n)	[bi'kini]
swimsuit, bikini	costum (n) de baie	[kos'tum de 'bae]
swim trunks	slipi (m pl)	[slipi]

swimming pool	bazin (n)	[ba'zin]
to swim (vi)	a înota	[a ino'ta]
shower	duş (n)	[duʃ]
to change (one's clothes)	a se schimba	[a se skim'ba]
towel	prosop (n)	[pro'sop]

| boat | barcă (f) | ['barkə] |
| motorboat | cuter (n) | ['kuter] |

water ski	**schiuri** (n pl) **pe apă**	['skjurⁱ pe 'apə]
pedalo	**bicicletă** (f) **pe apă**	[bitʃi'kletə pe 'apə]
surfing	**surfing** (n)	['serfing]
surfer	**surfer** (m)	['serfer]
scuba set	**acvalang** (n)	[akva'lang]
flippers (swim fins)	**labe** (f pl) **de înot**	['labe de i'not]
mask (diving ~)	**mască** (f)	['maskə]
diver	**scufundător** (m)	[skufundə'tor]
to dive (vi)	**a se scufunda**	[a se skufun'da]
underwater (adv)	**sub apă**	[sub 'apə]
beach umbrella	**umbrelă** (f)	[um'brelə]
beach chair (sun lounger)	**şezlong** (n)	[ʃez'long]
sunglasses	**ochelari** (m pl)	[oke'larⁱ]
air mattress	**saltea** (f) **de înot**	[sal'tⁱa de i'not]
to play (amuse oneself)	**a juca**	[a ʒu'ka]
to go for a swim	**a se scălda**	[a se skəl'da]
beach ball	**minge** (f)	['mindʒe]
to inflate (vt)	**a umfla**	[a um'fla]
inflatable, air (adj)	**pneumatic**	[pneu'matik]
wave	**val** (n)	[val]
buoy (line of ~s)	**baliză** (f)	[ba'lizə]
to drown (ab. person)	**a se îneca**	[a se ine'ka]
to save, to rescue	**a salva**	[a sal'va]
life jacket	**vestă** (f) **de salvare**	['vestə de sal'vare]
to observe, to watch	**a observa**	[a obser'va]
lifeguard	**salvator** (m)	[salva'tor]

TECHNICAL EQUIPMENT. TRANSPORT

Technical equipment

165. Computer

computer	calculator (n)	[kalkula'tor]
notebook, laptop	laptop (n)	[ləp'top]
to turn on	a deschide	[a des'kide]
to turn off	a închide	[a i'nkide]
keyboard	tastatură (f)	[tasta'turə]
key	tastă (f)	['tastə]
mouse	mouse (n)	['maus]
mouse mat	mousepad (n)	[maus'pad]
button	tastă (f)	['tastə]
cursor	cursor (m)	[kur'sor]
monitor	monitor (n)	[moni'tor]
screen	ecran (n)	[e'kran]
hard disk	hard disc (n)	[hard disk]
hard disk capacity	capacitatea (f) hard discului	[kapatʃi'tatʲa 'hard 'diskuluj]
memory	memorie (f)	[me'morie]
random access memory	memorie (f) operativă	[me'morie opera'tivə]
file	fișier (n)	[fiʃi'er]
folder	document (n)	[doku'ment]
to open (vt)	a deschide	[a des'kide]
to close (vt)	a închide	[a i'nkide]
to save (vt)	a păstra	[a pəs'tra]
to delete (vt)	a șterge	[a 'ʃterdʒe]
to copy (vt)	a copia	[a kopi'ja]
to sort (vt)	a sorta	[a sor'ta]
to transfer (copy)	a copia	[a kopi'ja]
programme	program (n)	[pro'gram]
software	programe (n) de aplicație	[pro'grame de apli'katsie]
programmer	programator (m)	[programa'tor]
to program (vt)	a programa	[a progra'ma]
hacker	hacker (m)	['haker]
password	parolă (f)	[pa'rolə]
virus	virus (m)	['virus]
to find, to detect	a găsi	[a gə'si]
byte	bait (m)	[bajt]

megabyte	**megabyte** (m)	[mega'bajt]
data	**date** (f pl)	['date]
database	**bază** (f) **de date**	['bazə de 'date]

cable (USB, etc.)	**cablu** (n)	['kablu]
to disconnect (vt)	**a deconecta**	[a dekonek'ta]
to connect (sth to sth)	**a conecta**	[a konek'ta]

166. Internet. E-mail

Internet	**internet** (n)	[inter'net]
browser	**browser** (n)	['brauzer]
search engine	**motor** (n) **de căutare**	[mo'tor de kəu'tare]
provider	**cablu** (n)	['kablu]

webmaster	**web master** (m)	[web 'master]
website	**web site** (n)	[web 'sajt]
web page	**pagină** (f) **web**	['padʒinə web]

address (e-mail ~)	**adresă** (f)	[a'dresə]
address book	**registru** (n) **de adrese**	[re'dʒistru de a'drese]

postbox	**cutie** (f) **poştală**	[ku'tie poʃ'talə]
post	**corespondenţă** (f)	[korespon'dentsə]

message	**mesaj** (n)	[me'saʒ]
sender	**expeditor** (m)	[ekspedi'tor]
to send (vt)	**a expedia**	[a ekspedi'ja]
sending (of mail)	**expediere** (f)	[ekspe'djere]

receiver	**destinatar** (m)	[destina'tar]
to receive (vt)	**a primi**	[a pri'mi]

correspondence	**corespondenţă** (f)	[korespon'dentsə]
to correspond (vi)	**a coresponda**	[a korespon'da]

file	**fişier** (n)	[fiʃi'er]
to download (vt)	**a copia**	[a kopi'ja]
to create (vt)	**a crea**	[a 'krʲa]
to delete (vt)	**a şterge**	[a 'ʃterdʒe]
deleted (adj)	**şters**	[ʃters]

connection (ADSL, etc.)	**conexiune** (f)	[koneksi'une]
speed	**viteză** (f)	[vi'tezə]
modem	**modem** (n)	[mo'dem]

access	**acces** (n)	[ak'tʃes]
port (e.g. input ~)	**port** (n)	[port]

connection (make a ~)	**conectare** (f)	[konek'tare]
to connect to … (vi)	**a se conecta**	[a se konek'ta]

to select (vt)	**a alege**	[a a'ledʒe]
to search (for …)	**a căuta**	[a kəu'ta]

167. Electricity

electricity	electricitate (f)	[elektritʃi'tate]
electric, electrical (adj)	electric	[e'lektrik]
electric power station	centrală (f) electrică	[tʃen'tralə e'lektrikə]
energy	energie (f)	[ener'dʒie]
electric power	energie (f) electrică	[ener'dʒie e'lektrikə]
light bulb	bec (n)	[bek]
torch	lanternă (f)	[lan'ternə]
street light	felinar (n)	[feli'nar]
light	lumină (f)	[lu'minə]
to turn on	a aprinde	[a a'prinde]
to turn off	a stinge	[a 'stindʒe]
to turn off the light	a stinge lumina	[a 'stindʒe lu'mina]
to burn out (vi)	a arde	[a 'arde]
short circuit	scurtcircuit (n)	['skurtʃirku'it]
broken wire	ruptură (f)	[rup'turə]
contact (electrical ~)	contact (n)	[kon'takt]
light switch	întrerupător (n)	[intrerupə'tor]
socket outlet	priză (f)	['prizə]
plug	furcă (f)	['furkə]
extension lead	prelungitor (n)	[prelundʒi'tor]
fuse	siguranță (f)	[sigu'rantsə]
cable, wire	fir (n) electric	[fir e'lektrik]
wiring	instalație (f) electrică	[insta'latsie e'lektrikə]
ampere	amper (m)	[am'per]
amperage	intensitatea (f) curentului	[intensi'tatʲa ku'rentuluj]
volt	volt (m)	[volt]
voltage	tensiune (f)	[tensi'une]
electrical device	aparat (n) electric	[apa'rat e'lektrik]
indicator	indicator (n)	[indika'tor]
electrician	electrician (m)	[elektritʃi'an]
to solder (vt)	a lipi	[a li'pi]
soldering iron	ciocan (n) de lipit	[tʃio'kan de li'pit]
electric current	curent (m)	[ku'rent]

168. Tools

tool, instrument	instrument (n)	[instru'ment]
tools	instrumente (n pl)	[instru'mente]
equipment (factory ~)	utilaj (n)	[uti'laʒ]
hammer	ciocan (n)	[tʃio'kan]
screwdriver	şurubelniţă (f)	[ʃuru'belnitsə]
axe	topor (n)	[to'por]

saw	ferăstrău (n)	[ferəstrəu]
to saw (vt)	a tăia cu ferăstrăul	[a tə'ja 'ku ferəstrəul]
plane (tool)	rindea (f)	[rin'dʲa]
to plane (vt)	a gelui	[a dʒelu'i]
soldering iron	ciocan (n) de lipit	[tʃio'kan de li'pit]
to solder (vt)	a lipi	[a li'pi]

file (tool)	pilă (f)	['pilə]
carpenter pincers	cleşte (m)	['kleʃte]
combination pliers	cleşte (m) patent	['kleʃte pa'tent]
chisel	daltă (f) de tâmplărie	['daltə de timplə'rie]

drill bit	burghiu (n)	[bur'gju]
electric drill	sfredel (n)	['sfredel]
to drill (vi, vt)	a sfredeli	[a sfrede'li]

| knife | cuţit (n) | [ku'tsit] |
| blade | lamă (f) | ['lamə] |

sharp (blade, etc.)	ascuţit	[asku'tsit]
dull, blunt (adj)	tocit	[to'tʃit]
to get blunt (dull)	a se toci	[a se to'tʃi]
to sharpen (vt)	a ascuţi	[a asku'tsi]

bolt	şurub (n)	[ʃu'rub]
nut	piuliţă (f)	[pju'litsə]
thread (of a screw)	filet (n)	[fi'let]
wood screw	şurub (n)	[ʃu'rub]

| nail | cui (n) | [kuj] |
| nailhead | bont (n) | [bont] |

ruler (for measuring)	linie (f)	['linie]
tape measure	ruletă (f)	[ru'letə]
spirit level	nivelă (f)	[ni'vela]
magnifying glass	lupă (f)	['lupə]

measuring instrument	aparat (n) de măsurat	[apa'rat de məsu'rat]
to measure (vt)	a măsura	[a məsu'ra]
scale (temperature ~, etc.)	scală (f)	['skalə]
readings	indicaţii (f pl)	[indi'katsij]

| compressor | compresor (n) | [kompre'sor] |
| microscope | microscop (n) | [mikro'skop] |

pump (e.g. water ~)	pompă (f)	['pompə]
robot	robot (m)	[ro'bot]
laser	laser (n)	['laser]

spanner	cheie (f) franceză	['kee fran'tʃezə]
adhesive tape	bandă (f) izolatoare	['bandə izolato'are]
glue	clei (n)	[klej]

sandpaper	hârtie (f) abrazivă	[hir'tie abra'zivə]
spring	arc (n)	[ark]
magnet	magnet (m)	[mag'net]

gloves	mănuşi (f pl)	[məˈnuʃ]
rope	funie (f)	[ˈfunie]
cord	şnur (n)	[ʃnur]
wire (e.g. telephone ~)	fir (n) electric	[fir eˈlektrik]
cable	cablu (n)	[ˈkablu]

sledgehammer	baros (m)	[baˈros]
prybar	rangă (f)	[ˈrangə]
ladder	scară (f)	[ˈskarə]
stepladder	scară (f) de frânghie	[ˈskarə de frinˈgie]

to screw (tighten)	a înşuruba	[a inʃuruˈba]
to unscrew (lid, filter, etc.)	a deşuruba	[a deʃuruˈba]
to tighten (e.g. with a clamp)	a strânge	[a ˈstrindʒe]
to glue, to stick	a lipi	[a liˈpi]
to cut (vt)	a tăia	[a təˈja]

malfunction (fault)	deranjament (n)	[deranʒaˈment]
repair (mending)	reparaţie (f)	[repaˈratsie]
to repair, to fix (vt)	a repara	[a repaˈra]
to adjust (machine, etc.)	a regla	[a reˈgla]

to check (to examine)	a verifica	[a verifiˈka]
checking	verificare (f)	[verifiˈkare]
readings	indicaţie (f)	[indiˈkatsie]

| reliable, solid (machine) | sigur | [ˈsigur] |
| complex (adj) | complex | [komˈpleks] |

to rust (get rusted)	a rugini	[a rudʒiˈni]
rusty (adj)	ruginit	[rudʒiˈnit]
rust	rugină (f)	[ruˈdʒinə]

Transport

aeroplane	**avion** (n)	[a'vjon]
air ticket	**bilet** (n) **de avion**	[bi'let de a'vjon]
airline	**companie** (f) **aeriană**	[kompa'nie aeri'anə]
airport	**aeroport** (n)	[aero'port]
supersonic (adj)	**supersonic**	[super'sonik]
captain	**comandant** (m) **de navă**	[koman'dant de 'navə]
crew	**echipaj** (n)	[eki'paʒ]
pilot	**pilot** (m)	[pi'lot]
stewardess	**stewardesă** (f)	[stjuar'desə]
navigator	**navigator** (m)	[naviga'tor]
wings	**aripi** (f pl)	[a'ripⁱ]
tail	**coadă** (f)	[ko'adə]
cockpit	**cabină** (f)	[ka'binə]
engine	**motor** (n)	[mo'tor]
undercarriage (landing gear)	**tren** (n) **de aterizare**	[tren de ateri'zare]
turbine	**turbină** (f)	[tur'binə]
propeller	**elice** (f)	[e'litʃe]
black box	**cutie** (f) **neagră**	[ku'tie 'nⁱagrə]
yoke (control column)	**manşă** (f)	['manʃə]
fuel	**combustibil** (m)	[kombus'tibil]
safety card	**instrucţiune** (f)	[instruktsi'une]
oxygen mask	**mască** (f) **cu oxigen**	['maskə 'ku oksi'dʒen]
uniform	**uniformă** (f)	[uni'formə]
lifejacket	**vestă** (f) **de salvare**	['vestə de sal'vare]
parachute	**paraşută** (f)	[para'ʃutə]
takeoff	**decolare** (f)	[deko'lare]
to take off (vi)	**a decola**	[a deko'la]
runway	**pistă** (f) **de decolare**	['pistə de deko'lare]
visibility	**vizibilitate** (f)	[vizibili'tate]
flight (act of flying)	**zbor** (n)	[zbor]
altitude	**înălţime** (f)	[inəl'tsime]
air pocket	**gol de aer** (n)	[gol de 'aer]
seat	**loc** (n)	[lok]
headphones	**căşti** (f pl)	[kəʃtⁱ]
folding tray (tray table)	**măsuţă** (f) **rabatabilă**	[mə'sutsə raba'tabilə]
airplane window	**hublou** (n)	[hu'blou]
aisle	**trecere** (f)	['tretʃere]

170. Train

train	**tren** (n)	[tren]
commuter train	**tren** (n) **electric**	['tren e'lektrik]
express train	**tren** (n) **accelerat**	['tren aktʃele'rat]
diesel locomotive	**locomotivă** (f) **cu motor diesel**	[lokomo'tivə ku mo'tor 'dizel]
steam locomotive	**locomotivă** (f)	[lokomo'tivə]
coach, carriage	**vagon** (n)	[va'gon]
buffet car	**vagon-restaurant** (n)	[va'gon restau'rant]
rails	**şine** (f pl)	['ʃine]
railway	**cale** (f) **ferată**	['kale fe'ratə]
sleeper (track support)	**traversă** (f)	[tra'versə]
platform (railway ~)	**peron** (n)	[pe'ron]
platform (~ 1, 2, etc.)	**linie** (f)	['linie]
semaphore	**semafor** (n)	[sema'for]
station	**staţie** (f)	['statsie]
train driver	**maşinist** (m)	[maʃi'nist]
porter (of luggage)	**hamal** (m)	[ha'mal]
carriage attendant	**însoţitor** (m)	[insotsi'tor]
passenger	**pasager** (m)	[pasa'dʒer]
ticket inspector	**controlor** (m)	[kontro'lor]
corridor (in train)	**coridor** (n)	[kori'dor]
emergency brake	**semnal** (n) **de alarmă**	[sem'nal de a'larmə]
compartment	**compartiment** (n)	[komparti'ment]
berth	**cuşetă** (f)	[ku'ʃetə]
upper berth	**patul** (n) **de sus**	['patul de sus]
lower berth	**patul** (n) **de jos**	['patul de ʒos]
bed linen, bedding	**lenjerie** (f) **de pat**	[lenʒe'rie de pat]
ticket	**bilet** (n)	[bi'let]
timetable	**orar** (n)	[o'rar]
information display	**panou** (n)	[pa'nou]
to leave, to depart	**a pleca**	[a ple'ka]
departure (of a train)	**plecare** (f)	[ple'kare]
to arrive (ab. train)	**a sosi**	[a so'si]
arrival	**sosire** (f)	[so'sire]
to arrive by train	**a veni cu trenul**	[a ve'ni ku 'trenul]
to get on the train	**a se aşeza în tren**	[a se aʃə'za in tren]
to get off the train	**a coborî din tren**	[a kobo'ri din tren]
train crash	**accident** (n) **de tren**	[aktʃi'dent de tren]
steam locomotive	**locomotivă** (f)	[lokomo'tivə]
stoker, fireman	**fochist** (m)	[fo'kist]
firebox	**focar** (n)	[fo'kar]
coal	**cărbune** (m)	[kər'bune]

171. Ship

ship	**corabie** (f)	[ko'rabie]
vessel	**navă** (f)	['navə]
steamship	**vapor** (n)	[va'por]
riverboat	**motonavă** (f)	[moto'navə]
cruise ship	**vas** (n) **de croazieră**	[vas de kroa'zjerə]
cruiser	**crucişător** (n)	[krutʃiʃə'tor]
yacht	**iaht** (n)	[jaht]
tugboat	**remorcher** (n)	[remor'ker]
barge	**şlep** (n)	[ʃlep]
ferry	**bac** (n)	[bak]
sailing ship	**velier** (n)	[ve'ljer]
brigantine	**brigantină** (f)	[brigan'tinə]
ice breaker	**spărgător** (n) **de gheaţă**	[spərgə'tor de 'gʲatsə]
submarine	**submarin** (n)	[subma'rin]
boat (flat-bottomed ~)	**barcă** (f)	['barkə]
dinghy (lifeboat)	**şalupă** (f)	[ʃa'lupə]
lifeboat	**şalupă** (f) **de salvare**	[ʃa'lupə de sal'vare]
motorboat	**cuter** (n)	['kuter]
captain	**căpitan** (m)	[kəpi'tan]
seaman	**marinar** (m)	[mari'nar]
sailor	**marinar** (m)	[mari'nar]
crew	**echipaj** (n)	[eki'paʒ]
boatswain	**şef** (m) **de echipaj**	[ʃef de eki'paʒ]
ship's boy	**mus** (m)	[mus]
cook	**bucătar** (m)	[bukə'tar]
ship's doctor	**medic** (m) **pe navă**	['medik pe 'navə]
deck	**teugă** (f)	[te'ugə]
mast	**catarg** (n)	[ka'targ]
sail	**velă** (f)	['velə]
hold	**cală** (f)	['kalə]
bow (prow)	**proră** (f)	['prorə]
stern	**pupă** (f)	['pupə]
oar	**vâslă** (f)	['vislə]
screw propeller	**elice** (f)	[e'litʃe]
cabin	**cabină** (f)	[ka'binə]
wardroom	**salonul** (n) **ofiţerilor**	[sa'lonul ofi'tserilor]
engine room	**sala** (f) **maşinilor**	['sala ma'ʃinilor]
bridge	**punte** (f) **de comandă**	['punte de ko'mandə]
radio room	**staţie** (f) **de radio**	['statsie de 'radio]
wave (radio)	**undă** (f)	['undə]
logbook	**jurnal** (n) **de bord**	[ʒur'nal de bord]
spyglass	**lunetă** (f)	[lu'netə]
bell	**clopot** (n)	['klopot]

flag	**steag** (n)	['st'ag]
hawser (mooring ~)	**parâmă** (f)	[pa'rimə]
knot (bowline, etc.)	**nod** (n)	[nod]
deckrails	**bară** (f)	['barə]
gangway	**pasarelă** (f)	[pasa'relə]
anchor	**ancoră** (f)	['ankorə]
to weigh anchor	**a ridica ancora**	[a ridi'ka 'ankora]
to drop anchor	**a ancora**	[a anko'ra]
anchor chain	**lanț** (n) **de ancoră**	[lants de 'ankorə]
port (harbour)	**port** (n)	[port]
quay, wharf	**acostare** (f)	[akos'tare]
to berth (moor)	**a acosta**	[a akos'ta]
to cast off	**a demara**	[a dema'ra]
trip, voyage	**călătorie** (f)	[kələto'rie]
cruise (sea trip)	**croazieră** (f)	[kroa'zjerə]
course (route)	**direcție** (f)	[di'rektsie]
route (itinerary)	**rută** (f)	['rutə]
fairway (safe water channel)	**cale** (f) **navigabilă**	['kale navi'gabilə]
shallows	**banc** (n) **de nisip**	[bank de ni'sip]
to run aground	**a se împotmoli**	[a se impotmo'li]
storm	**furtună** (f)	[fur'tunə]
signal	**semnal** (n)	[sem'nal]
to sink (vi)	**a se scufunda**	[a se skufun'da]
SOS (distress signal)	**SOS**	[sos]
ring buoy	**colac** (m) **de salvare**	[ko'lak de sal'vare]

172. Airport

airport	**aeroport** (n)	[aero'port]
aeroplane	**avion** (n)	[a'vjon]
airline	**companie** (f) **aeriană**	[kompa'nie aeri'anə]
air traffic controller	**dispecer** (n)	[dis'petʃer]
departure	**decolare** (f)	[deko'lare]
arrival	**aterizare** (f)	[ateri'zare]
to arrive (by plane)	**a ateriza**	[a ateri'za]
departure time	**ora** (f) **decolării**	['ora dekolərij]
arrival time	**ora** (f) **aterizării**	['ora aterizərij]
to be delayed	**a întârzia**	[a intir'zija]
flight delay	**întârzierea** (f) **zborului**	[intirzjer'a 'zboruluj]
information board	**panou** (n)	[pa'nou]
information	**informație** (f)	[infor'matsie]
to announce (vt)	**a anunța**	[a anun'tsa]
flight (e.g. next ~)	**cursă** (f)	['kursə]
customs	**vamă** (f)	['vamə]

customs officer	vameș (m)	['vameʃ]
customs declaration	declarație (f)	[dekla'ratsie]
to fill in (vt)	a completa	[a komple'ta]
to fill in the declaration	a completa declarația	[a komple'ta dekla'ratsija]
passport control	controlul (n) pașapoartelor	[kon'trolul paʃapo'artelor]

luggage	bagaj (n)	[ba'gaʒ]
hand luggage	bagaj (n) de mână	[ba'gaʒ de 'minə]
luggage trolley	cărucior (n) pentru bagaj	[kəru'tʃior 'pentru ba'gaʒ]

landing	aterizare (f)	[ateri'zare]
landing strip	pistă (f) de aterizare	['pistə de ateri'zare]
to land (vi)	a ateriza	[a ateri'za]
airstair (passenger stair)	scară (f)	['skarə]

check-in	înregistrare (f)	[inredʒis'trare]
check-in counter	birou (n) de înregistrare	[bi'rou de inredʒis'trare]
to check-in (vi)	a se înregistra	[a se inredʒis'tra]
boarding card	număr (n) de bord	['numər de bord]
departure gate	debarcare (f)	[debar'kare]

transit	tranzit (n)	['tranzit]
to wait (vt)	a aștepta	[a aʃtep'ta]
departure lounge	sală (f) de așteptare	['salə de aʃtep'tare]
to see off	a conduce	[a kon'dutʃe]
to say goodbye	a-și lua rămas bun	[aʃ lu'a rə'mas bun]

173. Bicycle. Motorcycle

bicycle	bicicletă (f)	[bitʃi'kletə]
scooter	scuter (n)	['skuter]
motorbike	motocicletă (f)	[mototʃi'kletə]

to go by bicycle	a merge cu bicicleta	[a 'merdʒe ku bitʃik'leta]
handlebars	ghidon (n)	[gi'don]
pedal	pedală (f)	[pe'dalə]
brakes	frână (f)	['frinə]
bicycle seat (saddle)	șa (f)	[ʃa]

pump	pompă (f)	['pompə]
pannier rack	portbagaj (n)	[portba'gaʒ]
front lamp	felinar (n)	[feli'nar]
helmet	cască (f)	['kaskə]

wheel	roată (f)	[ro'atə]
mudguard	aripă (f)	[a'ripə]
rim	obada (f) roții	[o'bada 'rotsij]
spoke	spiță (f)	['spitsə]

Cars

174. Types of cars

car	**automobil** (n)	[automo'bil]
sports car	**automobil** (n) **sport**	[automo'bil 'sport]
limousine	**limuzină** (f)	[limu'zinə]
off-road vehicle	**vehicul** (n) **de teren** (n)	[ve'hikul de te'ren]
drophead coupé (convertible)	**cabrioletă** (f)	[kabrio'letə]
minibus	**microbuz** (n)	[mikro'buz]
ambulance	**ambulanţă** (f)	[ambu'lantsə]
snowplough	**maşină** (f) **de deszăpezire**	[ma'ʃinə de deszəpe'zire]
lorry	**autocamion** (n)	[autoka'mjon]
road tanker	**autocisternă** (f) **pentru combustibil**	[autotʃis'ternə 'pentru kombus'tibil]
van (small truck)	**furgon** (n)	[fur'gon]
tractor unit	**remorcher** (n)	[remor'ker]
trailer	**remorcă** (f)	[re'morkə]
comfortable (adj)	**confortabil**	[konfor'tabil]
used (adj)	**uzat**	[u'zat]

175. Cars. Bodywork

bonnet	**capotă** (f)	[ka'potə]
wing	**aripă** (f)	[a'ripə]
roof	**acoperiş** (n)	[akope'riʃ]
windscreen	**parbriz** (n)	[par'briz]
rear-view mirror	**oglindă** (f) **retrovizoare**	[og'lində retrovizo'are]
windscreen washer	**ştergător** (n)	[ʃtergə'tor]
windscreen wipers	**ştergător** (n) **de parbriz**	[ʃtergə'tor de par'briz]
side window	**fereastră** (f) **laterală**	[fe'rɪastrə late'ralə]
electric window	**macara** (f) **de geam**	[maka'ra de dʒʲam]
aerial	**antenă** (f)	[an'tenə]
sunroof	**trapă** (f)	['trapə]
bumper	**amortizor** (n)	[amorti'zor]
boot	**portbagaj** (n)	[portba'gaʒ]
door	**portieră** (f)	[por'tjerə]
door handle	**mâner** (n)	[mi'ner]
door lock	**încuietoare** (f)	[inkueto'are]
number plate	**număr** (n)	['numər]
silencer	**tobă** (f)	['tobə]

| petrol tank | rezervor (n) de benzină | [rezer'vor de ben'zinə] |
| exhaust pipe | ţeavă (f) de eşapament | ['ts'avə de eʃapa'ment] |

accelerator	gaz (n)	[gaz]
pedal	pedală (f)	[pe'dalə]
accelerator pedal	pedală (f) de acceleraţie	[pe'dalə de aktʃele'ratsie]

brake	frână (f)	['frinə]
brake pedal	pedală (f) de frână	[pe'dalə de 'frinə]
to brake (use the brake)	a frâna	[a fri'na]
handbrake	frână (f) de staţionare	['frinə de statsio'nare]

clutch	ambreiaj (n)	[ambre'jaʒ]
clutch pedal	pedală (f) de ambreiaj	[pe'dalə de ambre'jaʒ]
clutch disc	disc (n) de ambreiaj	['disk de ambre'jaʒ]
shock absorber	amortizor (n)	[amorti'zor]

wheel	roată (f)	[ro'atə]
spare tyre	roată (f) de rezervă	[ro'atə de re'zervə]
wheel cover (hubcap)	capac (n)	[ka'pak]

driving wheels	roţi (f pl) de tracţiune	['rots' de traktsi'une]
front-wheel drive (as adj)	tracţiune (f) frontală	[traktsi'une fron'talə]
rear-wheel drive (as adj)	tracţiune (f) spate	[traktsi'une 'spate]
all-wheel drive (as adj)	tracţiune (f) integrală	[traktsi'une inte'gralə]

gearbox	cutie (f) de viteză	[ku'tie de vi'tezə]
automatic (adj)	automat	[auto'mat]
mechanical (adj)	mecanic	[me'kanik]
gear lever	manetă (f) de viteze	[ma'netə de vi'teze]

| headlamp | far (n) | [far] |
| headlights | faruri (n pl) | ['farur'] |

dipped headlights	fază (f) mică	['fazə 'mikə]
full headlights	fază (f) mare	['fazə 'mare]
brake light	semnal (n) de oprire	[sem'nal de o'prire]

sidelights	semn (n) de gabarit	[semn de gaba'rit]
hazard lights	lumini (f) de avarie	[lu'min' de a'varie]
fog lights	faruri (n pl) anticeaţă	['farur' anti'tʃatsə]
turn indicator	mecanism (n) de direcţie	[meka'nism de di'rektsie]
reversing light	marşarier (n)	[marʃari'er]

176. Cars. Passenger compartment

car interior	interior (n)	[inte'rjor]
leather (as adj)	de piele	[de 'pjele]
velour (as adj)	de catifea	[de kati'f'a]
upholstery	tapiţare (f)	[tapi'tsare]

instrument (gage)	dispozitiv (n)	[dispozi'tiv]
dashboard	panou (n) de comandă	[pa'nou de ko'mandə]
speedometer	vitezometru (n)	[vitezo'metru]

needle (pointer)	ac (n)	[ak]
mileometer	contor (n)	[kon'tor]
indicator (sensor)	indicator (n)	[indika'tor]
level	nivel (n)	[ni'vel]
warning light	bec (n)	[bek]

steering wheel	volan (n)	[vo'lan]
horn	claxon (n)	[klak'son]
button	buton (n)	[bu'ton]
switch	schimbător (n) de viteză	[skimbə'tor de vi'tezə]

seat	scaun (n)	['skaun]
backrest	spătar (n)	[spə'tar]
headrest	tetieră (f)	[te'tjerə]
seat belt	centură (f) de siguranţă	[tʃen'turə de sigu'rantsə]
to fasten the belt	a pune centura de siguranţă	[a 'pune tʃen'tura de sigu'rantsə]
adjustment (of seats)	reglare (f)	[re'glare]

| airbag | airbag (n) | ['erbeg] |
| air-conditioner | aer (n) condiţionat | ['aer konditsio'nat] |

radio	radio (n)	['radio]
CD player	CD player (n)	[si'di 'pleer]
to turn on	a deschide	[a des'kide]
aerial	antenă (f)	[an'tenə]
glove box	torpedou (m)	[torpe'dou]
ashtray	scrumieră (f)	[skru'mjerə]

177. Cars. Engine

engine, motor	motor (n)	[mo'tor]
diesel (as adj)	diesel	['dizel]
petrol (as adj)	pe benzină	[pe ben'zinə]

engine volume	capacitatea (n) motorului	[kapatʃi'tatʲa mo'toruluj]
power	putere (f)	[pu'tere]
horsepower	cal-putere (m)	[kal pu'tere]
piston	piston (m)	[pis'ton]
cylinder	cilindru (m)	[tʃi'lindru]
valve	supapă (f)	[su'papə]

injector	injector (n)	[inʒek'tor]
generator (alternator)	generator (n)	[dʒenera'tor]
carburettor	carburator (n)	[karbura'tor]
motor oil	ulei (n) pentru motor	[u'lej 'pentru mo'tor]

radiator	radiator (n)	[radia'tor]
coolant	antigel (n)	[anti'dʒel]
cooling fan	ventilator (n)	[ventila'tor]

battery (accumulator)	acumulator (n)	[akumula'tor]
starter	demaror (n)	[dema'ror]
ignition	aprindere (f)	[a'prindere]

sparking plug	bujie (f) de aprindere	[bu'ʒie de a'prindere]
terminal (battery ~)	bornă (f)	['bornə]
positive terminal	plus (n)	[plus]
negative terminal	minus (m)	['minus]
fuse	siguranță (f)	[sigu'rantsə]

air filter	filtru (n) de aer	['filtru de 'aer]
oil filter	filtru (n) pentru ulei	['filtru 'pentru u'lej]
fuel filter	filtru (n) pentru combustibil	['filtru 'pentru kombus'tibil]

178. Cars. Crash. Repair

car crash	accident (n)	[aktʃi'dent]
traffic accident	accident (n) rutier	[aktʃi'dent ru'tjer]
to crash (into the wall, etc.)	a se tampona	[a se tampo'na]
to get smashed up	a se sparge	[a se 'spardʒe]
damage	avariere (f)	[ava'rjere]
intact (unscathed)	întreg	[in'treg]

breakdown	pană (f)	['panə]
to break down (vi)	a se strica	[a se stri'ka]
towrope	cablu (n) de remorcaj	['kablu de remor'kaʒ]

puncture	găurire (f)	[gəu'rire]
to have a puncture	a se dezumfla	[a se dezum'fla]
to pump up	a pompa	[a pom'pa]
pressure	presiune (f)	[presi'une]
to check (to examine)	a verifica	[a verifi'ka]

repair	reparație (f)	[repa'ratsie]
garage (auto service shop)	service (n) auto	['servis 'auto]
spare part	detalii (f pl)	[de'talij]
part	detaliu (n)	[de'talju]

bolt (with nut)	şurub (n)	[ʃu'rub]
screw (fastener)	şurub (n)	[ʃu'rub]
nut	piuliță (f)	[pju'litsə]
washer	şaibă (f)	['ʃajbə]
bearing (e.g. ball ~)	rulment (m)	[rul'ment]

tube	tub (n)	[tub]
gasket (head ~)	garnitură (f)	[garni'turə]
cable, wire	cablu (n)	['kablu]

jack	cric (n)	[krik]
spanner	cheie (f) fixă	['kee 'fiksə]
hammer	ciocan (n)	[tʃio'kan]
pump	pompă (f)	['pompə]
screwdriver	şurubelniță (f)	[ʃuru'belnitsə]

fire extinguisher	stingător (n)	[stingə'tor]
warning triangle	semn (n) de avarie	[semn de a'varie]
to stall (vi)	a se opri	[a se o'pri]
stall (n)	oprire (f)	[o'prire]

to be broken	**a fi stricat**	[a fi stri'kat]
to overheat (vi)	**a se încălzi**	[a se inkəl'zi]
to be clogged up	**a se înfunda**	[a se infun'da]
to freeze up (pipes, etc.)	**a îngheța**	[a inge'tsa]
to burst (vi, ab. tube)	**a crăpa**	[a krə'pa]
pressure	**presiune** (f)	[presi'une]
level	**nivel** (n)	[ni'vel]
slack (~ belt)	**scăzut**	[skə'zut]
dent	**îndoitură** (f)	[indoi'turə]
knocking noise (engine)	**lovitură** (f)	[lovi'turə]
crack	**crăpătură** (f)	[krəpə'turə]
scratch	**zgârietură** (f)	[zgirie'turə]

179. Cars. Road

road	**drum** (n)	[drum]
motorway	**autostradă** (f)	[auto'stradə]
highway	**șosea** (f)	[ʃo'sʲa]
direction (way)	**direcție** (f)	[di'rektsie]
distance	**distanță** (f)	[dis'tantsə]
bridge	**pod** (n)	[pod]
car park	**loc** (n) **de parcare**	[lok de par'kare]
square	**piață** (f)	['pjatsə]
road junction	**răscruce** (f)	[rəs'krutʃe]
tunnel	**tunel** (n)	[tu'nel]
petrol station	**benzinărie** (f)	[benzinə'rie]
car park	**parcare** (f)	[par'kare]
petrol pump	**stație** (f) **de benzină**	['statsie de ben'zinə]
auto repair shop	**garaj** (n)	[ga'raʒ]
to fill up	**a alimenta**	[a alimen'ta]
fuel	**combustibil** (m)	[kombus'tibil]
jerrycan	**canistră** (f)	[ka'nistrə]
asphalt, tarmac	**asfalt** (n)	[as'falt]
road markings	**marcare** (f)	[mar'kare]
kerb	**bordură** (f)	[bor'durə]
crash barrier	**îngrădire** (f)	[ingrə'dire]
ditch	**șanț** (n) **de scurgere**	[ʃants de 'skurdʒere]
roadside (shoulder)	**margine** (f)	['mardʒine]
lamppost	**stâlp** (m)	[stilp]
to drive (a car)	**a conduce**	[a kon'dutʃe]
to turn (e.g., ~ left)	**a întoarce**	[a into'artʃe]
to make a U-turn	**a vira**	[a vi'ra]
reverse (~ gear)	**mers** (n) **înapoi**	['mers ina'poj]
to honk (vi)	**a semnaliza**	[a semnali'za]
honk (sound)	**semnal** (n) **acustic**	[sem'nal a'kustik]
to get stuck (in the mud, etc.)	**a se împotmoli**	[a se impotmo'li]
to spin the wheels	**a remorca**	[a remor'ka]

to cut, to turn off (vt)	a opri	[a op'ri]
speed	viteză (f)	[vi'tezə]
to exceed the speed limit	a depăşi viteza	[a depə'ʃi vi'teza]
to give a ticket	a amenda	[a amen'da]
traffic lights	semafor (n)	[sema'for]
driving licence	permis (n) de conducere	[per'mis de kon'dutʃere]
level crossing	traversare (f)	[traver'sare]
crossroads	intersecţie (f)	[inter'sektsie]
zebra crossing	trecere (f) de pietoni	['tretʃere de pie'tonʲ]
bend, curve	curbă (f)	['kurbə]
pedestrian precinct	zonă (f) pentru pietoni	['zonə 'pentru pie'tonʲ]

180. Signs

Highway Code	reguli (f pl) de circulaţie	['regulʲ de tʃirku'latsie]
road sign (traffic sign)	semn (n)	[semn]
overtaking	întrecere (f)	[in'tretʃere]
curve	viraj (n)	[vi'raʒ]
U-turn	întoarcere (f)	[intu'artʃerə]
roundabout	mişcare (f) circulară	[miʃ'kare tʃiru'larə]
No entry	intrarea interzisă	[in'trarʲa inter'zisə]
All vehicles prohibited	circulaţia interzisă	[tʃirku'latsia inter'zisə]
No overtaking	depăşirea interzisă	[depə'ʃirʲa inter'zisə]
No parking	parcarea interzisă	[par'karʲa inter'zisə]
No stopping	oprirea interzisă	[o'prirʲa inter'zisə]
dangerous curve	curbă (f) periculoasă	['kurbə perikulo'asə]
steep descent	pantă (f) abruptă	['pantə a'bruptə]
one-way traffic	într-o singură direcţie (f)	['intro 'singurə di'rektsie]
zebra crossing	trecere (f) de pietoni	['tretʃere de pie'tonʲ]
slippery road	drum (n) alunecos	[drum alune'kos]
GIVE WAY	cedează trecerea	[tʃe'dʲazə 'tretʃerʲa]

PEOPLE. LIFE EVENTS

181. Holidays. Event

celebration, holiday	sărbătoare (f)	[sərbəto'are]
national day	sărbătoare (f) naţională	[sərbəto'are natsio'nalə]
public holiday	zi (f) de sărbătoare	[zi de sərbəto'are]
to commemorate (vt)	a sărbători	[a sərbəto'ri]
event (happening)	eveniment (n)	[eveni'ment]
event (organized activity)	manifestare (f)	[manifes'tare]
banquet (party)	banchet (n)	[ban'ket]
reception (formal party)	recepţie (f)	[re'tʃeptsie]
feast	ospăţ (n)	[os'pəts]
anniversary	aniversare (f)	[aniver'sare]
jubilee	jubileu (n)	[ʒubi'leu]
to celebrate (vt)	a sărbători	[a sərbəto'ri]
New Year	Anul (m) Nou	['anul 'nou]
Happy New Year!	La Mulţi Ani!	[la 'mults^j an^j]
Christmas	Crăciun (n)	[krə'tʃiun]
Merry Christmas!	Crăciun Fericit!	[krə'tʃiun feri'tʃit]
Christmas tree	pom (m) de Crăciun	[pom de krə'tʃiun]
fireworks (fireworks show)	artificii (n)	[arti'fitʃij]
wedding	nuntă (f)	['nuntə]
groom	mire (m)	['mire]
bride	mireasă (f)	[mi'rʲasə]
to invite (vt)	a invita	[a invi'ta]
invitation card	invitaţie (f)	[invi'tatsie]
guest	oaspete (m)	[o'aspete]
to visit (~ your parents, etc.)	a merge în ospeţie	[a 'merdʒe in ospe'tsie]
to meet the guests	a întâmpina oaspeţii	[a intimpi'na o'aspetsij]
gift, present	cadou (n)	[ka'dou]
to give (sth as present)	a dărui	[a dəru'i]
to receive gifts	a primi cadouri	[a pri'mi ka'dour^j]
bouquet (of flowers)	buchet (n)	[bu'ket]
congratulations	urare (f)	[u'rare]
to congratulate (vt)	a felicita	[a felitʃi'ta]
greetings card	felicitare (f)	[felitʃi'tare]
to send a postcard	a expedia o felicitare	[a ekspedi'ja o felitʃi'tare]
to get a postcard	a primi o felicitare	[a pri'mi o felitʃi'tare]
toast	toast (n)	[tost]

| to offer (a drink, etc.) | a servi | [a ser'vi] |
| champagne | şampanie (f) | [ʃam'panie] |

to enjoy oneself	a se veseli	[a se vese'li]
merriment (gaiety)	veselie (f)	[vese'lie]
joy (emotion)	bucurie (f)	[buku'rie]

| dance | dans (n) | [dans] |
| to dance (vi, vt) | a dansa | [a dan'sa] |

| waltz | vals (n) | [vals] |
| tango | tangou (n) | [tan'gou] |

182. Funerals. Burial

cemetery	cimitir (n)	[tʃimi'tir]
grave, tomb	mormânt (n)	[mor'mint]
cross	cruce (f)	['krutʃe]
gravestone	piatră funerară (n)	['pjatrə fune'rarə]
fence	gard (n)	[gard]
chapel	capelă (f)	[ka'pelə]

death	moarte (f)	[mo'arte]
to die (vi)	a muri	[a mu'ri]
the deceased	mort (m)	[mort]
mourning	doliu (n)	['dolju]

to bury (vt)	a îngropa	[a ingro'pa]
undertakers	pompe (f pl) funebre	['pompe fu'nebre]
funeral	înmormântare (f)	[inmormin'tare]

wreath	cunună (f)	[ku'nunə]
coffin	sicriu (n)	[si'kriu]
hearse	dric (n)	[drik]
shroud	giulgiu (n)	['dʒiuldʒiu]

| funerary urn | urnă (f) funerară | ['urnə fune'rarə] |
| crematorium | crematoriu (n) | [krema'torju] |

obituary	necrolog (m)	[nekro'log]
to cry (weep)	a plânge	[a 'plindʒe]
to sob (vi)	a plânge în hohote	[a 'plindʒe in 'hohote]

183. War. Soldiers

platoon	pluton (n)	[plu'ton]
company	companie (f)	[kompa'nie]
regiment	regiment (n)	[redʒi'ment]
army	armată (f)	[ar'matə]
division	divizie (f)	[di'vizie]
section, squad	detaşament (n)	[detaʃa'ment]
host (army)	armată (f)	[ar'matə]

soldier	**soldat** (m)	[sol'dat]
officer	**ofiţer** (m)	[ofi'tser]
private	**soldat** (m)	[sol'dat]
sergeant	**sergent** (m)	[ser'dʒent]
lieutenant	**locotenent** (m)	[lokote'nent]
captain	**căpitan** (m)	[kəpi'tan]
major	**maior** (m)	[ma'jor]
colonel	**colonel** (m)	[kolo'nel]
general	**general** (m)	[dʒene'ral]
sailor	**marinar** (m)	[mari'nar]
captain	**căpitan** (m)	[kəpi'tan]
boatswain	**şef** (m) **de echipaj**	[ʃef de eki'paʒ]
artilleryman	**artilerist** (m)	[artile'rist]
paratrooper	**paraşutist** (m)	[paraʃu'tist]
pilot	**pilot** (m)	[pi'lot]
navigator	**navigator** (m)	[naviga'tor]
mechanic	**mecanic** (m)	[me'kanik]
pioneer (sapper)	**genist** (m)	[dʒe'nist]
parachutist	**paraşutist** (m)	[paraʃu'tist]
reconnaissance scout	**cercetaş** (m)	[tʃertʃe'taʃ]
sniper	**lunetist** (m)	[lune'tist]
patrol (group)	**patrulă** (f)	[pa'trulə]
to patrol (vt)	**a patrula**	[a patru'la]
sentry, guard	**santinelă** (f)	[santi'nelə]
warrior	**ostaş** (m)	[os'taʃ]
patriot	**patriot** (m)	[patri'ot]
hero	**erou** (m)	[e'rou]
heroine	**eroină** (f)	[ero'inə]
traitor	**trădător** (m)	[trədə'tor]
deserter	**dezertor** (m)	[dezer'tor]
to desert (vi)	**a dezerta**	[a dezer'ta]
mercenary	**mercenar** (m)	[mertʃe'nar]
recruit	**recrut** (m)	[re'krut]
volunteer	**voluntar** (m)	[volun'tar]
dead (n)	**ucis** (m)	[u'tʃis]
wounded (n)	**rănit** (m)	[rə'nit]
prisoner of war	**prizonier** (m)	[prizo'njer]

184. War. Military actions. Part 1

war	**război** (n)	[rəz'boj]
to be at war	**a lupta**	[a lup'ta]
civil war	**război** (n) **civil**	[rəz'boj tʃi'vil]
treacherously (adv)	**în mod perfid**	[in mod per'fid]
declaration of war	**declarare** (f)	[dekla'rare]

to declare (~ war)	a declara	[a dekla'ra]
aggression	agresiune (f)	[agresi'une]
to attack (invade)	a ataca	[a ata'ka]
to invade (vt)	a captura	[a kaptu'ra]
invader	cotropitor (m)	[kotropi'tor]
conqueror	cuceritor (m)	[kutʃeri'tor]
defence	apărare (f)	[apə'rare]
to defend (a country, etc.)	a apăra	[a apə'ra]
to defend (against …)	a se apăra	[a se apə'ra]
enemy	duşman (m)	[duʃ'man]
foe, adversary	adversar (m)	[adver'sar]
enemy (as adj)	duşmănos	[duʃmə'nos]
strategy	strategie (f)	[strate'dʒie]
tactics	tactică (f)	['taktikə]
order	ordin (n)	['ordin]
command (order)	comandă (f)	[ko'mandə]
to order (vt)	a ordona	[a ordo'na]
mission	misiune (f)	[misi'une]
secret (adj)	secret	[se'kret]
battle	bătălie (f)	[bətə'lie]
combat	luptă (f)	['luptə]
attack	atac (n)	[a'tak]
charge (assault)	asalt (n)	[a'salt]
to storm (vt)	a asalta	[a asal'ta]
siege (to be under ~)	asediu (n)	[a'sedju]
offensive (n)	atac (n)	[a'tak]
to go on the offensive	a ataca	[a ata'ka]
retreat	retragere (f)	[re'tradʒere]
to retreat (vi)	a se retrage	[a se re'tradʒe]
encirclement	încercuire (f)	[intʃerku'ire]
to encircle (vt)	a încercui	[a intʃerku'i]
bombing (by aircraft)	bombardament (n)	[bombarda'ment]
to drop a bomb	a arunca o bombă	[a arun'ka o 'bombə]
to bomb (vt)	a bombarda	[a bombar'da]
explosion	explozie (f)	[eks'plozie]
shot	împuşcătură (f)	[impuʃkə'turə]
to fire (~ a shot)	a împuşca	[a impuʃ'ka]
firing (burst of ~)	foc (n)	[fok]
to aim (to point a weapon)	a ţinti	[a tsin'ti]
to point (a gun)	a îndrepta	[a indrep'ta]
to hit (the target)	a nimeri	[a nime'ri]
to sink (~ a ship)	a scufunda	[a skufun'da]
hole (in a ship)	gaură (f)	['gaurə]

to founder, to sink (vi)	a se scufunda	[a se skufun'da]
front (war ~)	front (n)	[front]
evacuation	evacuare (f)	[evaku'are]
to evacuate (vt)	a evacua	[a evaku'a]

trench	tranşee (f)	[tran'ʃee]
barbed wire	sârmă (f) ghimpată	['sirmə gim'patə]
barrier (anti tank ~)	îngrădire (f)	[ingrə'dire]
watchtower	turlă (f)	['turlə]

military hospital	spital (n)	[spi'tal]
to wound (vt)	a răni	[a rə'ni]
wound	rană (f)	['ranə]
wounded (n)	rănit (m)	[rə'nit]
to be wounded	a fi rănit	[a fi rə'nit]
serious (wound)	serios	[se'rjos]

185. War. Military actions. Part 2

captivity	prizonierat (n)	[prizonie'rat]
to take captive	a lua prizonier	[a lu'a prizo'njer]
to be held captive	a fi prizonier	[a fi prizo'njer]
to be taken captive	a cădea prizonier	[a kə'dʲa prizo'njer]

concentration camp	lagăr (n) de concentrare	['lagər de kontʃen'trare]
prisoner of war	prizonier (m)	[prizo'njer]
to escape (vi)	a evada	[a eva'da]

to betray (vt)	a trăda	[a trə'da]
betrayer	trădător (m)	[trədə'tor]
betrayal	trădare (f)	[trə'dare]

| to execute (by firing squad) | a împuşca | [a impuʃ'ka] |
| execution (by firing squad) | împuşcare (f) | [impuʃ'kare] |

equipment (military gear)	echipare (f)	[eki'pare]
shoulder board	epolet (m)	[epo'let]
gas mask	mască (f) de gaze	['maskə de 'gaze]

field radio	staţie (f) de radio	['statsie de 'radio]
cipher, code	cifru (n)	['tʃifru]
secrecy	conspiraţie (f)	[konspi'ratsie]
password	parolă (f)	[pa'rolə]

land mine	mină (f)	['minə]
to mine (road, etc.)	a mina	[a mi'na]
minefield	câmp (n) minat	[kimp mi'nat]

air-raid warning	alarmă (f) aeriană	[a'larmə aeri'anə]
alarm (alert signal)	alarmă (f)	[a'larmə]
signal	semnal (n)	[sem'nal]
signal flare	rachetă (f) de semnalizare	[ra'ketə de semnali'zare]
headquarters	stat-major (n)	[stat ma'ʒor]
reconnaissance	cercetare (f)	[tʃertʃe'tare]

situation	condiții (f pl)	[kon'ditsij]
report	raport (n)	[ra'port]
ambush	ambuscadă (f)	[ambus'kadə]
reinforcement (army)	întărire (f)	[intə'rire]

target	țintă (f)	['tsintə]
training area	poligon (n)	[poli'gon]
military exercise	manevre (f pl)	[ma'nevre]

panic	panică (f)	['panikə]
devastation	ruină (f)	[ru'inə]
destruction, ruins	distrugere (f)	[dis'trudʒere]
to destroy (vt)	a distruge	[a dis'trudʒe]

to survive (vi, vt)	a scăpa cu viață	[a skə'pa ku 'vjatsə]
to disarm (vt)	a dezarma	[a dezar'ma]
to handle (~ a gun)	a mânui	[a minu'i]

| Attention! | Drepți! | [drepts] |
| At ease! | Pe loc repaus! | [pe lok re'paus] |

feat, act of courage	faptă (f) eroică	['faptə ero'ikə]
oath (vow)	jurământ (n)	[ʒurə'mint]
to swear (an oath)	a jura	[a ʒu'ra]

decoration (medal, etc.)	premiu (n)	['premju]
to award (give a medal to)	a premia	[a premi'ja]
medal	medalie (f)	[me'dalie]
order (e.g. ~ of Merit)	ordin (n)	['ordin]

victory	victorie (f)	[vik'torie]
defeat	înfrângere (f)	[in'frindʒere]
armistice	armistițiu (n)	[armis'titsju]

standard (battle flag)	drapel (n)	[dra'pel]
glory (honour, fame)	glorie (f)	['glorie]
parade	paradă (f)	[pa'radə]
to march (on parade)	a mărșălui	[a mərʃəlu'i]

186. Weapons

weapons	armă (f)	['armə]
firearms	armă (f) de foc	['armə de fok]
cold weapons (knives, etc.)	armă (f) albă	['armə 'albə]

chemical weapons	armă (f) chimică	['armə 'kimikə]
nuclear (adj)	nuclear	[nukle'ar]
nuclear weapons	armă (f) nucleară	['armə nukle'arə]

| bomb | bombă (f) | ['bombə] |
| atomic bomb | bombă (f) atomică | ['bombə a'tomikə] |

| pistol (gun) | pistol (n) | [pis'tol] |
| rifle | armă (f) | ['armə] |

| submachine gun | automat (n) | [auto'mat] |
| machine gun | mitralieră (f) | [mitra'ljerə] |

muzzle	gură (f)	['gurə]
barrel	ţeavă (f)	['tsʲavə]
calibre	calibru (n)	[ka'libru]

| trigger | cocoş (m) | [ko'koʃ] |
| sight (aiming device) | înălţător (n) | [inəltsə'tor] |

| magazine | magazie (f) | [maga'zie] |
| butt (shoulder stock) | patul (n) de puşcă | ['patul de 'puʃka] |

| hand grenade | grenadă (f) | [gre'nadə] |
| explosive | exploziv (n) | [eksplo'ziv] |

| bullet | glonţ (n) | [glonts] |
| cartridge | cartuş (n) | [kar'tuʃ] |

| charge | încărcătură (f) | [inkərkə'turə] |
| ammunition | muniţii (f pl) | [mu'nitsij] |

bomber (aircraft)	bombardier (n)	[bombar'djer]
fighter	distrugător (n)	[distrugə'tor]
helicopter	elicopter (n)	[elikop'ter]

anti-aircraft gun	tun (n) antiaerian	[tun antiaeri'an]
tank	tanc (n)	[tank]
tank gun	tun (n)	[tun]

| artillery | artilerie (f) | [artile'rie] |
| to lay (a gun) | a îndrepta | [a indrep'ta] |

| shell (projectile) | proiectil (n) | [proek'til] |
| mortar bomb | mină (f) | ['minə] |

| mortar | aruncător (n) de mine | [arunkə'tor de 'mine] |
| splinter (shell fragment) | schijă (f) | ['skiʒə] |

submarine	submarin (n)	[subma'rin]
torpedo	torpilă (f)	[tor'pilə]
missile	rachetă (f)	[ra'ketə]

| to load (gun) | a încărca | [a inkər'ka] |
| to shoot (vi) | a trage | [a 'tradʒe] |

| to point at (the cannon) | a ţinti | [a tsin'ti] |
| bayonet | baionetă (f) | [bajo'netə] |

rapier	spadă (f)	['spadə]
sabre (e.g. cavalry ~)	sabie (f)	['sabie]
spear (weapon)	suliţă (f)	['sulitsə]
bow	arc (n)	[ark]
arrow	săgeată (f)	[sə'dʒʲatə]
musket	flintă (f)	['flintə]
crossbow	arbaletă (f)	[arba'letə]

187. Ancient people

primitive (prehistoric)	**primitiv**	[primi'tiv]
prehistoric (adj)	**preistoric**	[preis'torik]
ancient (~ civilization)	**străvechi**	[strə'veki]
Stone Age	**Epoca** (f) **de piatră**	['epoka de 'pjatrə]
Bronze Age	**Epoca** (f) **de bronz**	['epoka de 'bronz]
Ice Age	**Epoca** (f) **glaciară**	['epoka glatʃi'arə]
tribe	**trib** (n)	[trib]
cannibal	**canibal** (m)	[kani'bal]
hunter	**vânător** (m)	[vinə'tor]
to hunt (vi, vt)	**a vâna**	[a vi'na]
mammoth	**mamut** (m)	[ma'mut]
cave	**peşteră** (f)	['peʃterə]
fire	**foc** (n)	[fok]
campfire	**foc** (n) **de tabără**	[fok də ta'bərə]
cave painting	**desen** (n) **pe piatră**	[de'sen pe 'pjatrə]
tool (e.g. stone axe)	**unealtă** (f)	[u'nʲaltə]
spear	**suliţă** (f)	['sulitsə]
stone axe	**topor** (n) **de piatră**	[to'por din 'pjatrə]
to be at war	**a lupta**	[a lup'ta]
to domesticate (vt)	**a domestici**	[a domesti'tʃi]
idol	**idol** (m)	['idol]
to worship (vt)	**a se închina**	[a se inki'na]
superstition	**superstiţie** (f)	[supers'titsie]
evolution	**evoluţie** (f)	[evo'lutsie]
development	**dezvoltare** (f)	[dezvol'tare]
disappearance (extinction)	**dispariţie** (f)	[dispa'ritsie]
to adapt oneself	**a se acomoda**	[a se akomo'da]
archaeology	**arheologie** (f)	[arheolo'dʒie]
archaeologist	**arheolog** (m)	[arheo'log]
archaeological (adj)	**arheologic**	[arheo'lodʒik]
excavation site	**săpături** (f pl)	[səpə'turʲ]
excavations	**săpături** (f pl)	[səpə'turʲ]
find (object)	**descoperire** (f)	[deskope'rire]
fragment	**fragment** (n)	[frag'ment]

188. Middle Ages

people (ethnic group)	**popor** (n)	[po'por]
peoples	**popoare** (n pl)	[popo'are]
tribe	**trib** (n)	[trib]
tribes	**triburi** (n pl)	['triburʲ]
barbarians	**barbari** (m pl)	[bar'barʲ]
Gauls	**gali** (m pl)	[galʲ]

Goths	**goți** (m pl)	[gotsʲ]
Slavs	**slavi** (m pl)	[slavʲ]
Vikings	**vikingi** (m pl)	['vikindʒʲ]

| Romans | **romani** (m pl) | [ro'manʲ] |
| Roman (adj) | **roman** | [ro'man] |

Byzantines	**bizantinieni** (m pl)	[bizantini'enʲ]
Byzantium	**Imperiul** (n) **Bizantin**	[im'perjul bizan'tin]
Byzantine (adj)	**bizantin**	[bizan'tin]

emperor	**împărat** (m)	[impə'rat]
leader, chief (tribal ~)	**căpetenie** (f)	[kəpe'tenie]
powerful (~ king)	**puternic**	[pu'ternik]
king	**rege** (m)	['redʒe]
ruler (sovereign)	**conducător** (m)	[kondukə'tor]

knight	**cavaler** (m)	[kava'ler]
feudal lord	**feudal** (m)	[feu'dal]
feudal (adj)	**feudal**	[feu'dal]
vassal	**vasal** (m)	[va'sal]

duke	**duce** (m)	['dutʃe]
earl	**conte** (m)	['konte]
baron	**baron** (m)	[ba'ron]
bishop	**episcop** (m)	[e'piskop]

armour	**armură** (f)	[ar'murə]
shield	**scut** (n)	[skut]
sword	**sabie** (f)	['sabie]
visor	**vizieră** (f)	[vi'zjerə]
chainmail	**zale** (f pl)	['zale]

| Crusade | **cruciadă** (f) | [krutʃi'adə] |
| crusader | **cruciat** (m) | [krutʃi'at] |

territory	**teritoriu** (n)	[teri'torju]
to attack (invade)	**a ataca**	[a ata'ka]
to conquer (vt)	**a cuceri**	[a kutʃe'ri]
to occupy (invade)	**a cotropi**	[a kotro'pi]

siege (to be under ~)	**asediu** (n)	[a'sedju]
besieged (adj)	**asediat** (m)	[asedi'at]
to besiege (vt)	**a asedia**	[a asedi'a]

inquisition	**inchiziție** (f)	[inki'zitsie]
inquisitor	**inchizitor** (m)	[inkizi'tor]
torture	**tortură** (f)	[tor'turə]
cruel (adj)	**crud**	[krud]
heretic	**eretic** (m)	[e'retik]
heresy	**erezie** (f)	[ere'zie]

seafaring	**navigație** (f) **maritimă**	[navi'gatsie ma'ritime]
pirate	**pirat** (m)	[pi'rat]
piracy	**piraterie** (f)	[pirate'rie]
boarding (attack)	**abordaj** (n)	[abor'daʒ]

loot, booty	**captură** (f)	[kap'turə]
treasure	**comoară** (f)	[komo'arə]

discovery	**descoperire** (f)	[deskope'rire]
to discover (new land, etc.)	**a descoperi**	[a deskope'ri]
expedition	**expediţie** (f)	[ekspe'diʦie]

musketeer	**muşchetar** (m)	[muʃke'tar]
cardinal	**cardinal** (m)	[kardi'nal]
heraldry	**heraldică** (f)	[he'raldikə]
heraldic (adj)	**heraldic**	[he'raldik]

189. Leader. Chief. Authorities

king	**rege** (m)	['reʤe]
queen	**regină** (f)	[re'ʤinə]
royal (adj)	**regal**	[re'gal]
kingdom	**regat** (n)	[re'gat]

prince	**prinţ** (m)	[prinʦ]
princess	**prinţesă** (f)	[prin'ʦesə]

president	**preşedinte** (m)	[preʃə'dinte]
vice-president	**vice-preşedinte** (m)	['viʧe preʃə'dinte]
senator	**senator** (m)	[sena'tor]

monarch	**monarh** (m)	[mo'narh]
ruler (sovereign)	**conducător** (m)	[kondukə'tor]
dictator	**dictator** (m)	[dikta'tor]
tyrant	**tiran** (m)	[ti'ran]
magnate	**magnat** (m)	[mag'nat]

director	**director** (m)	[di'rektor]
chief	**şef** (m)	[ʃef]
manager (director)	**manager** (m)	['menedʒə]

boss	**boss** (m)	[bos]
owner	**patron** (m)	[pa'tron]

head (~ of delegation)	**şef** (m)	[ʃef]
authorities	**autorităţi** (f pl)	[autoritəts']
superiors	**conducere** (f)	[kon'duʧere]

governor	**guvernator** (m)	[guverna'tor]
consul	**consul** (m)	['konsul]
diplomat	**diplomat** (m)	[diplo'mat]

mayor	**primar** (m)	[pri'mar]
sheriff	**şerif** (m)	[ʃə'rif]

emperor	**împărat** (m)	[impə'rat]
tsar, czar	**ţar** (m)	[ʦar]
pharaoh	**faraon** (m)	[fara'on]
khan	**han** (m)	[han]

190. Road. Way. Directions

road	**drum** (n)	[drum]
way (direction)	**cale** (f)	['kale]
highway	**şosea** (f)	[ʃo'sʲa]
motorway	**autostradă** (f)	[auto'stradə]
trunk road	**drum** (n) **naţional**	['drum natsio'nal]
main road	**drumul** (n) **principal**	['drumul printʃi'pal]
dirt road	**drum** (n) **vicinal**	['drum vitʃi'nal]
pathway	**potecă** (f)	[po'təkə]
footpath (troddenpath)	**cărare** (f)	[kə'rare]
Where?	**Unde?**	['unde]
Where (to)?	**Unde?**	['unde]
From where?	**De unde?**	[de 'unde]
direction (way)	**direcţie** (f)	[di'rektsie]
to point (~ the way)	**a arăta**	[a arə'ta]
to the left	**la stânga**	[la 'stinga]
to the right	**la dreapta**	[la 'drʲapta]
straight ahead (adv)	**înainte**	[ina'inte]
back (e.g. to turn ~)	**înapoi**	[ina'poj]
bend, curve	**curbă** (f)	['kurbə]
to turn (e.g., ~ left)	**a vira**	[a vi'ra]
to make a U-turn	**a întoarce**	[a into'artʃe]
to be visible	**a se zări**	[a se zə'ri]
(mountains, castle, etc.)		
to appear (come into view)	**a se arăta**	[a se arə'ta]
stop, halt (e.g., during a trip)	**oprire** (f)	[o'prire]
to rest, to pause (vi)	**a se odihni**	[a se odih'ni]
rest (pause)	**odihnă** (f)	[o'dihnə]
to lose one's way	**a se rătăci**	[a se rətə'tʃi]
to lead to ... (ab. road)	**a duce spre ...**	[a 'dutʃe spre]
to came out	**a ieşi la ...**	[a e'ʃi la]
(e.g., on the highway)		
stretch (of the road)	**porţiune** (f)	[portsi'une]
asphalt	**asfalt** (n)	[as'falt]
kerb	**bordură** (f)	[bor'durə]
ditch	**şanţ** (n)	[ʃants]
manhole	**capac** (n) **de canalizare**	[ka'pak de kanali'zare]
roadside (shoulder)	**margine** (f)	['mardʒine]
pit, pothole	**groapă** (f)	[gro'apə]
to go (on foot)	**a merge**	[a 'merdʒe]
to overtake (vt)	**a depăşi**	[a depə'ʃi]
step (footstep)	**pas** (m)	[pas]

on foot (adv)	pe jos	[pe ʒos]
to block (road)	a despărți	[a despər'tsi]
boom gate	barieră (f)	[ba'rjerə]
dead end	fundătură (f)	[fundə'turə]

191. Breaking the law. Criminals. Part 1

bandit	bandit (m)	[ban'dit]
crime	crimă (f)	['krimə]
criminal (person)	criminal (m)	[krimi'nal]

thief	hoț (m)	[hots]
to steal (vi, vt)	a fura	[a fu'ra]
stealing (larceny)	hoție (f)	[ho'tsie]
theft	furt (n)	[furt]

to kidnap (vt)	a răpi	[a rə'pi]
kidnapping	răpire (f)	[rə'pire]
kidnapper	răpitor (m)	[rəpi'tor]

| ransom | răscumpărare (f) | [rəskumpə'rare] |
| to demand ransom | a cere răscumpărare | [a 'tʃere rəskumpə'rare] |

to rob (vt)	a jefui	[a ʒefu'i]
robbery	jaf (n)	[ʒaf]
robber	jefuitor (m)	[ʒefui'tor]

to extort (vt)	a escroca	[a eskro'ka]
extortionist	escroc (m)	[es'krok]
extortion	escrocherie (f)	[eskroke'rie]

to murder, to kill	a ucide	[a u'tʃide]
murder	asasinat (n)	[asasi'nat]
murderer	asasin (m)	[asa'sin]

gunshot	împușcătură (f)	[impuʃkə'turə]
to fire (~ a shot)	a împușca	[a impuʃ'ka]
to shoot to death	a împușca	[a impuʃ'ka]
to shoot (vi)	a trage	[a 'tradʒə]
shooting	focuri (n) de armă	['fokurʲ de 'armə]

incident (fight, etc.)	întâmplare (f)	[intim'plare]
fight, brawl	bătaie (f)	[bə'tae]
victim	jertfă (f)	['ʒertfə]

to damage (vt)	a prejudicia	[a preʒuditʃi'a]
damage	daună (f)	['daunə]
dead body, corpse	cadavru (n)	[ka'davru]
grave (~ crime)	grav	[grav]

to attack (vt)	a ataca	[a ata'ka]
to beat (to hit)	a bate	[a 'bate]
to beat up	a snopi în bătăi	[a sno'pi in bətəj]
to take (rob of sth)	a lua	[a lu'a]

to stab to death	a înjunghia	[a inʒungi'ja]
to maim (vt)	a schilodi	[a skilo'di]
to wound (vt)	a răni	[a rə'ni]

blackmail	şantaj (n)	[ʃan'taʒ]
to blackmail (vt)	a şantaja	[a ʃanta'ʒa]
blackmailer	şantajist (m)	[ʃanta'ʒist]

protection racket	banditism (n)	[bandi'tizm]
racketeer	bandit (m)	[ban'dit]
gangster	gangster (m)	['gangster]
mafia	mafie (f)	['mafie]

pickpocket	hoţ (m) de buzunare	[hoʦ de buzu'nare]
burglar	spărgător (m)	[spərgə'tor]
smuggling	contrabandă (f)	[kontra'bandə]
smuggler	contrabandist (m)	[kontraban'dist]

forgery	falsificare (f)	[falsifi'kare]
to forge (counterfeit)	a falsifica	[a falsifi'ka]
fake (forged)	fals	[fals]

192. Breaking the law. Criminals. Part 2

rape	viol (n)	[vi'ol]
to rape (vt)	a viola	[a vio'la]
rapist	violator (m)	[viola'tor]
maniac	maniac (m)	[mani'ak]

prostitute (fem.)	prostituată (f)	[prostitu'atə]
prostitution	prostituţie (f)	[prosti'tuʦie]
pimp	proxenet (m)	[prokse'net]

| drug addict | narcoman (m) | [narko'man] |
| drug dealer | vânzător (m) de droguri | [vinzə'tor de 'drogurʲ] |

to blow up (bomb)	a arunca în aer	[a arun'ka in 'aer]
explosion	explozie (f)	[eks'plozie]
to set fire	a incendia	[a inʧendi'a]
arsonist	incendiator (m)	[inʧendia'tor]

terrorism	terorism (n)	[tero'rism]
terrorist	terorist (m)	[tero'rist]
hostage	ostatic (m)	[os'tatik]

to swindle (deceive)	a înşela	[a inʃə'la]
swindle, deception	înşelăciune (f)	[inʃələ'ʧiune]
swindler	şarlatan (m)	[ʃarla'tan]

to bribe (vt)	a mitui	[a mitu'i]
bribery	mituire (f)	[mitu'ire]
bribe	mită (f)	['mitə]
poison	otravă (f)	[o'travə]
to poison (vt)	a otrăvi	[a otrə'vi]

to poison oneself	**a se otrăvi**	[a se otrə'vi]
suicide (act)	**sinucidere** (f)	[sinu'tʃidere]
suicide (person)	**sinucigaş** (m)	[sinutʃi'gaʃ]

to threaten (vt)	**a ameninţa**	[a amenin'tsa]
threat	**ameninţare** (f)	[amenin'tsare]
to make an attempt	**a atenta la**	[a aten'ta la]
attempt (attack)	**atentat** (n)	[aten'tat]

to steal (a car)	**a goni**	[a go'ni]
to hijack (a plane)	**a goni**	[a go'ni]

revenge	**răzbunare** (f)	[rəzbu'nare]
to avenge (get revenge)	**a răzbuna**	[a rəzbu'na]

to torture (vt)	**a tortura**	[a tortu'ra]
torture	**tortură** (f)	[tor'turə]
to torment (vt)	**a chinui**	[a kinu'i]

pirate	**pirat** (m)	[pi'rat]
hooligan	**huligan** (m)	[huli'gan]
armed (adj)	**înarmat**	[inar'mat]
violence	**violenţă** (f)	[vio'lentsə]

spying (espionage)	**spionaj** (n)	[spio'naʒ]
to spy (vi)	**a spiona**	[a spio'na]

193. Police. Law. Part 1

justice	**justiţie** (f)	[ʒus'titsie]
court (see you in ~)	**curte** (f)	['kurte]

judge	**judecător** (m)	[ʒudekə'tor]
jurors	**juraţi** (m pl)	[ʒu'ratsʲ]
jury trial	**curte** (f) **de juraţi**	['kurte de ʒu'ratsʲ]
to judge, to try (vt)	**a judeca**	[a ʒude'ka]

lawyer, barrister	**avocat** (m)	[avo'kat]
defendant	**acuzat** (m)	[aku'zat]
dock	**banca** (f) **acuzaţilor**	['banka aku'zatsilor]

charge	**învinuire** (f)	[invinu'ire]
accused	**învinuit** (m)	[invinu'it]

sentence	**verdict** (n)	[ver'dikt]
to sentence (vt)	**a condamna**	[a kondam'na]

guilty (culprit)	**vinovat** (m)	[vino'vat]
to punish (vt)	**a pedepsi**	[a pedep'si]
punishment	**pedeapsă** (f)	[pe'dʲapsə]

fine (penalty)	**amendă** (f)	[a'mendə]
life imprisonment	**închisoare** (f) **pe viaţă**	[inkiso'are pe 'vjatsə]
death penalty	**pedeapsă** (f) **capitală**	[pe'dʲapsə kapi'talə]

electric chair	scaun (n) electric	['skaun e'lektrik]
gallows	spânzurătoare (f)	[spinzurəto'are]
to execute (vt)	a executa	[a egzeku'ta]
execution	execuţie (f)	[egze'kutsie]
prison	închisoare (f)	[inkiso'are]
cell	cameră (f)	['kamerə]
escort (convoy)	convoi (n)	[kon'voj]
prison officer	paznic (m)	['paznik]
prisoner	arestat (m)	[ares'tat]
handcuffs	cătuşe (f pl)	[kə'tuʃə]
to handcuff (vt)	a pune cătuşele	[a 'pune kə'tuʃəle]
prison break	evadare (f)	[eva'dare]
to break out (vi)	a evada	[a eva'da]
to disappear (vi)	a dispărea	[a dispə'r'a]
to release (from prison)	a elibera	[a elibe'ra]
amnesty	amnistie (f)	[am'nistie]
police	poliţie (f)	[po'litsie]
police officer	poliţist (m)	[poli'tsist]
police station	secţie (f) de poliţie	['sektsie de po'litsie]
truncheon	baston (n) de cauciuc	[bas'ton de kau'tʃiuk]
megaphone (loudhailer)	portavoce (f)	[porta'votʃe]
patrol car	maşină (f) de patrulă	[ma'ʃine de pa'trulə]
siren	sirenă (f)	[si'renə]
to turn on the siren	a conecta sirena	[a konek'ta si'rena]
siren call	alarma (f) sirenei	[a'larma si'renej]
crime scene	locul (n) faptei	['lokul 'faptej]
witness	martor (m)	['martor]
freedom	libertate (f)	[liber'tate]
accomplice	complice (m)	[kom'plitʃe]
to flee (vi)	a se ascunde	[a se as'kunde]
trace (to leave a ~)	urmă (f)	['urmə]

194. Police. Law. Part 2

search (investigation)	investigaţie (f)	[investi'gatsie]
to look for …	a căuta	[a kəu'ta]
suspicion	suspiciune (f)	[suspitʃi'une]
suspicious (e.g., ~ vehicle)	suspect	[sus'pekt]
to stop (cause to halt)	a opri	[a op'ri]
to detain (keep in custody)	a reţine	[a re'tsine]
case (lawsuit)	dosar (n)	[do'sar]
investigation	anchetă (f)	[an'ketə]
detective	detectiv (m)	[detek'tiv]
investigator	anchetator (m)	[anketa'tor]
hypothesis	versiune (f)	[versi'une]

motive	motiv (n)	[mo'tiv]
interrogation	interogatoriu (n)	[interoga'torju]
to interrogate (vt)	a interoga	[a intero'ga]
to question	a audia	[a audi'a]
(~ neighbors, etc.)		
check (identity ~)	verificare (f)	[verifi'kare]

round-up (raid)	razie (f)	['razie]
search (~ warrant)	percheziție (f)	[perke'zitsie]
chase (pursuit)	urmărire (f)	[urmə'rire]
to pursue, to chase	a urmări	[a urmə'ri]
to track (a criminal)	a urmări	[a urmə'ri]

arrest	arestare (f)	[ares'tare]
to arrest (sb)	a aresta	[a ares'ta]
to catch (thief, etc.)	a prinde	[a 'prinde]
capture	prindere (f)	['prindere]

document	act (n)	[akt]
proof (evidence)	dovadă (f)	[do'vadə]
to prove (vt)	a dovedi	[a dove'di]
footprint	amprentă (f)	[am'prentə]
fingerprints	amprente (f pl) digitale	[am'prente didʒi'tale]
piece of evidence	probă (f)	['probə]

alibi	alibi (n)	['alibi]
innocent (not guilty)	nevinovat (m)	[nevino'vat]
injustice	nedreptate (f)	[nedrep'tate]
unjust, unfair (adj)	nedrept	[ne'drept]

criminal (adj)	criminal (m)	[krimi'nal]
to confiscate (vt)	a confisca	[a konfis'ka]
drug (illegal substance)	narcotic (n)	[nar'kotik]
weapon, gun	armă (f)	['armə]
to disarm (vt)	a dezarma	[a dezar'ma]
to order (command)	a ordona	[a ordo'na]
to disappear (vi)	a dispărea	[a dispə'rʲa]

law	lege (f)	['ledʒe]
legal, lawful (adj)	legal	[le'gal]
illegal, illicit (adj)	ilegal	[ile'gal]

responsibility (blame)	responsabilitate (f)	[responsabili'tate]
responsible (adj)	responsabil	[respon'sabil]

NATURE

The Earth. Part 1

space	cosmos (n)	['kosmos]
space (as adj)	cosmic	['kosmik]
outer space	spaţiu (n) cosmic	['spatsju 'kosmik]
galaxy	galaxie (f)	[galak'sie]
star	stea (f)	[stʲa]
constellation	constelaţie (f)	[konste'latsie]
planet	planetă (f)	[pla'netə]
satellite	satelit (m)	[sate'lit]
meteorite	meteorit (m)	[meteo'rit]
comet	cometă (f)	[ko'metə]
asteroid	asteroid (m)	[astero'id]
orbit	orbită (f)	[or'bitə]
to revolve	a se roti	[a se ro'ti]
(~ around the Earth)		
atmosphere	atmosferă (f)	[atmos'ferə]
the Sun	soare (n)	[so'are]
solar system	sistem (n) solar	[sis'tem so'lar]
solar eclipse	eclipsă (f) de soare	[ek'lipsə de so'are]
the Earth	Pământ (n)	[pə'mint]
the Moon	Lună (f)	['lunə]
Mars	Marte (m)	['marte]
Venus	Venus (f)	['venus]
Jupiter	Jupiter (m)	['ʒupiter]
Saturn	Saturn (m)	[sa'turn]
Mercury	Mercur (m)	[mer'kur]
Uranus	Uranus (m)	[u'ranus]
Neptune	Neptun (m)	[nep'tun]
Pluto	Pluto (m)	['pluto]
Milky Way	Calea (f) Lactee	['kalʲa lak'tee]
Great Bear (Ursa Major)	Ursa (f) mare	['ursa 'mare]
North Star	Steaua (f) polară	['stʲawa po'larə]
Martian	marţian (m)	[martsi'an]
extraterrestrial (n)	extraterestru (m)	[ekstrate'restru]
alien	extraterestru (m)	[ekstrate'restru]

flying saucer	farfurie (f) zburătoare	[farfu'rie zburəto'are]
spaceship	navă (f) spaţială	['navə spatsi'alə]
space station	staţie (f) orbitală	['statsie orbi'talə]
blast-off	start (n)	[start]
engine	motor (n)	[mo'tor]
nozzle	ajutaj (n)	[aʒu'taʒ]
fuel	combustibil (m)	[kombus'tibil]
cockpit, flight deck	cabină (f)	[ka'binə]
aerial	antenă (f)	[an'tenə]
porthole	hublou (n)	[hu'blou]
solar panel	baterie (f) solară	[bate'rie so'larə]
spacesuit	scafandru (m)	[ska'fandru]
weightlessness	imponderabilitate (f)	[imponderabili'tate]
oxygen	oxigen (n)	[oksi'dʒen]
docking (in space)	unire (f)	[u'nire]
to dock (vi, vt)	a uni	[a u'ni]
observatory	observator (n) astronomic	[observa'tor astro'nomik]
telescope	telescop (n)	[tele'skop]
to observe (vt)	a observa	[a obser'va]
to explore (vt)	a cerceta	[a tʃertʃe'ta]

196. The Earth

the Earth	Pământ (n)	[pə'mint]
the globe (the Earth)	globul (n) pământesc	['globul pəmin'tesk]
planet	planetă (f)	[pla'netə]
atmosphere	atmosferă (f)	[atmos'ferə]
geography	geografie (f)	[dʒeogra'fie]
nature	natură (f)	[na'turə]
globe (table ~)	glob (n)	[glob]
map	hartă (f)	['hartə]
atlas	atlas (n)	[at'las]
Europe	Europa (f)	[eu'ropa]
Asia	Asia (f)	['asia]
Africa	Africa (f)	['afrika]
Australia	Australia (f)	[au'stralia]
America	America (f)	[a'merika]
North America	America (f) de Nord	[a'merika de nord]
South America	America (f) de Sud	[a'merika de sud]
Antarctica	Antarctida (f)	[antark'tida]
the Arctic	Arctica (f)	['arktika]

197. Cardinal directions

north	nord (n)	[nord]
to the north	la nord	[la nord]
in the north	la nord	[la nord]
northern (adj)	de nord	[de nord]

south	sud (n)	[sud]
to the south	la sud	[la sud]
in the south	la sud	[la sud]
southern (adj)	de sud	[de sud]

west	vest (n)	[vest]
to the west	la vest	[la vest]
in the west	la vest	[la vest]
western (adj)	de vest	[de vest]

east	est (n)	[est]
to the east	la est	[la est]
in the east	la est	[la est]
eastern (adj)	de est	[de est]

198. Sea. Ocean

sea	mare (f)	['mare]
ocean	ocean (n)	[otʃə'an]
gulf (bay)	golf (n)	[golf]
straits	strâmtoare (f)	[strimto'are]

continent (mainland)	continent (n)	[konti'nent]
island	insulă (f)	['insulə]
peninsula	peninsulă (f)	[pe'ninsulə]
archipelago	arhipelag (n)	[arhipe'lag]

bay, cove	golf (n)	[golf]
harbour	port (n)	[port]
lagoon	lagună (f)	[la'gunə]
cape	cap (n)	[kap]

atoll	atol (m)	[a'tol]
reef	recif (m)	[re'tʃif]
coral	coral (m)	[ko'ral]
coral reef	recif (m) de corali	[re'tʃif de ko'raliˈ]

deep (adj)	adânc	[a'dink]
depth (deep water)	adâncime (f)	[adin'tʃime]
abyss	abis (n)	[a'bis]
trench (e.g. Mariana ~)	groapă (f)	[gro'apə]

current (Ocean ~)	curent (n)	[ku'rent]
to surround (bathe)	a spăla	[a spə'la]
shore	mal (n)	[mal]
coast	litoral (n)	[lito'ral]

flow (flood tide)	**flux** (n)	[fluks]
ebb (ebb tide)	**reflux** (n)	[re'fluks]
shoal	**banc** (n) **de nisip**	[bank de ni'sip]
bottom (~ of the sea)	**fund** (n)	[fund]
wave	**val** (n)	[val]
crest (~ of a wave)	**creasta** (f) **valului**	['kriasta 'valuluj]
spume (sea foam)	**spumă** (f)	['spumə]
storm (sea storm)	**furtună** (f)	[fur'tunə]
hurricane	**uragan** (m)	[ura'gan]
tsunami	**tsunami** (n)	[ʦu'nami]
calm (dead ~)	**timp** (n) **calm**	[timp kalm]
quiet, calm (adj)	**liniştit**	[liniʃ'tit]
pole	**pol** (n)	[pol]
polar (adj)	**polar**	[po'lar]
latitude	**longitudine** (f)	[londʒi'tudine]
longitude	**latitudine** (f)	[lati'tudine]
parallel	**paralelă** (f)	[para'lelə]
equator	**ecuator** (n)	[ekua'tor]
sky	**cer** (n)	[ʧer]
horizon	**orizont** (n)	[ori'zont]
air	**aer** (n)	['aer]
lighthouse	**far** (n)	[far]
to dive (vi)	**a se scufunda**	[a se skufun'da]
to sink (ab. boat)	**a se duce la fund**	[a se duʧə lʲa fund]
treasure	**comoară** (f)	[komo'arə]

199. Seas & Oceans names

Atlantic Ocean	**Oceanul** (n) **Atlantic**	[oʧə'anul at'lantik]
Indian Ocean	**Oceanul** (n) **Indian**	[oʧə'anul indi'an]
Pacific Ocean	**Oceanul** (n) **Pacific**	[oʧə'anul pa'ʧifik]
Arctic Ocean	**Oceanul** (n) **Îngheţat de Nord**	[oʧə'anul inge'ʦat de nord]
Black Sea	**Marea** (f) **Neagră**	['marʲa 'nʲagrə]
Red Sea	**Marea** (f) **Roşie**	['marʲa 'roʃie]
Yellow Sea	**Marea** (f) **Galbenă**	['marʲa 'galbenə]
White Sea	**Marea** (f) **Albă**	['marʲa 'albə]
Caspian Sea	**Marea** (f) **Caspică**	['marʲa 'kaspikə]
Dead Sea	**Marea** (f) **Moartă**	['marʲa mo'artə]
Mediterranean Sea	**Marea** (f) **Mediterană**	['marʲa medite'ranə]
Aegean Sea	**Marea** (f) **Egee**	['marʲa e'dʒee]
Adriatic Sea	**Marea** (f) **Adriatică**	['marʲa adri'atikə]
Arabian Sea	**Marea** (f) **Arabiei**	['marʲa a'rabiej]
Sea of Japan	**Marea** (f) **Japoneză**	['marʲa ʒapo'nezə]

Bering Sea	Marea (f) Bering	['maria 'bering]
South China Sea	Marea (f) Chinei de Sud	['maria 'kinej de sud]
Coral Sea	Marea (f) Coral	['maria ko'ral]
Tasman Sea	Marea (f) Tasmaniei	['maria tas'maniej]
Caribbean Sea	Marea (f) Caraibelor	['maria kara'ibelor]
Barents Sea	Marea (f) Barents	['maria ba'rents]
Kara Sea	Marea (f) Kara	['maria 'kara]
North Sea	Marea (f) Nordului	['maria 'norduluj]
Baltic Sea	Marea (f) Baltică	['maria 'baltikə]
Norwegian Sea	Marea (f) Norvegiei	['maria nor'vedʒiej]

200. Mountains

mountain	munte (m)	['munte]
mountain range	lanț (n) muntos	[lants mun'tos]
mountain ridge	lanț (n) de munți	[lants de munts]
summit, top	vârf (n)	[virf]
peak	culme (f)	['kulmə]
foot (~ of the mountain)	poale (f pl)	[po'ale]
slope (mountainside)	pantă (f)	['pantə]
volcano	vulcan (n)	[vul'kan]
active volcano	vulcan (n) activ	[vul'kan ak'tiv]
dormant volcano	vulcan (n) stins	[vul'kan stins]
eruption	erupție (f)	[e'ruptsie]
crater	crater (n)	['krater]
magma	magmă (f)	['magmə]
lava	lavă (f)	['lavə]
molten (~ lava)	încins	[in'tʃins]
canyon	canion (n)	[kani'on]
gorge	defileu (n)	[defi'leu]
crevice	pas (n)	[pas]
pass, col	trecătoare (f)	[trekəto'are]
plateau	podiş (n)	[po'diʃ]
cliff	stâncă (f)	['stinkə]
hill	deal (n)	['dial]
glacier	ghețar (m)	[ge'tsar]
waterfall	cascadă (f)	[kas'kadə]
geyser	gheizer (m)	['gejzer]
lake	lac (n)	[lak]
plain	şes (n)	[ʃəs]
landscape	peisaj (n)	[pej'saʒ]
echo	ecou (n)	[e'kou]
alpinist	alpinist (m)	[alpi'nist]
rock climber	căţărător (m)	[kətsərə'tor]

| to conquer (in climbing) | a cuceri | [a kutʃe'ri] |
| climb (an easy ~) | ascensiune (f) | [astʃensi'une] |

201. Mountains names

The Alps	Alpi (m pl)	['alpʲ]
Mont Blanc	Mont Blanc (m)	[mon 'blan]
The Pyrenees	Pirinei (m)	[piri'nej]

The Carpathians	Carpați (m pl)	[kar'patsʲ]
The Ural Mountains	Munții (m pl) Ural	['muntsij u'ral]
The Caucasus Mountains	Caucaz (m)	[kau'kaz]
Mount Elbrus	Elbrus (m)	['elbrus]

The Altai Mountains	Altai (m)	[al'taj]
The Tian Shan	Tian-Şan (m)	['tjan 'ʃan]
The Pamirs	Pamir (m)	[pa'mir]
The Himalayas	Himalaya	[hima'laja]
Mount Everest	Everest (m)	[eve'rest]

| The Andes | Anzi | ['anzʲ] |
| Mount Kilimanjaro | Kilimanjaro (m) | [kiliman'ʒaro] |

202. Rivers

river	râu (n)	['riu]
spring (natural source)	izvor (n)	[iz'vor]
riverbed (river channel)	matcă (f)	['matkə]
basin (river valley)	bazin (n)	[ba'zin]
to flow into …	a se vărsa	[a se vər'sa]

| tributary | afluent (m) | [aflu'ent] |
| bank (river ~) | mal (n) | [mal] |

current (stream)	curs (n)	[kurs]
downstream (adv)	în josul apei	[in 'ʒosul 'apej]
upstream (adv)	în susul apei	[in 'susul 'apej]

inundation	inundaţie (f)	[inun'datsie]
flooding	revărsare (f) a apelor	[revər'sare a 'apelor]
to overflow (vi)	a se revărsa	[a se revər'sa]
to flood (vt)	a inunda	[a inun'da]

| shallow (shoal) | banc (n) de nisip | [bank de ni'sip] |
| rapids | prag (n) | [prag] |

dam	baraj (n)	[ba'raʒ]
canal	canal (n)	[ka'nal]
reservoir (artificial lake)	bazin (n)	[ba'zin]
sluice, lock	ecluză (f)	[e'kluzə]
water body (pond, etc.)	bazin (n)	[ba'zin]
swamp (marshland)	mlaştină (f)	['mlaʃtinə]

| bog, marsh | mlaştină (f), smârc (n) | ['mlaʃtinə], [smirk] |
| whirlpool | vârtej (n) de apă | [vir'teʒ de 'apə] |

stream (brook)	pârâu (n)	[pi'riu]
drinking (ab. water)	potabil	[po'tabil]
fresh (~ water)	nesărat	[nesə'rat]

| ice | gheață (f) | ['gʲatsə] |
| to freeze over (ab. river, etc.) | a îngheța | [a inge'tsa] |

203. Rivers names

| Seine | Sena (f) | ['sena] |
| Loire | Loara (f) | [lo'ara] |

Thames	Tamisa (f)	[ta'misa]
Rhine	Rin (m)	[rin]
Danube	Dunăre (f)	['dunəre]

Volga	Volga (f)	['volga]
Don	Don (m)	[don]
Lena	Lena (f)	['lena]

Yellow River	Huang He (m)	[huan 'he]
Yangtze	Yangtze (m)	[janʦ'zi]
Mekong	Mekong (m)	[me'kong]
Ganges	Gang (m)	[gang]

Nile River	Nil (m)	[nil]
Congo River	Congo (m)	['kongo]
Okavango River	Okavango (m)	[oka'vango]
Zambezi River	Zambezi (m)	[zam'bezi]
Limpopo River	Limpopo (m)	[limpo'po]
Mississippi River	Mississippi (m)	[misi'sipi]

204. Forest

| forest, wood | pădure (f) | [pə'dure] |
| forest (as adj) | de pădure | [de pə'dure] |

thick forest	desiş (n)	[de'siʃ]
grove	pădurice (f)	[pədu'riʧe]
forest clearing	poiană (f)	[po'janə]

| thicket | tufiş (n) | [tu'fiʃ] |
| scrubland | arbust (m) | [ar'bust] |

| footpath (troddenpath) | cărare (f) | [kə'rare] |
| gully | râpă (f) | ['ripə] |

| tree | copac (m) | [ko'pak] |
| leaf | frunză (f) | ['frunzə] |

leaves (foliage)	frunziş (n)	[frun'ziʃ]
fall of leaves	cădere (f) a frunzelor	[kə'dere a 'frunzelor]
to fall (ab. leaves)	a cădea	[a kə'dʲa]
top (of the tree)	vârf (n)	[virf]

branch	ramură (f)	['ramurə]
bough	creangă (f)	['krʲangə]
bud (on shrub, tree)	mugur (m)	['mugur]
needle (of the pine tree)	ac (n)	[ak]
fir cone	con (n)	[kon]

tree hollow	scorbură (f)	['skorburə]
nest	cuib (n)	[kujb]
burrow (animal hole)	vizuină (f)	[vizu'inə]

trunk	trunchi (n)	[trunkʲ]
root	rădăcină (f)	[rədə'tʃinə]
bark	scoarţă (f)	[sko'artsə]
moss	muşchi (m)	[muʃkʲ]

to uproot (remove trees or tree stumps)	a defrişa	[a defri'ʃa]
to chop down	a tăia	[a tə'ja]
to deforest (vt)	a doborî	[a dobo'ri]
tree stump	buturugă (f)	[butu'rugə]

campfire	foc (n)	[fok]
forest fire	incendiu (n)	[in'tʃendju]
to extinguish (vt)	a stinge	[a 'stindʒe]

forest ranger	pădurar (m)	[pədu'rar]
protection	protecţie (f)	[pro'tektsie]
to protect (~ nature)	a ocroti	[a okro'ti]
poacher	braconier (m)	[brako'njer]
steel trap	capcană (f)	[kap'kanə]

| to gather, to pick (vt) | a strânge | [a 'strindʒe] |
| to lose one's way | a se rătăci | [a se rətə'tʃi] |

205. Natural resources

natural resources	resurse (f pl) naturale	[re'surse natu'rale]
minerals	bogăţii (f pl) minerale	[bogə'tsij mine'rale]
deposits	depozite (n pl)	[de'pozite]
field (e.g. oilfield)	zăcământ (n)	[zəkə'mint]

to mine (extract)	a extrage	[a eks'tradʒe]
mining (extraction)	obţinere (f)	[ob'tsinere]
ore	minereu (n)	[mine'reu]
mine (e.g. for coal)	mină (f)	['minə]
shaft (mine ~)	puţ (n)	['puts]
miner	miner (m)	[mi'ner]
gas (natural ~)	gaz (n)	[gaz]
gas pipeline	conductă (f) de gaze	[kon'duktə de 'gaze]

oil (petroleum)	petrol (n)	[pe'trol]
oil pipeline	conductă (f) de petrol	[kon'duktə de pe'trol]
oil well	sondă (f) de ţiţei (n)	['sondə de tsi'tsej]
derrick (tower)	turlă (f) de foraj	['turlə de fo'raʒ]
tanker	tanc (n) petrolier	['tank petro'ljer]

sand	nisip (n)	[ni'sip]
limestone	calcar (n)	[kal'kar]
gravel	pietriş (n)	[pe'triʃ]
peat	turbă (f)	['turbə]
clay	argilă (f)	[ar'dʒilə]
coal	cărbune (m)	[kər'bune]

iron (ore)	fier (m)	[fier]
gold	aur (n)	['aur]
silver	argint (n)	[ar'dʒint]
nickel	nichel (n)	['nikel]
copper	cupru (n)	['kupru]

zinc	zinc (n)	[zink]
manganese	mangan (n)	[man'gan]
mercury	mercur (n)	[mer'kur]
lead	plumb (n)	[plumb]

mineral	mineral (n)	[mine'ral]
crystal	cristal (n)	[kris'tal]
marble	marmură (f)	['marmurə]
uranium	uraniu (n)	[u'ranju]

The Earth. Part 2

weather	timp (n)	[timp]
weather forecast	prognoză (f) meteo	[prog'nozə 'meteo]
temperature	temperatură (f)	[tempera'turə]
thermometer	termometru (n)	[termo'metru]
barometer	barometru (n)	[baro'metru]
humidity	umiditate (f)	[umidi'tate]
heat (extreme ~)	caniculă (f)	[ka'nikulə]
hot (torrid)	fierbinte	[fier'binte]
it's hot	e foarte cald	[e fo'arte kald]
it's warm	e cald	[e kald]
warm (moderately hot)	cald	[kald]
it's cold	e frig	[e frig]
cold (adj)	rece	['retʃe]
sun	soare (n)	[so'are]
to shine (vi)	a străluci	[a strəlu'tʃi]
sunny (day)	însorit	[inso'rit]
to come up (vi)	a răsări	[a rəsə'ri]
to set (vi)	a apune	[a a'pune]
cloud	nor (m)	[nor]
cloudy (adj)	înnorat	[inno'rat]
rain cloud	nor (m)	[nor]
somber (gloomy)	mohorât	[moho'rît]
rain	ploaie (f)	[plo'ae]
it's raining	plouă	['plowə]
rainy (~ day, weather)	ploios	[plo'jos]
to drizzle (vi)	a bura	[a bu'ra]
pouring rain	ploaie (f) torenţială	[plo'ae toren'tsjalə]
downpour	rupere (f) de nori	['rupere de 'nori]
heavy (e.g. ~ rain)	puternic	[pu'ternik]
puddle	băltoacă (f)	[bəlto'akə]
to get wet (in rain)	a se uda	[a se u'da]
fog (mist)	ceaţă (f)	['tʃatsə]
foggy	ceţos	[tʃe'tsos]
snow	zăpadă (f)	[zə'padə]
it's snowing	ninge	['nindʒe]

207. Severe weather. Natural disasters

thunderstorm	furtună (f)	[fur'tunə]
lightning (~ strike)	fulger (n)	['fuldʒer]
to flash (vi)	a fulgera	[a fuldʒe'ra]
thunder	tunet (n)	['tunet]
to thunder (vi)	a tuna	[a tu'na]
it's thundering	tună	['tunə]
hail	grindină (f)	[grin'dinə]
it's hailing	plouă cu gheață	['plowə ku 'gʲatsə]
to flood (vt)	a inunda	[a inun'da]
flood, inundation	inundaţie (f)	[inun'datsie]
earthquake	cutremur (n)	[ku'tremur]
tremor, shoke	zguduire (f)	[zgudu'ire]
epicentre	epicentru (m)	[epi'tʃentru]
eruption	erupţie (f)	[e'ruptsie]
lava	lavă (f)	['lavə]
twister	vârtej (n)	[vir'teʒ]
tornado	tornadă (f)	[tor'nadə]
typhoon	taifun (n)	[taj'fun]
hurricane	uragan (m)	[ura'gan]
storm	furtună (f)	[fur'tunə]
tsunami	tsunami (n)	[tsu'nami]
cyclone	ciclon (m)	[tʃi'klon]
bad weather	vreme (f) rea	['vreme rʲa]
fire (accident)	incendiu (n)	[in'tʃendju]
disaster	catastrofă (f)	[katas'trofə]
meteorite	meteorit (m)	[meteo'rit]
avalanche	avalanşă (f)	[ava'lanʃə]
snowslide	prăbuşire (f)	[prəbu'ʃire]
blizzard	viscol (n)	['viskol]
snowstorm	viscol (n)	['viskol]

208. Noises. Sounds

silence (quiet)	tăcere (f)	[tə'tʃere]
sound	sunet (n)	['sunet]
noise	zgomot (n)	['zgomot]
to make noise	a face zgomot	[a 'fatʃe 'zgomot]
noisy (adj)	zgomotos	[zgomo'tos]
loudly (to speak, etc.)	tare	['tare]
loud (voice, etc.)	tare	['tare]
constant (e.g., ~ noise)	permanent	[perma'nent]

cry, shout (n)	**strigăt** (n)	['strigət]
to cry, to shout (vi)	**a striga**	[a stri'ga]
whisper	**şoaptă** (f)	[ʃo'aptə]
to whisper (vi, vt)	**a şopti**	[a ʃop'ti]
barking (dog's ~)	**lătrat** (n)	[lə'trat]
to bark (vi)	**a lătra**	[a lə'tra]
groan (of pain, etc.)	**geamăt** (n)	['dʒamət]
to groan (vi)	**a geme**	[a 'dʒeme]
cough	**tuse** (f)	['tuse]
to cough (vi)	**a tuşi**	[a tu'ʃi]
whistle	**fluierat** (n)	[flue'rat]
to whistle (vi)	**a fluiera**	[a flue'ra]
knock (at the door)	**lovitură** (f)	[lovi'turə]
to knock (on the door)	**a bate**	[a 'bate]
to crack (vi)	**a trosni**	[a tros'ni]
crack (cracking sound)	**trosnitură** (f)	[trosni'ture]
siren	**sirenă** (f)	[si'renə]
whistle (factory ~, etc.)	**fluier** (n)	['flujer]
to whistle (ab. train)	**a vui**	[a vu'i]
honk (car horn sound)	**claxon** (n)	[klak'son]
to honk (vi)	**a semnaliza**	[a semnali'za]

209. Winter

winter (n)	**iarnă** (f)	['jarnə]
winter (as adj)	**de iarnă**	[de 'jarnə]
in winter	**iarna**	['jarna]
snow	**zăpadă** (f)	[zə'padə]
it's snowing	**ninge**	['nindʒe]
snowfall	**ninsoare** (f)	[ninso'are]
snowdrift	**troian** (n)	[tro'jan]
snowflake	**fulg** (m) **de zăpadă**	[fulg de zə'padə]
snowball	**bulgăre** (m) **de zăpadă**	['bulgəre de zə'padə]
snowman	**om** (m) **de zăpadă**	[om de zə'padə]
icicle	**ţurţur** (m)	['tsurtsur]
December	**decembrie** (m)	[de'tʃembrie]
January	**ianuarie** (m)	[janu'arie]
February	**februarie** (m)	[febru'arie]
frost (severe ~, freezing cold)	**ger** (n)	[dʒer]
frosty (weather, air)	**geros**	[dʒe'ros]
below zero (adv)	**sub zero grade**	[sub 'zero 'grade]
first frost	**îngheţ** (n) **uşor**	[i'ngets u'ʃor]
hoarfrost	**brumă** (f)	['brumə]
cold (cold weather)	**frig** (n)	[frig]

it's cold	frig	[frig]
fur coat	şubă (f)	['ʃubə]
mittens	mănuşi (f pl)	[mə'nuʃ
	cu un singur deget	ku un 'singur 'dedʒet]

to fall ill	a se îmbolnăvi	[a se imbolnə'vi]
cold (illness)	răceală (f)	[rə'tʃalə]
to catch a cold	a răci	[a rə'tʃi]

ice	gheață (f)	['gʲatsə]
black ice	polei (n)	[po'lej]
to freeze over (ab. river, etc.)	a îngheța	[a inge'tsa]
ice floe	sloi (n)	[sloj]

skis	schiuri (n pl)	['skjurʲ]
skier	schior (m)	['skjor]
to ski (vi)	a schia	[a ski'a]
to skate (vi)	a patina	[a pati'na]

Fauna

predator	**prădător** (n)	[prədə'tor]
tiger	**tigru** (m)	['tigru]
lion	**leu** (m)	['leu]
wolf	**lup** (m)	[lup]
fox	**vulpe** (f)	['vulpe]
jaguar	**jaguar** (m)	[ʒagu'ar]
leopard	**leopard** (m)	[leo'pard]
cheetah	**ghepard** (m)	[ge'pard]
black panther	**panteră** (f)	[pan'terə]
puma	**pumă** (f)	['pumə]
snow leopard	**ghepard** (m)	[ge'pard]
lynx	**râs** (m)	[ris]
coyote	**coiot** (m)	[ko'jot]
jackal	**şacal** (m)	[ʃa'kal]
hyena	**hienă** (f)	[hi'enə]

animal	**animal** (n)	[ani'mal]
beast (animal)	**animal** (n) **sălbatic**	[ani'mal səl'batik]
squirrel	**veveriță** (f)	[veve'ritsə]
hedgehog	**arici** (m)	[a'ritʃi]
hare	**iepure** (m)	['jepure]
rabbit	**iepure** (m) **de casă**	['jepure de 'kasə]
badger	**bursuc** (m)	[bur'suk]
raccoon	**enot** (m)	[e'not]
hamster	**hârciog** (m)	[hir'tʃiog]
marmot	**marmotă** (f)	[mar'motə]
mole	**cârtiță** (f)	['kirtitsə]
mouse	**şoarece** (m)	[ʃo'aretʃe]
rat	**şobolan** (m)	[ʃobo'lan]
bat	**liliac** (m)	[lili'ak]
ermine	**hermină** (f)	[her'minə]
sable	**samur** (m)	[sa'mur]
marten	**jder** (m)	[ʒder]
weasel	**nevăstuică** (f)	[nevəs'tujkə]
mink	**nurcă** (f)	['nurkə]

| beaver | castor (m) | ['kastor] |
| otter | vidră (f) | ['vidrə] |

horse	cal (m)	[kal]
moose	elan (m)	[e'lan]
deer	cerb (m)	[tʃerb]
camel	cămilă (f)	[kə'milə]

bison	bizon (m)	[bi'zon]
wisent	zimbru (m)	['zimbru]
buffalo	bivol (m)	['bivol]

zebra	zebră (f)	['zebrə]
antelope	antilopă (f)	[anti'lopə]
roe deer	căprioară (f)	[kəprio'arə]
fallow deer	ciută (f)	['tʃiutə]
chamois	capră (f) neagră	['kaprə 'niagrə]
wild boar	mistreț (m)	[mis'treʦ]

whale	balenă (f)	[ba'lenə]
seal	focă (f)	['fokə]
walrus	morsă (f)	['morsə]
fur seal	urs (m) de mare	[urs de 'mare]
dolphin	delfin (m)	[del'fin]

bear	urs (m)	[urs]
polar bear	urs (m) polar	[urs po'lar]
panda	panda (m)	['panda]

monkey	maimuță (f)	[maj'muʦə]
chimpanzee	cimpanzeu (m)	[tʃimpan'zeu]
orangutan	urangutan (m)	[urangu'tan]
gorilla	gorilă (f)	[go'rilə]
macaque	macac (m)	[ma'kak]
gibbon	gibon (m)	[dʒi'bon]

elephant	elefant (m)	[ele'fant]
rhinoceros	rinocer (m)	[rino'tʃer]
giraffe	girafă (f)	[dʒi'rafə]
hippopotamus	hipopotam (m)	[hipopo'tam]

| kangaroo | cangur (m) | ['kangur] |
| koala (bear) | koala (f) | [ko'ala] |

mongoose	mangustă (f)	[man'gustə]
chinchilla	şinşilă (f)	[ʃin'ʃilə]
skunk	sconcs (m)	[skonks]
porcupine	porc (m) spinos	[pork spi'nos]

212. Domestic animals

cat	pisică (f)	[pi'sikə]
tomcat	motan (m)	[mo'tan]
horse	cal (m)	[kal]

stallion (male horse)	armăsar (m)	[armə'sar]
mare	iapă (f)	['japə]
cow	vacă (f)	['vakə]
bull	taur (m)	['taur]
ox	bou (m)	['bou]
sheep (ewe)	oaie (f)	[o'ae]
ram	berbec (m)	[ber'bek]
goat	capră (f)	['kaprə]
billy goat, he-goat	ţap (m)	[ʦap]
donkey	măgar (m)	[mə'gar]
mule	catâr (m)	[ka'tir]
pig	porc (m)	[pork]
piglet	purcel (m)	[pur'ʧel]
rabbit	iepure (m) de casă	['jepure de 'kasə]
hen (chicken)	găină (f)	[gə'inə]
cock	cocoș (m)	[ko'koʃ]
duck	rață (f)	['raʦə]
drake	rățoi (m)	[rə'ʦoj]
goose	gâscă (f)	['giskə]
tom turkey, gobbler	curcan (m)	[kur'kan]
turkey (hen)	curcă (f)	['kurkə]
domestic animals	animale (n pl) domestice	[ani'male do'mestiʧe]
tame (e.g. ~ hamster)	domestic	[do'mestik]
to tame (vt)	a domestici	[a domesti'ʧi]
to breed (vt)	a crește	[a 'kreʃte]
farm	fermă (f)	['fermə]
poultry	păsări (f pl) de curte	[pəsərɪ de 'kurte]
cattle	vite (f pl)	['vite]
herd (cattle)	turmă (f)	['turmə]
stable	grajd (n)	[graʒd]
pigsty	cocină (f) de porci	[ko'ʧinə de 'porʧi]
cowshed	grajd (n) pentru vaci	['graʒd 'pentru 'vaʧi]
rabbit hutch	cușcă (f) pentru iepuri	['kuʃkə 'pentru 'epurɪ]
hen house	coteț (n) de găini	[ko'teʦ de gə'inɪ]

213. Dogs. Dog breeds

dog	câine (m)	['kijne]
sheepdog	câine (m) ciobănesc	['kijne ʧiobə'nesk]
poodle	pudel (m)	[pu'del]
dachshund	teckel (m)	['tekel]
bulldog	buldog (m)	[bul'dog]
boxer	boxer (m)	[bok'ser]

mastiff	mastif (m)	[mas'tif]
Rottweiler	rottweiler (m)	[rot'wejler]
Doberman	doberman (m)	[dober'man]

basset	basset (m)	[ba'set]
bobtail	bobtail (m)	[bob'tejl]
Dalmatian	dalmaţian (m)	[dalmaţsi'an]
cocker spaniel	cocker spaniel (m)	['koker spani'el]

| Newfoundland | newfoundland (m) | [nju'faundlend] |
| Saint Bernard | sentbernar (m) | [senber'nar] |

husky	huski (m)	['haski]
Chow Chow	chow chow (m)	['ʧau 'ʧau]
spitz	spitz (m)	[ʃpiʦ]
pug	mops (m)	[mops]

214. Sounds made by animals

barking (n)	lătrat (n)	[lə'trat]
to bark (vi)	a lătra	[a lə'tra]
to miaow (vi)	a mieuna	[a meu'na]
to purr (vi)	a toarce	[a to'arʧe]

to moo (vi)	a mugi	[a mu'ʤi]
to bellow (bull)	a rage	[a 'raʤe]
to growl (vi)	a mârâi	[a miri'i]

howl (n)	urlet (n)	['urlet]
to howl (vi)	a urla	[a ur'la]
to whine (vi)	a scheuna	[a skeu'na]

to bleat (sheep)	a behăi	[a behə'i]
to oink, to grunt (pig)	a grohăi	[a grohə'i]
to squeal (vi)	a ţipa	[a ʦi'pa]

to croak (vi)	a orăcăi	[a orəkə'i]
to buzz (insect)	a bâzâi	[a bizi'i]
to chirp (crickets, grasshopper)	a ţârâi	[a ʦiri'i]

215. Young animals

cub	pui (m) de animal	[puj de ani'mal]
kitten	motănaş (m)	[motə'naʃ]
baby mouse	şoricel (m)	[ʃori'ʧel]
puppy	căţeluş (m)	[kəʦe'luʃ]

leveret	iepuraş (m)	[jepu'raʃ]
baby rabbit	iepuraş (m)	[jepu'raʃ]
wolf cub	pui (m) de lup	[puj de lup]
fox cub	pui (m) de vulpe	[puj de 'vulpe]

bear cub	ursuleţ (m)	[ursu'lets]
lion cub	pui (m) de leu	[puj de 'leu]
tiger cub	pui (m) de tigru	[puj de 'tigru]
elephant calf	pui (m) de elefant	[puj de ele'fant]

piglet	purcel (m)	[pur'tʃel]
calf (young cow, bull)	viţel (m)	[vi'tsel]
kid (young goat)	ied (m)	[jed]
lamb	miel (m)	[mjel]
fawn (young deer)	pui (m) de cerb	[puj de tʃerb]
young camel	pui (m) de cămilă	[puj de kə'milə]

| snakelet (baby snake) | pui (m) de şarpe | [puj de 'ʃarpe] |
| froglet (baby frog) | broscuţă (f) | [bros'kutsə] |

baby bird	pui (m) de pasăre	[puj de 'pasəre]
chick (of chicken)	pui (m)	[puj]
duckling	răţuşcă (f)	[rə'tsuʃkə]

216. Birds

bird	pasăre (f)	['pasəre]
pigeon	porumbel (m)	[porum'bel]
sparrow	vrabie (f)	['vrabie]
tit (great tit)	piţigoi (m)	[pitsi'goj]
magpie	coţofană (f)	[kotso'fanə]

raven	corb (m)	[korb]
crow	cioară (f)	[tʃio'arə]
jackdaw	stancă (f)	['stankə]
rook	cioară (f) de câmp	[tʃio'arə de 'kimp]

duck	raţă (f)	['ratsə]
goose	gâscă (f)	['giskə]
pheasant	fazan (m)	[fa'zan]

eagle	acvilă (f)	['akvilə]
hawk	uliu (m)	['ulju]
falcon	şoim (m)	[ʃojm]
vulture	vultur (m)	['vultur]
condor (Andean ~)	condor (m)	[kon'dor]

swan	lebădă (f)	['lebədə]
crane	cocor (m)	[ko'kor]
stork	cocostârc (m)	[kokos'tirk]

parrot	papagal (m)	[papa'gal]
hummingbird	pasărea (f) colibri	['pasər'a ko'libri]
peacock	păun (m)	[pə'un]

ostrich	struţ (m)	[struts]
heron	stârc (m)	[stirk]
flamingo	flamingo (m)	[fla'mingo]
pelican	pelican (m)	[peli'kan]

nightingale	privighetoare (f)	[priviɡeto'are]
swallow	rândunică (f)	[rindu'nikə]
thrush	mierlă (f)	['merlə]
song thrush	sturz-cântător (m)	[sturz kintə'tor]
blackbird	mierlă (f) sură	['merlə 'surə]
swift	lăstun (m)	[ləs'tun]
lark	ciocârlie (f)	[ʧiokɨr'lie]
quail	prepeliță (f)	[prepe'liʦə]
woodpecker	ciocănitoare (f)	[ʧiokənito'are]
cuckoo	cuc (m)	[kuk]
owl	bufniță (f)	['bufniʦə]
eagle owl	buha mare (f)	['buhə 'mare]
wood grouse	cocoș (m) de munte	[ko'koʃ de 'munte]
black grouse	cocoș (m) sălbatic	[ko'koʃ səlba'tik]
partridge	potârniche (f)	[potir'nike]
starling	graur (m)	['graur]
canary	canar (m)	[ka'nar]
hazel grouse	găinușă de alun (f)	[gəi'nuʃə de a'lun]
chaffinch	cinteză (f)	[ʧin'tezə]
bullfinch	botgros (m)	[bot'gros]
seagull	pescăruș (m)	[peskə'ruʃ]
albatross	albatros (m)	[alba'tros]
penguin	pinguin (m)	[piɡu'in]

217. Birds. Singing and sounds

to sing (vi)	a cânta	[a kin'ta]
to call (animal, bird)	a striga	[a stri'ga]
to crow (cock)	a cânta cucurigu	[a kin'ta kuku'rigu]
cock-a-doodle-doo	cucurigu (m)	[kuku'rigu]
to cluck (hen)	a cotcodăci	[a kotkodə'ʧi]
to caw (crow call)	a croncăni	[a kronkə'ni]
to quack (duck call)	a măcăi	[a məkə'i]
to cheep (vi)	a piui	[a pju'i]
to chirp, to twitter	a ciripi	[a ʧiri'pi]

218. Fish. Marine animals

bream	plătică (f)	[plə'tikə]
carp	crap (m)	[krap]
perch	biban (m)	[bi'ban]
catfish	somn (m)	[somn]
pike	știucă (f)	['ʃtjukə]
salmon	somon (m)	[so'mon]
sturgeon	nisetru (m)	[ni'setru]

herring	scrumbie (f)	[skrum'bie]
Atlantic salmon	somon (m)	[so'mon]
mackerel	macrou (n)	[ma'krou]
flatfish	cambulă (f)	[kam'bulə]

zander, pike perch	şalău (m)	[ʃa'ləu]
cod	batog (m)	[ba'tog]
tuna	ton (m)	[ton]
trout	păstrăv (m)	[pəs'trəv]

eel	ţipar (m)	[tsi'par]
electric ray	peşte-torpilă (m)	['peʃte tor'pilə]
moray eel	murenă (f)	[mu'renə]
piranha	piranha (f)	[pi'ranija]

shark	rechin (m)	[re'kin]
dolphin	delfin (m)	[del'fin]
whale	balenă (f)	[ba'lenə]

crab	crab (m)	[krab]
jellyfish	meduză (f)	[me'duzə]
octopus	caracatiţă (f)	[kara'katitsə]

starfish	stea de mare (f)	[stʲa de 'mare]
sea urchin	arici de mare (m)	[a'ritʃi de 'mare]
seahorse	căluţ (m) de mare (f)	[ka'luts de 'mare]

oyster	stridie (f)	['stridie]
prawn	crevetă (f)	[kre'vetə]
lobster	stacoj (m)	[sta'koʒ]
spiny lobster	langustă (f)	[lan'gustə]

219. Amphibians. Reptiles

snake	şarpe (m)	['ʃarpe]
venomous (snake)	veninos	[veni'nos]

viper	viperă (f)	['viperə]
cobra	cobră (f)	['kobrə]
python	piton (m)	[pi'ton]
boa	şarpe (m) boa	['ʃarpe bo'a]

grass snake	şarpe (m) de casă	['ʃarpe de 'kasə]
rattle snake	şarpe (m) cu clopoţei	['ʃarpe ku klopo'tsej]
anaconda	anacondă (f)	[ana'kondə]

lizard	şopârlă (f)	[ʃo'pirlə]
iguana	iguană (f)	[igu'anə]
monitor lizard	şopârlă (f)	[ʃo'pirlə]
salamander	salamandră (f)	[sala'mandrə]
chameleon	cameleon (m)	[kamele'on]
scorpion	scorpion (m)	[skorpi'on]
turtle	broască (f) ţestoasă	[bro'askə tsesto'asə]
frog	broască (f)	[bro'askə]

| toad | broască (f) râioasă | [bro'askə rijo'asə] |
| crocodile | crocodil (m) | [kroko'dil] |

220. Insects

insect	insectă (f)	[in'sektə]
butterfly	fluture (m)	['fluture]
ant	furnică (f)	[fur'nikə]
fly	muscă (f)	['muskə]
mosquito	țânțar (m)	[tsin'tsar]
beetle	gândac (m)	[gin'dak]

wasp	viespe (f)	['vespe]
bee	albină (f)	[al'binə]
bumblebee	bondar (m)	[bon'dar]
gadfly (botfly)	tăun (m)	[tə'un]

| spider | păianjen (m) | [pə'janʒen] |
| spider's web | pânză (f) de păianjen | ['pinzə de pə'janʒen] |

dragonfly	libelulă (f)	[libe'lulə]
grasshopper	greier (m)	['greer]
moth (night butterfly)	fluture (m)	['fluture]

cockroach	gândac (m)	[gin'dak]
tick	căpușă (f)	[kə'puʃə]
flea	purice (m)	['puritʃe]
midge	musculiță (f)	[musku'litsə]

locust	lăcustă (f)	[lə'kustə]
snail	melc (m)	[melk]
cricket	greier (m)	['greer]
firefly	licurici (m)	[liku'ritʃi]
ladybird	buburuză (f)	[bubu'ruzə]
cockchafer	cărăbuș (m)	[kərə'buʃ]

leech	lipitoare (f)	[lipito'are]
caterpillar	omidă (f)	[o'midə]
earthworm	vierme (m)	['verme]
larva	larvă (f)	['larvə]

221. Animals. Body parts

beak	cioc (n)	[tʃiok]
wings	aripi (f pl)	[a'ripʲ]
foot (of the bird)	labă (f)	['labə]
feathers (plumage)	penaj (n)	[pe'naʒ]
feather	pană (f)	['panə]
crest	moț (n)	[mots]

| gills | branhii (f pl) | [bran'hij] |
| spawn | icre (f pl) | ['ikre] |

larva	larvă (f)	['larvə]
fin	aripioară (f)	[ari'pjoarə]
scales (of fish, reptile)	solzi (m pl)	[solzʲ]

fang (canine)	dinte (m) canin	['dinte ka'nin]
paw (e.g. cat's ~)	labă (f)	['labə]
muzzle (snout)	bot (n)	[bot]
mouth (cat's ~)	bot (n)	[bot]
tail	coadă (f)	[ko'adə]
whiskers	mustăţi (f pl)	[mus'tətsʲ]

| hoof | copită (f) | [ko'pitə] |
| horn | corn (n) | [korn] |

carapace	carapace (f)	[kara'patʃe]
shell (mollusk ~)	schelet (n)	[ske'let]
eggshell	găoace (f)	[gəo'atʃe]

| animal's hair (pelage) | blană (f) | ['blanə] |
| pelt (hide) | piele (f) | ['pjele] |

222. Actions of animals

| to fly (vi) | a zbura | [a zbu'ra] |
| to fly in circles | a se roti | [a se ro'ti] |

| to fly away | a-şi lua zborul | [aʃ lu'a 'zborul] |
| to flap (~ the wings) | a bate din aripi | [a 'bate din 'aripʲ] |

| to peck (vi) | a ciuguli | [a tʃiugu'li] |
| to sit on eggs | a cloci | [a klo'tʃi] |

| to hatch out (vi) | a ieşi din ou | [a e'ʃi din ow] |
| to build a nest | a face cuib | [a 'fatʃe kujb] |

to slither, to crawl	a se târî	[a se ti'rɨ]
to sting, to bite (insect)	a înţepa	[a intse'pa]
to bite (ab. animal)	a muşca	[a muʃ'ka]

to sniff (vt)	a mirosi	[a miro'si]
to bark (vi)	a lătra	[a lə'tra]
to hiss (snake)	a sâsâi	[a sisi'i]

| to scare (vt) | a speria | [a speri'ja] |
| to attack (vt) | a ataca | [a ata'ka] |

to gnaw (bone, etc.)	a roade	[a ro'ade]
to scratch (with claws)	a zgâria	[a zgiri'ja]
to hide (vi)	a se ascunde	[a se as'kunde]

to play (kittens, etc.)	a juca	[a ʒu'ka]
to hunt (vi, vt)	a vâna	[a vi'na]
to hibernate (vi)	a hiberna	[a hiber'na]
to go extinct	a dispărea	[a dispə'rʲa]

223. Animals. Habitats

habitat	mediu (n) ambiant	['medju am'bjant]
migration	migraţie (f)	[mi'graʦie]
mountain	munte (m)	['munte]
reef	recif (m)	[re'ʧif]
cliff	stâncă (f)	['stinkə]
forest	pădure (f)	[pə'dure]
jungle	junglă (f)	['ʒunglə]
savanna	savană (f)	[sa'vanə]
tundra	tundră (f)	['tundrə]
steppe	stepă (f)	['stepə]
desert	deşert (n)	[de'ʃərt]
oasis	oază (f)	[o'azə]
sea	mare (f)	['mare]
lake	lac (n)	[lak]
ocean	ocean (n)	[oʧə'an]
swamp (marshland)	mlaştină (f)	['mlaʃtinə]
freshwater (adj)	de apă dulce	[de 'apə 'dulʧe]
pond	iaz (n)	[jaz]
river	râu (n)	['riu]
den (bear's ~)	bârlog (n)	[bir'log]
nest	cuib (n)	[kujb]
tree hollow	scorbură (f)	['skorburə]
burrow (animal hole)	vizuină (f)	[vizu'inə]
anthill	furnicar (n)	[furni'kar]

224. Animal care

zoo	grădină (f) zoologică	[grə'dinə zoo'loʤikə]
nature reserve	rezervaţie (f) naturală	[rezer'vaʦie natu'ralə]
breeder (cattery, kennel, etc.)	pepinieră (f)	[pepi'njerə]
open-air cage	volieră (f)	[voli'erə]
cage	cuşcă (f)	['kuʃkə]
kennel	coteţ (n) de câine	[ko'teʦ de 'kinə]
dovecot	porumbărie (f)	[porumbə'rie]
aquarium (fish tank)	acvariu (n)	[ak'varju]
dolphinarium	delfinariu (n)	[delfi'narju]
to breed (animals)	a creşte	[a 'kreʃte]
brood, litter	pui (m pl)	[puj]
to tame (vt)	a domestici	[a domesti'ʧi]
to train (animals)	a dresa	[a dre'sa]
feed (fodder, etc.)	hrană (f)	['hranə]
to feed (vt)	a hrăni	[a hrə'ni]

pet shop	magazin (n) zoo	[maga'zin 'zoo]
muzzle (for dog)	botniță (f)	['botnitsə]
collar (e.g., dog ~)	zgardă (f)	['zgardə]
name (of an animal)	porecla (f)	[po'reklə]
pedigree (dog's ~)	genealogie (f)	[dʒenealo'dʒie]

225. Animals. Miscellaneous

pack (wolves)	haită (f)	['hajtə]
flock (birds)	stol (n)	[stol]
shoal, school (fish)	banc (n)	[bank]
herd (horses)	herghelie (f)	[herge'lie]

male (n)	mascul (m)	[mas'kul]
female (n)	femelă (f)	[fe'melə]

hungry (adj)	flămând	[flə'mind]
wild (adj)	sălbatic	[səl'batik]
dangerous (adj)	periculos	[periku'los]

226. Horses

horse	cal (m)	[kal]
breed (race)	rasă (f)	['rasə]

foal	mânz (m)	[minz]
mare	iapă (f)	['japə]

mustang	mustang (m)	[mus'tang]
pony	ponei (m)	['ponej]
draught horse	cal (m) de tracțiune	[kal de trakʦi'une]

mane	coamă (f)	[ko'amə]
tail	coadă (f)	[ko'adə]

hoof	copită (f)	[ko'pitə]
horseshoe	potcoavă (f)	[potko'avə]
to shoe (vt)	a potcovi	[a potko'vi]
blacksmith	fierar (m)	[fe'rar]

saddle	șa (f)	[ʃa]
stirrup	scară (f)	['skarə]
bridle	frâu (n)	['friu]
reins	hățuri (n pl)	[həʦurʲ]
whip (for riding)	bici (n)	[bitʃi]

rider	călăreț (m)	[kələ'reʦ]
to saddle up (vt)	a înșeua	[a inʃeu'a]
to mount a horse	a se așeza în șa	[a se aʃə'za 'in 'ʃa]

gallop	galop (n)	[ga'lop]
to gallop (vi)	a galopa	[a galo'pa]

| trot (n) | **trap** (n) | [trap] |
| at a trot (adv) | **la trap** | [la trap] |

| racehorse | **cal** (m) **de curse** | [kal de 'kurse] |
| horse racing | **cursă** (f) **de cai** | ['kursə de kaj] |

stable	**grajd** (n)	[graʒd]
to feed (vt)	**a hrăni**	[a hrə'ni]
hay	**fân** (n)	[fin]
to water (animals)	**a adăpa**	[a adə'pa]
to wash (horse)	**a ţesăla**	[a ʦesə'la]

to graze (vi)	**a paşte**	[a 'paʃte]
to neigh (vi)	**a necheza**	[a neke'za]
to kick (to buck)	**a zvârli cu copita**	[a zvir'li ku ko'pita]

Flora

tree	copac (m)	[ko'pak]
deciduous (adj)	foios	[fo'jos]
coniferous (adj)	conifer	[koni'fere]
evergreen (adj)	veşnic verde	['veʃnik 'verde]

apple tree	măr (m)	[mər]
pear tree	păr (m)	[pər]
sweet cherry tree	cireş (m)	[ʧi'reʃ]
sour cherry tree	vişin (m)	['viʃin]
plum tree	prun (m)	[prun]

birch	mesteacăn (m)	[mes't'akən]
oak	stejar (m)	[ste'ʒar]
linden tree	tei (m)	[tej]
aspen	plop tremurător (m)	['plop tremurə'tor]
maple	arţar (m)	[ar'tsar]
spruce	brad (m)	[brad]
pine	pin (m)	[pin]
larch	zadă (f)	['zadə]
fir tree	brad (m) alb	['brad 'alb]
cedar	cedru (m)	['ʧedru]

poplar	plop (m)	[plop]
rowan	sorb (m)	[sorb]
willow	salcie (f)	['salʧie]
alder	arin (m)	[a'rin]
beech	fag (m)	[fag]
elm	ulm (m)	[ulm]
ash (tree)	frasin (m)	['frasin]
chestnut	castan (m)	[kas'tan]

magnolia	magnolie (f)	[mag'nolie]
palm tree	palmier (m)	[palmi'er]
cypress	chiparos (m)	[kipa'ros]

mangrove	manglier (m)	[mangli'jer]
baobab	baobab (m)	[bao'bab]
eucalyptus	eucalipt (m)	[euka'lipt]
sequoia	secvoia (m)	[sek'voja]

| bush | tufă (f) | ['tufə] |
| shrub | arbust (m) | [ar'bust] |

| grapevine | viță (f) de vie | ['vitsə de 'vie] |
| vineyard | vie (f) | ['vie] |

raspberry bush	zmeură (f)	['zmeurə]
redcurrant bush	coacăz (m) roşu	[ko'akəz 'roʃu]
gooseberry bush	agriş (m)	[a'griʃ]

acacia	salcâm (m)	[sal'kim]
barberry	lemn (m) galben	['lemn 'galben]
jasmine	iasomie (f)	[jaso'mie]

juniper	ienupăr (m)	[je'nupər]
rosebush	tufă (f) de trandafir	['tufə de tranda'fir]
dog rose	măceş (m)	[mə'tʃeʃ]

229. Mushrooms

mushroom	ciupercă (f)	[tʃiu'perkə]
edible mushroom	ciupercă (f) comestibilă	[tʃiu'perkə komes'tibilə]
poisonous mushroom	ciupercă (f) otrăvitoare	[tʃiu'perkə otrəvito'are]
cap	pălărie (f)	[pələ'rie]
stipe	picior (n)	[pi'tʃior]

cep, penny bun	hrib (m)	[hrib]
orange-cap boletus	pitărcuţă (f)	[pitər'kutsə]
birch bolete	pitarcă (f)	[pi'tarkə]
chanterelle	gălbior (m)	[gəlbi'or]
russula	vineţică (f)	[vine'tsikə]

morel	zbârciog (m)	[zbir'tʃiog]
fly agaric	burete (m) pestriţ	[bu'rete pes'trits]
death cap	ciupercă (f) otrăvitoare	[tʃiu'perkə otrəvito'are]

230. Fruits. Berries

apple	măr (n)	[mər]
pear	pară (f)	['parə]
plum	prună (f)	['prunə]

strawberry (garden ~)	căpşună (f)	[kəp'ʃunə]
sour cherry	vişină (f)	['viʃinə]
sweet cherry	cireaşă (f)	[tʃi'rʲaʃə]
grape	struguri (m pl)	['struguri]

raspberry	zmeură (f)	['zmeurə]
blackcurrant	coacăză (f) neagră	[ko'akəzə 'nʲagrə]
redcurrant	coacăză (f) roşie	[ko'akəzə 'roʃie]
gooseberry	agrişă (f)	[a'griʃə]
cranberry	răchiţele (f pl)	[rəki'tsele]

| orange | portocală (f) | [porto'kalə] |
| tangerine | mandarină (f) | [manda'rinə] |

pineapple	ananas (m)	[ana'nas]
banana	banană (f)	[ba'nanə]
date	curmală (f)	[kur'malə]

lemon	lămâie (f)	[lə'mie]
apricot	caisă (f)	[ka'isə]
peach	piersică (f)	['pjersikə]
kiwi	kiwi (n)	['kivi]
grapefruit	grepfrut (n)	['grepfrut]

berry	boabă (f)	[bo'abə]
berries	fructe (n pl) de pădure	['frukte de pə'dure]
cowberry	merişor (m)	[meri'ʃor]
wild strawberry	frag (m)	[frag]
bilberry	afină (f)	[a'finə]

231. Flowers. Plants

| flower | floare (f) | [flo'are] |
| bouquet (of flowers) | buchet (n) | [bu'ket] |

rose (flower)	trandafir (m)	[tranda'fir]
tulip	lalea (f)	[la'l'a]
carnation	garoafă (f)	[garo'afə]
gladiolus	gladiolă (f)	[gladi'olə]

cornflower	albăstrea (f)	[albəs'tr'a]
harebell	clopoţel (m)	[klopo'tsel]
dandelion	păpădie (f)	[pəpə'die]
camomile	romaniţă (f)	[roma'nitsə]

aloe	aloe (f)	[a'loe]
cactus	cactus (m)	['kaktus]
rubber plant, ficus	ficus (m)	['fikus]

lily	crin (m)	[krin]
geranium	muşcată (f)	[muʃ'katə]
hyacinth	zambilă (f)	[zam'bilə]

mimosa	mimoză (f)	[mi'mozə]
narcissus	narcisă (f)	[nar'tʃisə]
nasturtium	condurul-doamnei (m)	[kon'durul do'amnej]

orchid	orhidee (f)	[orhi'dee]
peony	bujor (m)	[bu'ʒor]
violet	toporaş (m)	[topo'raʃ]

pansy	pansele (f)	[pan'sele]
forget-me-not	nu-mă-uita (f)	[nu mə uj'ta]
daisy	margaretă (f)	[marga'retə]

poppy	mac (m)	[mak]
hemp	cânepă (f)	['kinepə]
mint	mentă (f)	['mentə]

lily of the valley	lăcrămioară (f)	[ləkrəmjo'arə]
snowdrop	ghiocel (m)	[gio'tʃel]
nettle	urzică (f)	[ur'zikə]
sorrel	măcriş (m)	[mə'kriʃ]
water lily	nufăr (m)	['nufər]
fern	ferigă (f)	['ferigə]
lichen	lichen (m)	[li'ken]
conservatory (greenhouse)	seră (f)	['serə]
lawn	gazon (n)	[ga'zon]
flowerbed	strat (n) de flori	[strat de 'florʲ]
plant	plantă (f)	['plantə]
grass	iarbă (f)	['jarbə]
blade of grass	fir (n) de iarbă	[fir de 'jarbə]
leaf	frunză (f)	['frunzə]
petal	petală (f)	[pe'talə]
stem	tulpină (f)	[tul'pinə]
tuber	tubercul (m)	[tu'berkul]
young plant (shoot)	mugur (m)	['mugur]
thorn	ghimpe (m)	['gimpe]
to blossom (vi)	a înflori	[a inflo'ri]
to fade, to wither	a se ofili	[a se ofe'li]
smell (odour)	miros (n)	[mi'ros]
to cut (flowers)	a tăia	[a tə'ja]
to pick (a flower)	a rupe	[a 'rupe]

232. Cereals, grains

grain	grăunţe (n pl)	[grə'untse]
cereal crops	cereale (f pl)	[tʃere'ale]
ear (of barley, etc.)	spic (n)	[spik]
wheat	grâu (n)	['griu]
rye	secară (f)	[se'karə]
oats	ovăz (n)	[ovəz]
millet	mei (m)	[mej]
barley	orz (n)	[orz]
maize	porumb (m)	[po'rumb]
rice	orez (n)	[o'rez]
buckwheat	hrişcă (f)	['hriʃkə]
pea plant	mazăre (f)	['mazəre]
kidney bean	fasole (f)	[fa'sole]
soya	soia (f)	['soja]
lentil	linte (n)	['linte]
beans (pulse crops)	boabe (f pl)	[bo'abe]

233. Vegetables. Greens

vegetables	legume (f pl)	[le'gume]
greens	verdeață (f)	[ver'dʲatsə]
tomato	roşie (f)	['roʃie]
cucumber	castravete (m)	[kastra'vete]
carrot	morcov (m)	['morkov]
potato	cartof (m)	[kar'tof]
onion	ceapă (f)	['tʃapə]
garlic	usturoi (m)	[ustu'roj]
cabbage	varză (f)	['varzə]
cauliflower	conopidă (f)	[kono'pidə]
Brussels sprouts	varză (f) de Bruxelles	['varzə de bruk'sel]
beetroot	sfeclă (f)	['sfeklə]
aubergine	vânătă (f)	['vinətə]
marrow	dovlecel (m)	[dovle'tʃel]
pumpkin	dovleac (m)	[dov'lʲak]
turnip	nap (m)	[nap]
parsley	pătrunjel (m)	[pətrun'ʒel]
dill	mărar (m)	[mə'rar]
lettuce	salată (f)	[sa'latə]
celery	ţelină (f)	['tselinə]
asparagus	sparanghel (m)	[sparan'gel]
spinach	spanac (m)	[spa'nak]
pea	mazăre (f)	['mazəre]
beans	boabe (f pl)	[bo'abe]
maize	porumb (m)	[po'rumb]
kidney bean	fasole (f)	[fa'sole]
pepper	piper (m)	[pi'per]
radish	ridiche (f)	[ri'dike]
artichoke	anghinare (f)	[angi'nare]

REGIONAL GEOGRAPHY

234. Western Europe

Europe	**Europa** (f)	[eu'ropa]
European Union	**Uniunea** (f) **Europeană**	[uni'una euro'panə]
European (n)	**european** (m)	[euro'pan]
European (adj)	**european**	[euro'pan]
Austria	**Austria** (f)	[a'ustrija]
Austrian (masc.)	**austriac** (m)	[austri'ak]
Austrian (fem.)	**austriacă** (f)	[austri'akə]
Austrian (adj)	**austriac**	[austri'ak]
Great Britain	**Marea Britanie** (f)	['mara bri'tanie]
England	**Anglia** (f)	['anglija]
British (masc.)	**englez** (m)	[en'glez]
British (fem.)	**englezoaică** (f)	[englezo'ajkə]
English, British (adj)	**englez**	[en'glez]
Belgium	**Belgia** (f)	['beldʒia]
Belgian (masc.)	**belgian** (m)	[beldʒi'an]
Belgian (fem.)	**belgiană** (f)	[beldʒi'anə]
Belgian (adj)	**belgian**	[beldʒi'an]
Germany	**Germania** (f)	[dʒer'manija]
German (masc.)	**neamț** (m)	['namts]
German (fem.)	**nemțoaică** (f)	[nemtso'ajkə]
German (adj)	**nemțesc**	[nem'tsesk]
Netherlands	**Țările de Jos** (f pl)	['tsərile de ʒos]
Holland	**Olanda** (f)	[o'landa]
Dutch (masc.)	**olandez** (m)	[olan'dez]
Dutch (fem.)	**olandeză** (f)	[olan'dezə]
Dutch (adj)	**olandez**	[olan'dez]
Greece	**Grecia** (f)	['gretʃia]
Greek (masc.)	**grec** (m)	[grek]
Greek (fem.)	**grecoaică** (f)	[greko'ajkə]
Greek (adj)	**grecesc**	[gre'tʃesk]
Denmark	**Danemarca** (f)	[dane'marka]
Dane (masc.)	**danez** (m)	[da'nez]
Dane (fem.)	**daneză** (f)	[dɑ'nezə]
Danish (adj)	**danez**	[da'nez]
Ireland	**Irlanda** (f)	[ir'landa]
Irish (masc.)	**irlandez** (m)	[irlan'dez]
Irish (fem.)	**irlandeză** (f)	[irlan'dezə]
Irish (adj)	**irlandez**	[irlan'dez]

Iceland	Islanda (f)	[is'landa]
Icelander (masc.)	islandez (m)	[islan'dez]
Icelander (fem.)	islandeză (f)	[islan'dezə]
Icelandic (adj)	islandez	[islan'dez]

Spain	Spania (f)	['spania]
Spaniard (masc.)	spaniol (m)	[spa'njol]
Spaniard (fem.)	spanioloaică (f)	[spanjolo'ajkə]
Spanish (adj)	spaniol	[spa'njol]

Italy	Italia (f)	[i'talia]
Italian (masc.)	italian (m)	[itali'an]
Italian (fem.)	italiancă (f)	[itali'ankə]
Italian (adj)	italian	[itali'an]

Cyprus	Cipru (n)	['tʃipru]
Cypriot (masc.)	cipriot (m)	[tʃipri'ot]
Cypriot (fem.)	cipriotă (f)	[tʃipri'otə]
Cypriot (adj)	cipriot	[tʃipri'ot]

Malta	Malta (f)	['malta]
Maltese (masc.)	maltez (m)	[mal'tez]
Maltese (fem.)	malteză (f)	[mal'tezə]
Maltese (adj)	maltez	[mal'tez]

Norway	Norvegia (f)	[nor'vedʒia]
Norwegian (masc.)	norvegian (m)	[norvedʒi'an]
Norwegian (fem.)	norvegiancă (f)	[norvedʒi'ankə]
Norwegian (adj)	norvegian	[norvedʒi'an]

Portugal	Portugalia (f)	[portu'galia]
Portuguese (masc.)	portughez (m)	[portu'gez]
Portuguese (fem.)	portugheză (f)	[portu'gezə]
Portuguese (adj)	portughez	[portu'gez]

Finland	Finlanda (f)	[fin'landa]
Finn (masc.)	finlandez (m)	[finlan'dez]
Finn (fem.)	finlandeză (f)	[finlan'dezə]
Finnish (adj)	finlandez	[finlan'dez]

France	Franța (f)	['frantsa]
French (masc.)	francez (m)	[fran'tʃez]
French (fem.)	franțuzoaică (f)	[frantsuzo'ajkə]
French (adj)	francez	[fran'tʃez]

Sweden	Suedia (f)	[su'edia]
Swede (masc.)	suedez (m)	[sue'dez]
Swede (fem.)	suedeză (f)	[sue'dezə]
Swedish (adj)	suedez	[sue'dez]

Switzerland	Elveția (f)	[el'vetsia]
Swiss (masc.)	elvețian (m)	[elvetsi'an]
Swiss (fem.)	elvețiancă (f)	[elvetsi'ankə]
Swiss (adj)	elvețian	[elvetsi'an]
Scotland	Scoția (f)	['skotsia]
Scottish (masc.)	scoțian (m)	[skotsi'an]

| Scottish (fem.) | scoțiancă (f) | [skoțsi'ankə] |
| Scottish (adj) | scoțian | [skoțsi'an] |

Vatican City	Vatican (m)	[vati'kan]
Liechtenstein	Liechtenstein (m)	[lihten'ʃtajn]
Luxembourg	Luxemburg (m)	[luksem'burg]
Monaco	Monaco (m)	[mo'nako]

235. Central and Eastern Europe

Albania	Albania (f)	[al'banija]
Albanian (masc.)	albanez (m)	[alba'nez]
Albanian (fem.)	albaneză (f)	[alba'nezə]
Albanian (adj)	albanez	[alba'nez]

Bulgaria	Bulgaria (f)	[bul'garia]
Bulgarian (masc.)	bulgar (m)	[bul'gar]
Bulgarian (fem.)	bulgăroaică (f)	[bulgəro'ajkə]
Bulgarian (adj)	bulgăresc	[bulgə'resk]

Hungary	Ungaria (f)	[un'garia]
Hungarian (masc.)	ungur (m)	['ungur]
Hungarian (fem.)	unguroaică (f)	[unguro'ajkə]
Hungarian (adj)	unguresc	[ungu'resk]

Latvia	Letonia (f)	[le'tonia]
Latvian (masc.)	leton (m)	[le'ton]
Latvian (fem.)	letonă (f)	[le'tonə]
Latvian (adj)	leton	[le'ton]

Lithuania	Lituania (f)	[litu'ania]
Lithuanian (masc.)	lituanian (m)	[lituani'an]
Lithuanian (fem.)	lituaniană (f)	[lituani'anə]
Lithuanian (adj)	lituanian	[lituani'an]

Poland	Polonia (f)	[po'lonia]
Pole (masc.)	polonez (m)	[polo'nez]
Pole (fem.)	poloneză (f)	[polo'nezə]
Polish (adj)	polonez	[polo'nez]

Romania	România (f)	[rominia]
Romanian (masc.)	român (m)	[ro'min]
Romanian (fem.)	româncă (f)	[ro'minkə]
Romanian (adj)	român	[ro'min]

Serbia	Serbia (f)	['serbija]
Serbian (masc.)	sârb (m)	[sirb]
Serbian (fem.)	serbă (f)	['serbə]
Serbian (adj)	sârb	[sirb]

Slovakia	Slovacia (f)	[slo'vatʃia]
Slovak (masc.)	slovac (m)	[slo'vak]
Slovak (fem.)	slovacă (f)	[slo'vakə]
Slovak (adj)	slovac	[slo'vak]

Croatia	Croația (f)	[kro'atsia]
Croatian (masc.)	croat (m)	[kro'at]
Croatian (fem.)	croată (f)	[kro'atə]
Croatian (adj)	croat	[kro'at]

Czech Republic	Cehia (f)	['tʃehija]
Czech (masc.)	ceh (m)	[tʃeh]
Czech (fem.)	cehă (f)	['tʃehə]
Czech (adj)	ceh	[tʃeh]

Estonia	Estonia (f)	[es'tonia]
Estonian (masc.)	estonian (m)	[estoni'an]
Estonian (fem.)	estoniană (f)	[estoni'anə]
Estonian (adj)	estonian	[estoni'an]

Bosnia and Herzegovina	Bosnia și Herțegovina (f)	['bosnia ʃi hertsego'vina]
North Macedonia	Macedonia (f)	[matʃe'donia]
Slovenia	Slovenia (f)	[slo'venia]
Montenegro	Muntenegru (m)	[munte'negru]

236. Former USSR countries

Azerbaijan	Azerbaidjan (m)	[azerbaj'dʒan]
Azerbaijani (masc.)	azerbaidjan (m)	[azerbaj'dʒan]
Azerbaijani (fem.)	azerbaidjană (f)	[azerbaj'dʒanə]
Azerbaijani, Azeri (adj)	azerbaidjan	[azerbaj'dʒan]

Armenia	Armenia (f)	[ar'menia]
Armenian (masc.)	armean (m)	[ar'mʲan]
Armenian (fem.)	armeancă (f)	[ar'mʲankə]
Armenian (adj)	armenesc	[arme'nesk]

Belarus	Belarus (f)	[bela'rus]
Belarusian (masc.)	bielorus (m)	[belo'rus]
Belarusian (fem.)	bielorusă (f)	[belo'rusə]
Belarusian (adj)	bielorus	[belo'rus]

Georgia	Georgia (f)	['dʒordʒia]
Georgian (masc.)	gruzin (m)	[gru'zin]
Georgian (fem.)	georgiană (f)	[dʒordʒi'anə]
Georgian (adj)	gruzin	[gru'zin]

Kazakhstan	Kazahstan (n)	[kazah'stan]
Kazakh (masc.)	kazah (m)	[ka'zah]
Kazakh (fem.)	kazahă (f)	[ka'zahə]
Kazakh (adj)	kazah	[ka'zah]

Kirghizia	Kîrgîstan (m)	[kirgiz'stan]
Kirghiz (masc.)	kirghiz (m)	[kir'giz]
Kirghiz (fem.)	kirghiză (f)	[kir'gize]
Kirghiz (adj)	kirghiz	[kir'giz]

| Moldova, Moldavia | Moldova (f) | [mol'dova] |
| Moldavian (masc.) | moldovean (m) | [moldo'vʲan] |

| Moldavian (fem.) | moldoveancă (f) | [moldo'vɪankə] |
| Moldavian (adj) | moldovenesc | [moldove'nesk] |

Russia	Rusia (f)	['rusia]
Russian (masc.)	rus (m)	[rus]
Russian (fem.)	rusoaică (f)	[ruso'ajkə]
Russian (adj)	rusesc	[ru'sesk]

Tajikistan	Tadjikistan (m)	[tadʒiki'stan]
Tajik (masc.)	tadjic (m)	[ta'dʒik]
Tajik (fem.)	tadjică (f)	[ta'dʒikə]
Tajik (adj)	tadjic	[ta'dʒik]

Turkmenistan	Turkmenistan (n)	[turkmeni'stan]
Turkmen (masc.)	turkmen (m)	[turk'men]
Turkmen (fem.)	turkmenă (f)	[turk'menə]
Turkmenian (adj)	turkmen	[turk'men]

Uzbekistan	Uzbekistan (n)	[uzbeki'stan]
Uzbek (masc.)	uzbec (m)	[uz'bek]
Uzbek (fem.)	uzbecă (f)	[uz'bekə]
Uzbek (adj)	uzbec	[uz'bek]

Ukraine	Ucraina (f)	[ukra'ina]
Ukrainian (masc.)	ucrainean (m)	[ukrai'nɪan]
Ukrainian (fem.)	ucraineancă (f)	[ukrai'nɪankə]
Ukrainian (adj)	ucrainean	[ukrai'nɪan]

237. Asia

| Asia | Asia (f) | ['asia] |
| Asian (adj) | asiatic | [asi'atik] |

Vietnam	Vietnam (n)	[viet'nam]
Vietnamese (masc.)	vietnamez (m)	[vetna'mez]
Vietnamese (fem.)	vietnameză (f)	[vetna'mezə]
Vietnamese (adj)	vietnamez	[vetna'mezə]

India	India (f)	['india]
Indian (masc.)	indian (m)	[indi'an]
Indian (fem.)	indiancă (f)	[indi'ankə]
Indian (adj)	indian	[indi'an]

Israel	Israel (n)	[isra'el]
Israeli (masc.)	israelian (m)	[israeli'an]
Israeli (fem.)	israeliană (f)	[israeli'anə]
Israeli (adj)	israelit	[israe'lit]

Jew (n)	evreu (m)	[e'vreu]
Jewess (n)	evreică (f)	[e'vrejkə]
Jewish (adj)	evreiesc	[evre'esk]

| China | China (f) | ['kina] |
| Chinese (masc.) | chinez (m) | [ki'nez] |

Chinese (fem.)	chineză (f)	[ki'neze]
Chinese (adj)	chinezesc	[kine'zesk]
Korean (masc.)	coreean (m)	[kore'an]
Korean (fem.)	coreeancă (f)	[kore'ankə]
Korean (adj)	coreean	[kore'an]
Lebanon	Liban (n)	[li'ban]
Lebanese (masc.)	libanez (m)	[liba'nez]
Lebanese (fem.)	libaneză (f)	[liba'nezə]
Lebanese (adj)	libanez	[liba'nez]
Mongolia	Mongolia (f)	[mon'golia]
Mongolian (masc.)	mongol (m)	[mon'gol]
Mongolian (fem.)	mongolă (f)	[mon'golə]
Mongolian (adj)	mongol	[mon'gol]
Malaysia	Malaezia (f)	[mala'ezia]
Malaysian (masc.)	malaezian (f)	[malaezi'an]
Malaysian (fem.)	malaeziană (f)	[malaezi'anə]
Malaysian (adj)	malaez	[mala'ez]
Pakistan	Pakistan (n)	[paki'stan]
Pakistani (masc.)	pakistanez (m)	[pakista'nez]
Pakistani (fem.)	pakistaneză (f)	[pakista'nezə]
Pakistani (adj)	pakistanez	[pakista'nez]
Saudi Arabia	Arabia (f) Saudită	[a'rabia sau'ditə]
Arab (masc.)	arab (m)	[a'rab]
Arab (fem.)	arăboaică (f)	[arəbo'ajkə]
Arabic, Arabian (adj)	arab	[a'rab]
Thailand	Thailanda (f)	[taj'landa]
Thai (masc.)	thailandez (m)	[tajlan'dez]
Thai (fem.)	thailandeză (f)	[tajlan'dezə]
Thai (adj)	thailandez	[tajlan'dez]
Taiwan	Taiwan (m)	[taj'van]
Taiwanese (masc.)	taiwanez (m)	[tajva'nez]
Taiwanese (fem.)	taiwaneză (f)	[tajva'nezə]
Taiwanese (adj)	taiwanez	[tajva'nez]
Turkey	Turcia (f)	['turtʃia]
Turk (masc.)	turc (m)	[turk]
Turk (fem.)	turcoaică (f)	[turko'ajkə]
Turkish (adj)	turcesc	[tur'tʃesk]
Japan	Japonia (f)	[ʒa'ponia]
Japanese (masc.)	japonez (m)	[ʒapo'nez]
Japanese (fem.)	japoneză (f)	[ʒapo'nezə]
Japanese (adj)	japonez	[ʒapo'nez]
Afghanistan	Afganistan (n)	[afganis'tan]
Bangladesh	Bangladeş (m)	[bangla'deʃ]
Indonesia	Indonezia (f)	[indo'nezia]
Jordan	Iordania (f)	[jor'dania]

Iraq	**Irak** (n)	[i'rak]
Iran	**Iran** (n)	[i'ran]
Cambodia	**Cambodgia** (f)	[kam'bodʒia]
Kuwait	**Kuweit** (n)	[kuve'it]

Laos	**Laos** (n)	['laos]
Myanmar	**Myanmar** (m)	[mjan'mar]
Nepal	**Nepal** (n)	[ne'pal]
United Arab Emirates	**Emiratele** (n pl) **Arabe Unite**	[emi'ratele a'rabe u'nite]

Syria	**Siria** (f)	['sirija]
Palestine	**Palestina** (f)	[pales'tina]
South Korea	**Coreea** (f) **de Sud**	[ko'rea de 'sud]
North Korea	**Coreea** (f) **de Nord**	[ko'rea de 'nord]

238. North America

United States of America	**Statele** (n pl) **Unite ale Americii**	['statele u'nite 'ale a'meritʃij]
American (masc.)	**american** (m)	[ameri'kan]
American (fem.)	**americancă** (f)	[ameri'kankə]
American (adj)	**american**	[ameri'kan]

Canada	**Canada** (f)	[ka'nada]
Canadian (masc.)	**canadian** (m)	[kanadi'an]
Canadian (fem.)	**canadiancă** (f)	[kanadi'ankə]
Canadian (adj)	**canadian**	[kanadi'an]

Mexico	**Mexic** (n)	['meksik]
Mexican (masc.)	**mexican** (m)	[meksi'kan]
Mexican (fem.)	**mexicancă** (f)	[meksi'kankə]
Mexican (adj)	**mexican**	[meksi'kan]

239. Central and South America

Argentina	**Argentina** (f)	[arʒen'tina]
Argentinian (masc.)	**argentinian** (m)	[arʒentini'an]
Argentinian (fem.)	**argentiniană** (f)	[ardʒentini'anə]
Argentinian (adj)	**argentinian**	[arʒentini'an]

Brazil	**Brazilia** (f)	[bra'zilia]
Brazilian (masc.)	**brazilian** (m)	[brazili'an]
Brazilian (fem.)	**braziliancă** (f)	[brazili'ankə]
Brazilian (adj)	**brazilian**	[brazili'an]

Colombia	**Columbia** (f)	[ko'lumbia]
Colombian (masc.)	**columbian** (m)	[kolumbi'an]
Colombian (fem.)	**columbiană** (f)	[kolumbi'anə]
Colombian (adj)	**columbian**	[kolumbi'an]

| Cuba | **Cuba** (f) | ['kuba] |
| Cuban (masc.) | **cubanez** (m) | [kuba'nez] |

| Cuban (fem.) | cubaneză (f) | [kuba'nezə] |
| Cuban (adj) | cubanez | [kuba'nez] |

Chile	Chile (n)	['ʧile]
Chilean (masc.)	chilian (m)	[ʧili'an]
Chilean (fem.)	chiliană (f)	[ʧili'anə]
Chilean (adj)	chilian	[ʧili'an]

Bolivia	Bolivia (f)	[bo'livia]
Venezuela	Venezuela (f)	[venezu'ela]
Paraguay	Paraguay (n)	[paragu'aj]
Peru	Peru (n)	['peru]

Suriname	Surinam (n)	[suri'nam]
Uruguay	Uruguay (n)	[urugu'aj]
Ecuador	Ecuador (m)	[ekua'dor]

The Bahamas	Insulele (f pl) Bahamas	['insulele ba'hamas]
Haiti	Haiti (n)	[ha'iti]
Dominican Republic	Republica (f) Dominicană	[re'publika domini'kanə]
Panama	Panama (f)	[pana'ma]
Jamaica	Jamaica (f)	[ʒa'majka]

240. Africa

Egypt	Egipt (n)	[e'ʤipt]
Egyptian (masc.)	egiptean (m)	[edʒip'tˌan]
Egyptian (fem.)	egipteancă (f)	[edʒip'tˌankə]
Egyptian (adj)	egiptean	[edʒip'tˌan]

Morocco	Maroc (n)	[ma'rok]
Moroccan (masc.)	marocan (m)	[maro'kan]
Moroccan (fem.)	marocană (f)	[maro'kanə]
Moroccan (adj)	marocan	[maro'kan]

Tunisia	Tunisia (f)	[tu'nisia]
Tunisian (masc.)	tunisian (m)	[tunisi'an]
Tunisian (fem.)	tunisiancă (f)	[tunisi'ankə]
Tunisian (adj)	tunisian	[tunisi'an]

Ghana	Ghana (f)	['gana]
Zanzibar	Zanzibar (n)	[zanzi'bar]
Kenya	Kenia (f)	['kenia]
Libya	Libia (f)	['libia]
Madagascar	Madagascar (n)	[madagas'kar]

Namibia	Namibia (f)	[na'mibia]
Senegal	Senegal (n)	[sene'gal]
Tanzania	Tanzania (f)	[tan'zania]
South Africa	Africa de Sud (f)	['afrika de sud]

African (masc.)	african (m)	[afri'kan]
African (fem.)	africană (f)	[afri'kanə]
African (adj)	african	[afri'kan]

241. Australia. Oceania

Australia	Australia (f)	[au'stralia]
Australian (masc.)	australian (m)	[australi'an]
Australian (fem.)	australiană (f)	[australi'anə]
Australian (adj)	australian	[australi'an]

New Zealand	Noua Zeelandă (f)	['nowa zee'landə]
New Zealander (masc.)	neozeelandez (m)	[neozeelan'dez]
New Zealander (fem.)	neozeelandeză (f)	[neozeelan'dezə]
New Zealand (as adj)	neozeelandez	[neozeelan'dez]

Tasmania	Tasmania (f)	[tas'mania]
French Polynesia	Polinezia (f)	[poli'nezia]

242. Cities

Amsterdam	Amsterdam (n)	['amsterdam]
Ankara	Ankara (f)	[an'kara]
Athens	Atena (f)	[a'tena]
Baghdad	Bagdad (n)	[bag'dad]
Bangkok	Bangkok (m)	[ba'nkok]
Barcelona	Barcelona (f)	[barse'lona]

Beijing	Beijing (n)	[bej'ʒing]
Beirut	Beirut (n)	[bej'rut]
Berlin	Berlin (n)	[ber'lin]
Mumbai (Bombay)	Bombay (n)	[bom'bej]
Bonn	Bonn (n)	[bon]

Bordeaux	Bordeaux (n)	[bor'do]
Bratislava	Bratislava (f)	[bratislava]
Brussels	Bruxelles (n)	[bruk'sel]
Bucharest	Bucureşti (n)	[buku'reʃtʲ]
Budapest	Budapesta (f)	[buda'pesta]

Cairo	Cairo (n)	[ka'iro]
Kolkata (Calcutta)	Calcutta (f)	[kal'kuta]
Chicago	Chicago (n)	[ʧi'kago]
Copenhagen	Copenhaga (f)	[kopen'haga]

Dar-es-Salaam	Dar es Salaam (n)	[dar es sala'am]
Delhi	Delhi, New Delhi (m)	['deli], [nju 'deli]
Dubai	Dubai (n)	[du'baj]
Dublin	Dublin (n)	[dub'lin]
Düsseldorf	Düsseldorf (m)	[djusel'dorf]

Florence	Florenţa (f)	[flo'renʦa]
Frankfurt	Frankfurt (m)	['frankfurt]
Geneva	Geneva (f)	[dʒe'neva]

The Hague	Haga (f)	['haga]
Hamburg	Hamburg (n)	['hamburg]

Hanoi	Hanoi (n)	[ha'noj]
Havana	Havana (f)	[ha'vana]
Helsinki	Helsinki (n)	['helsinki]
Hiroshima	Hiroşima (f)	[hiro'ʃima]
Hong Kong	Hong-Kong (n)	['hong 'kong]

Istanbul	Istanbul (n)	[istan'bul]
Jerusalem	Ierusalim (n)	[jerusa'lim]
Kyiv	Kiev (n)	[ki'ev]
Kuala Lumpur	Kuala Lumpur (m)	[ku'ala lum'pur]
Lisbon	Lisabona (f)	[lisa'bona]
London	Londra (f)	['londra]
Los Angeles	Los Angeles (n)	['los 'andʒeles]
Lyons	Lyon (m)	[li'on]

Madrid	Madrid (n)	[ma'drid]
Marseille	Marsilia (f)	[mar'silia]
Mexico City	Mexico City (n)	['meksiko 'siti]
Miami	Miami (n)	[ma'jami]
Montreal	Montreal (m)	[monre'al]
Moscow	Moscova (f)	['moskova]
Munich	Munchen (m)	['mʲunhen]

Nairobi	Nairobi (n)	[naj'robi]
Naples	Napoli (m)	['napoli]
New York	New York (n)	[nju 'jork]
Nice	Nisa (f)	['nisa]
Oslo	Oslo (n)	['oslo]
Ottawa	Ottawa (f)	[ot'tava]

Paris	Paris (n)	[pa'ris]
Prague	Praga (f)	['praga]
Rio de Janeiro	Rio de Janeiro (n)	['rio de ʒa'nejro]
Rome	Roma (f)	['roma]

Saint Petersburg	Sankt Petersburg (n)	['sankt peters'burg]
Seoul	Seul (n)	[se'ul]
Shanghai	Shanghai (m)	[ʃan'haj]
Singapore	Singapore (n)	[singa'pore]
Stockholm	Stockholm (m)	['stokholm]
Sydney	Sydney (m)	['sidnej]

Taipei	Taipei (m)	[taj'pej]
Tokyo	Tokio (n)	['tokio]
Toronto	Toronto (n)	[to'ronto]
Venice	Veneţia (f)	[ve'neʦia]
Vienna	Viena (f)	[vi'ena]
Warsaw	Varşovia (f)	[var'ʃovia]
Washington	Washington (n)	['waʃington]

243. Politics. Government. Part 1

| politics | politică (f) | [po'litikə] |
| political (adj) | politic | [po'litik] |

politician	politician (m)	[politit͡ʃi'an]
state (country)	stat (n)	[stat]
citizen	cetăţean (m)	[t͡ʃetə'ts'an]
citizenship	cetăţenie (f)	[t͡ʃetətse'nie]
national emblem	stemă (f) naţională	['stemə natsio'nalə]
national anthem	imn (n) de stat	[imn de stat]
government	guvern (n)	[gu'vern]
head of state	conducătorul (m) ţării	[kondukə'torul tsərij]
parliament	parlament (n)	[parla'ment]
party	partid (n)	[par'tid]
capitalism	capitalism (n)	[kapita'lism]
capitalist (adj)	capitalist	[kapita'list]
socialism	socialism (n)	[sot͡ʃia'lizm]
socialist (adj)	socialist	[sot͡ʃia'list]
communism	comunism (n)	[komu'nizm]
communist (adj)	comunist	[komu'nist]
communist (n)	comunist (m)	[komu'nist]
democracy	democraţie (f)	[demokra'tsie]
democrat	democrat (m)	[demo'krat]
democratic (adj)	democrat	[demo'krat]
Democratic party	partid (n) democrat	[par'tid demo'krat]
liberal (n)	liberal (m)	[libe'ral]
Liberal (adj)	liberal	[libe'ral]
conservative (n)	conservator (m)	[konserva'tor]
conservative (adj)	conservator	[konserva'tor]
republic (n)	republică (f)	[re'publikə]
republican (n)	republican (m)	[republi'kan]
Republican party	partid (n) republican	[par'tid republi'kan]
elections	alegeri (f pl)	[a'ledʒer']
to elect (vt)	a alege	[a a'ledʒe]
elector, voter	alegător (m)	[alegə'tor]
election campaign	campanie (f) electorală	[kam'panie elekto'ralə]
voting (n)	votare (f)	[vo'tare]
to vote (vi)	a vota	[a vo'ta]
suffrage, right to vote	drept (n) de vot	[drept de vot]
candidate	candidat (m)	[kandi'dat]
to run for (~ President)	a candida	[ə kandi'da]
campaign	campanie (f)	[kam'panie]
opposition (as adj)	de opoziţie	[de opo'zitsie]
opposition (n)	opoziţie (f)	[opo'zitsie]
visit	vizită (f)	['vizitə]
official visit	vizită (f) oficială	['vizitə ofit͡ʃi'alə]

international (adj)	internaţional	[internatsio'nal]
negotiations	tratative (n pl)	[trata'tive]
to negotiate (vi)	a purta tratative	[a pur'ta trata'tive]

244. Politics. Government. Part 2

society	societate (f)	[sotʃie'tate]
constitution	constituţie (f)	[konsti'tutsie]
power (political control)	autoritate (f)	[autori'tate]
corruption	corupţie (f)	[ko'ruptsie]

| law (justice) | lege (f) | ['ledʒe] |
| legal (legitimate) | legal | [le'gal] |

| justice (fairness) | dreptate (f) | [drep'tate] |
| just (fair) | echitabil | [eki'tabil] |

committee	comitet (n)	[komi'tet]
bill (draft law)	proiect (n) de lege	[pro'ekt de 'ledʒe]
budget	buget (n)	[bu'dʒet]
policy	politică (f)	[po'litikə]
reform	reformă (f)	[re'formə]
radical (adj)	radical	[radi'kal]

power (strength, force)	putere (f)	[pu'tere]
powerful (adj)	puternic	[pu'ternik]
supporter	adept (m)	[a'dept]
influence	influenţă (f)	[influ'entsə]

regime (e.g. military ~)	regim (n)	[re'dʒim]
conflict	conflict (n)	[kon'flikt]
conspiracy (plot)	conspiraţie (f)	[konspi'ratsie]
provocation	provocare (f)	[provo'kare]

to overthrow (regime, etc.)	a răsturna	[a rəstur'na]
overthrow (of a government)	răsturnare (f)	[rəstur'nare]
revolution	revoluţie (f)	[revo'lutsie]

| coup d'état | lovitură (f) de stat | [lovi'tura də stat] |
| military coup | lovitură (f) de stat militară | [lovi'tura də stat mili'tarə] |

crisis	criză (f)	['krizə]
economic recession	scădere (f) economică	[skə'dere eko'nomikə]
demonstrator (protester)	manifestant (m)	[manifes'tant]
demonstration	manifestaţie (f)	[manifes'tatsie]
martial law	stare (f) de război	['stare de rəz'boj]
military base	bază (f) militară	['bazə mili'tarə]

| stability | stabilitate (f) | [stabili'tatə] |
| stable (adj) | stabil | [sta'bil] |

exploitation	exploatare (f)	[ekploa'tare]
to exploit (workers)	a exploata	[a eksploa'ta]
racism	rasism (n)	[ra'sism]

racist	rasist (m)	[ra'sist]
fascism	fascism (n)	[fas'tʃism]
fascist	fascist (m)	[fas'tʃist]

245. Countries. Miscellaneous

foreigner	cetăţean (m) străin	[tʃetə'tsʲan strə'in]
foreign (adj)	străin	[strə'in]
abroad (in a foreign country)	peste hotare	['peste ho'tare]

emigrant	emigrant (m)	[emi'grant]
emigration	emigrare (f)	[emi'grare]
to emigrate (vi)	a emigra	[a emi'gra]

the West	Vest (n)	[vest]
the East	Est (n)	[est]
the Far East	Extremul Orient (n)	[eks'tremul o'rjent]
civilization	civilizaţie (f)	[tʃivili'zatsie]
humanity (mankind)	umanitate (f)	[umani'tate]
the world (earth)	lume (f)	['lume]
peace	pace (f)	['patʃe]
worldwide (adj)	mondial	[mon'djal]

homeland	patrie (f)	['patrie]
people (population)	popor (n)	[po'por]
population	populaţie (f)	[popu'latsie]
people (a lot of ~)	oameni (m pl)	[o'amenʲ]
nation (people)	naţiune (f)	[natsi'une]
generation	generaţie (f)	[dʒene'ratsie]
territory (area)	teritoriu (n)	[teri'torju]
region	regiune (f)	[redʒi'une]
state (part of a country)	stat (n)	[stat]

tradition	tradiţie (f)	[tra'ditsie]
custom (tradition)	obicei (n)	[obi'tʃej]
ecology	ecologie (f)	[ekolo'dʒie]

Indian (Native American)	indian (m)	[indi'an]
Gypsy (masc.)	ţigan (m)	[tsi'gan]
Gypsy (fem.)	ţigancă (f)	[tsi'gankə]
Gypsy (adj)	ţigănesc	[tsigə'nesk]

empire	imperiu (n)	[im'perju]
colony	colonie (f)	[kolo'nie]
slavery	sclavie (f)	[skla'vie]
invasion	invazie (f)	[in'vazie]
famine	foamete (f)	[fo'amete]

246. Major religious groups. Confessions

| religion | religie (f) | [re'lidʒie] |
| religious (adj) | religios | [relidʒi'os] |

faith, belief	credință (f)	[kre'dintsə]
to believe (in God)	a crede	[a 'krede]
believer	credincios (m)	[kredin'tʃios]

| atheism | ateism (n) | [ate'izm] |
| atheist | ateu (m) | [a'teu] |

Christianity	creştinism (n)	[kreʃti'nism]
Christian (n)	creştin (m)	[kreʃ'tin]
Christian (adj)	creştin	[kreʃ'tin]

Catholicism	Catolicism (n)	[katoli'tʃism]
Catholic (n)	catolic (m)	[ka'tolik]
Catholic (adj)	catolic	[ka'tolik]

Protestantism	Protestantism (n)	[protestan'tizm]
Protestant Church	Biserica (f) Protestantă	[bi'serika protes'tantə]
Protestant (n)	protestant (m)	[protes'tant]

Orthodoxy	Ortodoxie (f)	[ortodok'sie]
Orthodox Church	Biserica (f) Ortodoxă	[bi'serika orto'doksə]
Orthodox (n)	ortodox (m)	[orto'doks]

Presbyterianism	calvinism (n)	[kalvi'nism]
Presbyterian Church	Biserica (f) Calvinistă	[bi'serika kalvi'nistə]
Presbyterian (n)	calvinist (m)	[kalvi'nist]

| Lutheranism | Biserica (f) Luterană | [bi'serika lute'ranə] |
| Lutheran (n) | luteran (m) | [lute'ran] |

| Baptist Church | Baptism (n) | [bap'tism] |
| Baptist (n) | baptist (m) | [bap'tist] |

| Anglican Church | Biserica (f) Anglicană | [bi'serika angli'kanə] |
| Anglican (n) | anglican (m) | [angli'kan] |

| Mormonism | Mormonism (n) | [mormo'nism] |
| Mormon (n) | mormon (m) | [mor'mon] |

| Judaism | Iudaism (n) | [juda'izm] |
| Jew (n) | iudeu (m) | [ju'deu] |

| Buddhism | Budism (n) | [bu'dizm] |
| Buddhist (n) | budist (m) | [bu'dist] |

| Hinduism | Hinduism (n) | [hindu'izm] |
| Hindu (n) | hindus (m) | [hin'dus] |

Islam	Islamism (n)	[isla'mizm]
Muslim (n)	musulman (m)	[musul'man]
Muslim (adj)	musulman	[musul'man]

Shiah Islam	Şiism (n)	[ʃi'ism]
Shiite (n)	şiit (m)	[ʃi'it]
Sunni Islam	Sunnism (n)	[su'nism]
Sunnite (n)	sunnit (m)	[su'nit]

247. Religions. Priests

| priest | preot (m) | ['preot] |
| the Pope | Papa Romei (m) | ['papa 'romej] |

monk, friar	călugăr (m)	[kə'lugər]
nun	călugăriţă (f)	[kə'lugəritsə]
pastor	pastor (m)	['pastor]

abbot	abate (m)	[a'bate]
vicar (parish priest)	vicar (m)	[vi'kar]
bishop	episcop (m)	[e'piskop]
cardinal	cardinal (m)	[kardi'nal]

preacher	propovăduitor (m)	[propovədui'tor]
preaching	predică (f)	['predikə]
parishioners	enoriaşi (m pl)	[enori'aʃ]

| believer | credincios (m) | [kredin'tʃios] |
| atheist | ateu (m) | [a'teu] |

248. Faith. Christianity. Islam

| Adam | Adam (m) | [a'dam] |
| Eve | Eva (f) | ['eva] |

God	Dumnezeu (m)	[dumne'zeu]
the Lord	Domnul (m)	['domnulʲ]
the Almighty	Atotputernic (m)	[atotpu'ternik]

sin	păcat (n)	[pə'kat]
to sin (vi)	a păcătui	[a pəkətu'i]
sinner (masc.)	păcătos (m)	[pəkə'tos]
sinner (fem.)	păcătoasă (f)	[pəkəto'asə]

| hell | iad (n) | [jad] |
| paradise | rai (f) | [raj] |

| Jesus | Isus (m) | [i'sus] |
| Jesus Christ | Isus Hristos (m) | [i'sus hris'tos] |

the Holy Spirit	Sfântul Duh (m)	['sfintul 'duh]
the Saviour	Salvator (m)	[salva'tor]
the Virgin Mary	Maica Domnului (f)	['majka 'domnuluj]

the Devil	Diavol (m)	['djavol]
devil's (adj)	diavolesc	[djavo'lesk]
Satan	Satana (f)	[sa'tana]
satanic (adj)	satanic	[sa'tanik]

angel	înger (m)	['indʒer]
guardian angel	înger (m) păzitor	['indʒer pəzi'tor]
angelic (adj)	îngeresc	[indʒe'resk]

apostle	**apostol** (m)	[a'postol]
archangel	**arhanghel** (m)	[ar'hangel]
the Antichrist	**antihrist** (m)	[anti'hrist]
Church	**Biserică** (f)	[bi'serikə]
Bible	**Biblie** (f)	['biblie]
biblical (adj)	**biblic**	['biblik]
Old Testament	**Vechiul Testament** (n)	['vekjul testa'ment]
New Testament	**Noul testament** (n)	['noul testa'ment]
Gospel	**Evanghelie** (f)	[eva'ngelie]
Holy Scripture	**Sfânta Scriptură** (f)	['sfinta skrip'turə]
Heaven	**Împărăția Cerului** (f)	[impərə'tsia 'tʃeruluj]
Commandment	**poruncă** (f)	[po'runkə]
prophet	**profet** (m)	[pro'fet]
prophecy	**profeție** (f)	[profe'tsie]
Allah	**Allah** (m)	[al'lah]
Mohammed	**Mohamed** (m)	[moha'med]
the Koran	**Coran** (n)	[ko'ran]
mosque	**moschee** (f)	[mos'kee]
mullah	**hoge** (m)	['hodʒe]
prayer	**rugăciune** (f)	[rugə'tʃiune]
to pray (vi, vt)	**a se ruga**	[a se ru'ga]
pilgrimage	**pelerinaj** (n)	[peleri'naʒ]
pilgrim	**pelerin** (m)	[pele'rin]
Mecca	**Mecca** (f)	['meka]
church	**biserică** (f)	[bi'serikə]
temple	**templu** (n)	['templu]
cathedral	**catedrală** (f)	[kate'dralə]
Gothic (adj)	**gotic**	['gotik]
synagogue	**sinagogă** (f)	[sina'gogə]
mosque	**moschee** (f)	[mos'kee]
chapel	**capelă** (f)	[ka'pelə]
abbey	**abație** (f)	[a'batsie]
convent	**mănăstire** (f) **de călugărițe**	[mənəs'tire de kə'lugəritse]
monastery	**mănăstire** (f) **de călugări**	[mənəs'tire de kə'lugərʲ]
bell (church ~s)	**clopot** (n)	['klopot]
bell tower	**clopotniță** (f)	[klo'potnitsə]
to ring (ab. bells)	**a bate**	[a 'bate]
cross	**cruce** (f)	['krutʃe]
cupola (roof)	**boltă** (f)	['boltə]
icon	**icoană** (f)	[iko'anə]
soul	**suflet** (n)	['suflet]
fate (destiny)	**soartă** (f)	[so'artə]
evil (n)	**rău** (n)	[rəu]
good (n)	**bine** (n)	['bine]
vampire	**vampir** (m)	[vam'pir]

witch (evil ~)	vrăjitoare (f)	[vrəʒito'are]
demon	demon (m)	['demon]
spirit	spirit (n)	['spirit]

| redemption (giving us ~) | ispăşire (f) | [ispə'ʃire] |
| to redeem (vt) | a ispăşi | [a ispə'ʃi] |

church service	slujbă (f)	['sluʒbə]
to say mass	a sluji	[a slu'ʒi]
confession	spovedanie (f)	[spove'danie]
to confess (vi)	a se spovedi	[a se spove'di]

saint (n)	sfânt (m)	[sfint]
sacred (holy)	sfânt	[sfint]
holy water	apă (f) sfinţită	['apə sfin'tsitə]

ritual (n)	ritual (n)	[ritu'al]
ritual (adj)	de rit	[de rit]
sacrifice	jertfă (f)	['ʒertfə]

superstition	superstiţie (f)	[supers'titsie]
superstitious (adj)	superstiţios	[superstitsi'os]
afterlife	viaţa (f) de după moarte	['vjatsa de 'dupə mo'arte]
eternal life	viaţă (f) veşnică	['vjatsə 'veʃnikə]

MISCELLANEOUS

249. Various useful words

background (green ~)	**fundal** (n)	[fun'dal]
balance (of the situation)	**balanţă** (f)	[ba'lantsə]
barrier (obstacle)	**barieră** (f)	[ba'rjerə]
base (basis)	**bază** (f)	['bazə]
beginning	**început** (n)	[intʃe'put]
category	**categorie** (f)	[katego'rie]
cause (reason)	**cauză** (f)	['kauzə]
choice	**alegere** (f)	[a'ledʒere]
coincidence	**coincidenţă** (f)	[kointʃi'dentsə]
comfortable (~ chair)	**confortabil**	[konfor'tabil]
comparison	**comparaţie** (f)	[kompa'ratsie]
compensation	**compensaţie** (f)	[kompen'satsie]
degree (extent, amount)	**grad** (n)	[grad]
development	**dezvoltare** (f)	[dezvol'tare]
difference	**deosebire** (f)	[deose'bire]
effect (e.g. of drugs)	**efect** (n)	[e'fekt]
effort (exertion)	**efort** (n)	[e'fort]
element	**element** (n)	[ele'ment]
end (finish)	**sfârşit** (n)	[sfir'ʃit]
example (illustration)	**exemplu** (n)	[e'gzemplu]
fact	**fapt** (n)	[fapt]
frequent (adj)	**des**	[des]
growth (development)	**creştere** (f)	['kreʃtere]
help	**ajutor** (n)	[aʒu'tor]
ideal	**ideal** (n)	[ide'al]
kind (sort, type)	**aspect** (n)	[as'pekt]
labyrinth	**labirint** (n)	[labi'rint]
mistake, error	**greşeală** (f)	[gre'ʃalə]
moment	**moment** (n)	[mo'mənt]
object (thing)	**obiect** (n)	[o'bjekt]
obstacle	**obstacol** (n)	[ob'stakol]
original (original copy)	**original** (n)	[oridʒi'nal]
part (~ of sth)	**parte** (f)	['parte]
particle, small part	**bucată** (f)	[bu'katə]
pause (break)	**pauză** (f)	['pauzə]
position	**poziţie** (f)	[po'zitsie]
principle	**principiu** (n)	[prin'tʃipju]
problem	**problemă** (f)	[pro'blemə]
process	**proces** (n)	[pro'tʃes]

progress	progres (n)	[pro'gres]
property (quality)	însușire (f)	[insu'ʃire]
reaction	reacție (f)	[re'aktsie]
risk	risc (n)	[risk]

secret	taină (f)	['tajnə]
series	serie (f)	['serie]
shape (outer form)	formă (f)	['formə]
situation	situație (f)	[situ'atsie]
solution	soluție (f)	[so'lutsie]

standard (adj)	standardizat	[standardi'zat]
standard (level of quality)	standard (n)	[stan'dard]
stop (pause)	pauză (f)	['pauzə]
style	stil (n)	[stil]

system	sistem (n)	[sis'tem]
table (chart)	tabel (n)	[ta'bel]
tempo, rate	ritm (n)	[ritm]
term (word, expression)	termen (n)	['termen]
thing (object, item)	obiect (n)	[o'bjekt]

truth (e.g. moment of ~)	adevăr (n)	[ade'vər]
turn (please wait your ~)	rând (n)	[rind]
type (sort, kind)	tip (n)	[tip]
urgent (adj)	urgent	[ur'dʒent]
urgently	urgent	[ur'dʒent]

utility (usefulness)	folos (n)	[fo'los]
variant (alternative)	variantă (f)	[vari'antə]
way (means, method)	mod (n)	[mod]
zone	zonă (f)	['zonə]

250. Modifiers. Adjectives. Part 1

additional (adj)	suplimentar	[suplimen'tar]
ancient (~ civilization)	antic	['antik]
artificial (adj)	artificial	[artifitʃi'al]
back, rear (adj)	posterior	[posteri'or]
bad (adj)	rău	['rəu]

beautiful (~ palace)	minunat	[minu'nat]
beautiful (person)	frumos	[fru'mos]
big (in size)	mare	['mare]
bitter (taste)	amar	[a'mar]
blind (sightless)	orb	[orb]

calm, quiet (adj)	liniștit	[liniʃ'tit]
careless (negligent)	neglijent	[negli'ʒent]
caring (~ father)	grijuliu	[griʒu'lju]
central (adj)	central	[tʃen'tral]

cheap (low-priced)	ieftin	['jeftin]
cheerful (adj)	vesel	['vesel]

children's (adj)	pentru copii	['pentru ko'pij]
civil (~ law)	civil	[ʧi'vil]
clandestine (secret)	ilegal	[ile'gal]
clean (free from dirt)	curat	[ku'rat]
clear (explanation, etc.)	clar	[klar]
clever (intelligent)	deştept	[deʃ'tept]
close (near in space)	vecin	[ve'ʧin]
closed (adj)	închis	[in'kis]
cloudless (sky)	fără nori	['fərə 'norʲ]
cold (drink, weather)	rece	['reʧe]
compatible (adj)	compatibil	[kompa'tibil]
contented (satisfied)	mulţumit	[mulʦu'mit]
continuous (uninterrupted)	neîntrerupt	[neintre'rupt]
cool (weather)	răcoros	[rəko'ros]
dangerous (adj)	periculos	[periku'los]
dark (room)	întunecat	[intune'kat]
dead (not alive)	mort	[mort]
dense (fog, smoke)	des	[des]
destitute (extremely poor)	sărac	[sə'rak]
different (not the same)	diferit	[dife'rit]
difficult (decision)	greu	['greu]
difficult (problem, task)	complex	[kom'pleks]
dim, faint (light)	şters	[ʃters]
dirty (not clean)	murdar	[mur'dar]
distant (in space)	îndepărtat	[indepər'tat]
dry (clothes, etc.)	uscat	[us'kat]
easy (not difficult)	simplu	['simplu]
empty (glass, room)	gol	[gol]
even (e.g. ~ surface)	neted	['neted]
exact (amount)	exact	[e'gzakt]
excellent (adj)	excelent	[eksʧe'lent]
excessive (adj)	excesiv	[eksʧe'siv]
expensive (adj)	scump	[skump]
exterior (adj)	exterior	[eksteri'or]
far (the ~ East)	îndepărtat	[indepər'tat]
fast (quick)	rapid	[ra'pid]
fatty (food)	gras	[gras]
fertile (land, soil)	roditor	[rodi'tor]
flat (~ panel display)	neted	['neted]
foreign (adj)	străin	[strə'in]
fragile (china, glass)	fragil	[fra'dʒil]
free (at no cost)	gratis	['gratis]
free (unrestricted)	liber	['liber]
fresh (~ water)	nesărat	[nesə'rat]
fresh (e.g. ~ bread)	proaspăt	[pro'aspət]
frozen (food)	congelat	[kondʒe'lat]
full (completely filled)	plin	[plin]

gloomy (house, forecast)	întunecat	[intune'kat]
good (book, etc.)	bun	[bun]
good, kind (kindhearted)	bun	[bun]
grateful (adj)	recunoscător	[rekunoskə'tor]

happy (adj)	fericit	[feri'tʃit]
hard (not soft)	tare	['tare]
heavy (in weight)	greu	['greu]
hostile (adj)	duşmănos	[duʃmə'nos]
hot (adj)	fierbinte	[fier'binte]

huge (adj)	uriaş	[uri'aʃ]
humid (adj)	umed	['umed]
hungry (adj)	flămând	[flə'mind]
ill (sick, unwell)	bolnav	[bol'nav]
immobile (adj)	imobil	[imo'bil]

important (adj)	important	[impor'tant]
impossible (adj)	imposibil	[impo'sibil]
incomprehensible	neclar	[ne'klar]
indispensable (adj)	necesar	[netʃe'sar]
inexperienced (adj)	lipsit de experienţă	[lip'sit de ekspe'rjentsə]

insignificant (adj)	neînsemnat	[neinsem'nat]
interior (adj)	interior	[interi'or]
joint (~ decision)	comun	[ko'mun]
last (e.g. ~ week)	trecut	[tre'kut]

last (final)	ultimul	['ultimul]
left (e.g. ~ side)	stâng	[sting]
legal (legitimate)	legal	[le'gal]
light (in weight)	uşor	[u'ʃor]
light (pale color)	de nuanţă deschisă	[de nu'antsə des'kisə]

limited (adj)	limitat	[limi'tat]
liquid (fluid)	lichid	[li'kid]
long (e.g. ~ hair)	lung	[lung]
loud (voice, etc.)	cu voce tare	[ku 'votʃe 'tare]
low (voice)	încet	[in'tʃet]

251. Modifiers. Adjectives. Part 2

main (principal)	principal	[printʃi'pal]
matt, matte	mat	[mat]
meticulous (job)	ordonat	[ordo'nat]
mysterious (adj)	enigmatic	[enig'matik]
narrow (street, etc.)	îngust	[in'gust]

native (~ country)	natal	[na'tal]
nearby (adj)	apropiat	[apropi'jat]
needed (necessary)	necesar	[netʃe'sar]
negative (~ response)	negativ	[nega'tiv]
neighbouring (adj)	vecin	[ve'tʃin]
nervous (adj)	nervos	[ner'vos]

new (adj)	nou	['nou]
next (e.g. ~ week)	următor	[urmə'tor]
nice (agreeable)	simpatic	[sim'patik]

pleasant (voice)	plăcut	[plə'kut]
normal (adj)	normal	[nor'mal]
not big (adj)	nu prea mare	['nu prʲa 'mare]
not difficult (adj)	uşor	[u'ʃor]

obligatory (adj)	obligatoriu	[obliga'torju]
old (house)	bătrân	[bə'trin]
open (adj)	deschis	[des'kis]
opposite (adj)	opus	[o'pus]
ordinary (usual)	obişnuit	[obiʃnu'it]

original (unusual)	original	[oridʒi'nal]
past (recent)	trecut	[tre'kut]
permanent (adj)	stabil	[sta'bil]
personal (adj)	personal	[perso'nal]
polite (adj)	politicos	[politi'kos]

poor (not rich)	sărac	[sə'rak]
possible (adj)	posibil	[po'sibil]
present (current)	prezent	[pre'zent]
principal (main)	fundamental	[fundamen'tal]

private (~ jet)	personal	[perso'nal]
probable (adj)	probabil	[pro'babil]
prolonged (e.g. ~ applause)	îndelungat	[indelu'ngat]
public (open to all)	social	[sotʃi'al]

punctual (person)	punctual	[punktu'al]
quiet (tranquil)	liniştit	[liniʃ'tit]
rare (adj)	rar	[rar]
raw (uncooked)	crud	[krud]

right (not left)	drept	[drept]
right, correct (adj)	corect	[ko'rekt]
ripe (fruit)	copt	[kopt]
risky (adj)	riscant	[ris'kant]
sad (~ look)	trist	[trist]

sad (depressing)	trist	[trist]
safe (not dangerous)	neprimejdios	[neprimeʒdi'os]
salty (food)	sărat	[sə'rat]
satisfied (customer)	satisfăcut	[satisfə'kut]

second hand (adj)	la mâna a doua	[la 'mina a 'dowa]
shallow (water)	mărunt	[mə'runt]
sharp (blade, etc.)	ascuţit	[asku'tsit]
short (in length)	scurt	[skurt]

short, short-lived (adj)	de scurtă durată	[de 'skurtə du'ratə]
short-sighted (adj)	miop	[mi'op]
significant (notable)	considerabil	[konside'rabil]
similar (adj)	asemănător	[asemənə'tor]

simple (easy)	**simplu**	['simplu]
skinny	**slab**	[slab]
small (in size)	**mic**	[mik]
smooth (surface)	**neted**	['neted]
soft (~ toys)	**moale**	[mo'ale]
solid (~ wall)	**durabil**	[du'rabil]
sour (flavour, taste)	**acru**	['akru]
spacious (house, etc.)	**spaţios**	[spatsi'os]
special (adj)	**special**	[spetʃi'al]
straight (line, road)	**drept**	[drept]
strong (person)	**puternic**	[pu'ternik]
stupid (foolish)	**prost**	[prost]
suitable (e.g. ~ for drinking)	**folositor**	[folosi'tor]
sunny (day)	**însorit**	[inso'rit]
superb, perfect (adj)	**superb**	[su'perb]
swarthy (dark-skinned)	**negricios**	[negri'tʃios]
sweet (sugary)	**dulce**	['dultʃe]
tanned (adj)	**bronzat**	[bron'zat]
tasty (delicious)	**gustos**	[gus'tos]
tender (affectionate)	**gingaş**	['dʒingaʃ]
the highest (adj)	**cel mai înalt**	[tʃel maj i'nalt]
the most important	**cel mai important**	[tʃel maj impor'tant]
the nearest	**cel mai apropiat**	['tʃel 'maj apropi'at]
the same, equal (adj)	**asemenea**	[a'semenıa]
thick (e.g. ~ fog)	**des**	[des]
thick (wall, slice)	**gras**	[gras]
thin (person)	**slab**	[slab]
tired (exhausted)	**obosit**	[obo'sit]
tiring (adj)	**obositor**	[obosi'tor]
transparent (adj)	**transparent**	[transpa'rent]
unclear (adj)	**neclar**	[ne'klar]
unique (exceptional)	**unic**	['unik]
various (adj)	**distinct**	[dis'tinkt]
warm (moderately hot)	**cald**	[kald]
wet (e.g. ~ clothes)	**ud**	[ud]
whole (entire, complete)	**întreg**	[in'treg]
wide (e.g. ~ road)	**larg**	[larg]
young (adj)	**tânăr**	['tinər]

MAIN 500 VERBS

to accompany (vt)	a acompania	[a akompani'ja]
to accuse (vt)	a învinui	[a invinu'i]
to acknowledge (admit)	a recunoaşte	[a rekuno'aʃte]
to act (take action)	a acţiona	[a akʦio'na]
to add (supplement)	a adăuga	[a adəu'ga]
to address (speak to)	a se adresa	[a se adre'sa]
to admire (vi)	a fi încântat	[a fi inkin'tat]
to advertise (vt)	a face reclamă	[a 'fatʃe re'klamə]
to advise (vt)	a sfătui	[a sfətu'i]
to affirm (assert)	a susţine	[a sus'ʦine]
to agree (say yes)	a fi de acord	[a fi de a'kord]
to aim (to point a weapon)	a ţinti	[a ʦin'ti]
to allow (sb to do sth)	a permite	[a per'mite]
to amputate (vt)	a amputa	[a ampu'ta]
to answer (vi, vt)	a răspunde	[a rəs'punde]
to apologize (vi)	a cere scuze	[a 'tʃere 'skuze]
to appear (come into view)	a apărea	[a apə'rʲa]
to applaud (vi, vt)	a aplauda	[a aplau'da]
to appoint (assign)	a numi	[a nu'mi]
to approach (come closer)	a se apropia	[a se apropi'a]
to arrive (ab. train)	a sosi	[a so'si]
to ask (~ sb to do sth)	a cere	[a 'tʃere]
to aspire to …	a aspira	[a aspi'ra]
to assist (help)	a asista	[a asis'ta]
to attack (mil.)	a ataca	[a ata'ka]
to attain (objectives)	a reuşi	[a reu'ʃi]
to avenge (get revenge)	a răzbuna	[a rəzbu'na]
to avoid (danger, task)	a evita	[a evi'ta]
to award (give a medal to)	a decora	[a deko'ra]
to battle (vi)	a se lupta	[a se lup'ta]
to be (vi)	a fi	[a fi]
to be a cause of …	a cauza …	[a kau'za]
to be afraid	a se teme	[a se 'teme]
to be angry (with …)	a se supăra	[a se supə'ra]
to be at war	a lupta	[a lup'ta]
to be based (on …)	a se baza pe	[a se ba'za pe]
to be bored	a se plictisi	[a se plikti'si]

to be convinced	a se convinge	[a se kon'vindʒe]
to be enough	a ajunge	[a a'ʒundʒe]
to be envious	a invidia	[a invidi'a]
to be indignant	a se indigna	[a se indig'na]
to be interested in …	a se interesa	[a se intere'sa]
to be lost in thought	a cădea pe gânduri	[a kə'dʲa pe 'gindurʲ]
to be lying (~ on the table)	a sta	[a sta]
to be needed	a fi nevoie	[a fi ne'voje]
to be perplexed (puzzled)	a fi nedumerit	[a fi nedume'rit]
to be preserved	a se păstra	[a se pəs'tra]
to be required	a fi necesar	[a fi netʃe'sar]
to be surprised	a se mira	[a se mi'ra]
to be worried	a se nelinişti	[a se neliniʃ'ti]
to beat (to hit)	a bate	[a 'bate]
to become (e.g. ~ old)	a deveni	[a deve'ni]
to behave (vi)	a se comporta	[a se kompor'ta]
to believe (think)	a crede	[a 'krede]
to belong to …	a aparţine	[a apar'tsine]
to berth (moor)	a acosta	[a akos'ta]
to blind (other drivers)	a orbi	[a or'bi]
to blow (wind)	a sufla	[a su'fla]
to blush (vi)	a se înroşi	[a se inro'ʃi]
to boast (vi)	a se lăuda	[a se ləu'da]
to borrow (money)	a împrumuta	[a imprumu'ta]
to break (branch, toy, etc.)	a rupe	[a 'rupe]
to breathe (vi)	a respira	[a respi'ra]
to bring (sth)	a aduce	[a a'dutʃe]
to burn (paper, logs)	a arde	[a 'arde]
to buy (purchase)	a cumpăra	[a kumpə'ra]
to call (~ for help)	a chema	[a ke'ma]
to call (yell for sb)	a chema	[a ke'ma]
to calm down (vt)	a linişti	[a liniʃ'ti]
can (v aux)	a putea	[a pu'tʲa]
to cancel (call off)	a anula	[a anu'la]
to cast off (of a boat or ship)	a demara	[a dema'ra]
to catch (e.g. ~ a ball)	a prinde	[a 'prinde]
to change (~ one's opinion)	a schimba	[a skim'ba]
to change (exchange)	a schimba	[a skim'ba]
to charm (vt)	a fermeca	[a ferme'ka]
to choose (select)	a alege	[a a'ledʒe]
to chop off (with an axe)	a tăia	[a tə'ja]
to clean (e.g. kettle from scale)	a curăţa	[a kurə'tsa]
to clean (shoes, etc.)	a curăţa	[a kurə'tsa]
to clean up (tidy)	a face ordine	[a 'fatʃe 'ordine]
to close (vt)	a închide	[a i'nkide]

to comb one's hair	a se pieptăna	[a se peptə'na]
to come down (the stairs)	a coborî	[a kobo'ri]
to come out (book)	a apărea	[a apə'rʲa]
to compare (vt)	a compara	[a kompa'ra]
to compensate (vt)	a compensa	[a kompen'sa]
to compete (vi)	a concura	[a konku'ra]
to compile (~ a list)	a alcătui	[a alkətu'i]
to complain (vi, vt)	a se plânge	[a se 'plindʒe]
to complicate (vt)	a complica	[a kompli'ka]
to compose (music, etc.)	a crea	[a 'krʲa]
to compromise (reputation)	a compromite	[a kompro'mite]
to concentrate (vi)	a se concentra	[a se kontʃen'tra]
to confess (criminal)	a mărturisi	[a mərturi'si]
to confuse (mix up)	a încurca	[a inkur'ka]
to congratulate (vt)	a felicita	[a felitʃi'ta]
to consult (doctor, expert)	a se consulta cu ...	[a se konsul'ta 'ku]
to continue (~ to do sth)	a continua	[a kontinu'a]
to control (vt)	a controla	[a kontro'la]
to convince (vt)	a convinge	[a kon'vindʒe]
to cooperate (vi)	a colabora	[a kolabo'ra]
to coordinate (vt)	a coordona	[a koordo'na]
to correct (an error)	a corecta	[a korek'ta]
to cost (vt)	a costa	[a kos'ta]
to count (money, etc.)	a calcula	[a kalku'la]
to count on ...	a conta pe ...	[a kon'ta pe]
to crack (ceiling, wall)	a crăpa	[a krə'pa]
to create (vt)	a crea	[a 'krʲa]
to crush, to squash (~ a bug)	a strivi	[a stri'vi]
to cry (weep)	a plânge	[a 'plindʒe]
to cut off (with a knife)	a tăia	[a tə'ja]

253. Verbs D-G

to dare (~ to do sth)	a îndrăzni	[a indrəz'ni]
to date from ...	a data	[a da'ta]
to deceive (vi, vt)	a minți	[a min'tsi]
to decide (~ to do sth)	a hotărî	[a hotə'ri]
to decorate (tree, street)	a decora	[a deko'ra]
to dedicate (book, etc.)	a dedica	[a dedi'ka]
to defend (a country, etc.)	a apăra	[a apə'ra]
to defend oneself	a se apăra	[a se apə'ra]
to demand (request firmly)	a cere	[a 'tʃere]
to denounce (vt)	a denunța	[a denun'tsa]
to deny (vt)	a nega	[a ne'ga]
to depend on ...	a depinde de ...	[a de'pinde de]
to deprive (vt)	a priva	[a pri'va]

to deserve (vt)	a merita	[a meri'ta]
to design (machine, etc.)	a proiecta	[a proek'ta]
to desire (want, wish)	a dori	[a do'ri]
to despise (vt)	a dispreţui	[a dispreţsu'i]

to destroy (documents, etc.)	a distruge	[a dis'trudʒe]
to differ (from sth)	a se deosebi de …	[a se deose'bi de]
to dig (tunnel, etc.)	a săpa	[a sə'pa]
to direct (point the way)	a îndrepta spre …	[a indrep'ta spre]

to disappear (vi)	a dispărea	[a dispə'rɪa]
to discover (new land, etc.)	a descoperi	[a deskope'ri]
to discuss (vt)	a discuta	[a disku'ta]
to distribute (leaflets, etc.)	a răspândi	[a rəspin'di]

to disturb (vt)	a deranja	[a deran'ʒa]
to dive (vi)	a se cufunda	[a se kufun'da]
to divide (math)	a împărţi	[a impər'ţsi]
to do (vt)	a face	[a 'fatʃe]

to do the laundry	a spăla	[a spə'la]
to double (increase)	a dubla	[a dub'la]
to doubt (have doubts)	a se îndoi	[a se indo'i]
to draw a conclusion	a trage o concluzie	[a 'tradʒe o kon'kluzie]

to dream (daydream)	a visa	[a vi'sa]
to dream (in sleep)	a visa	[a vi'sa]
to drink (vi, vt)	a bea	[a bɪa]
to drive a car	a conduce maşina	[a kon'dutʃe ma'ʃina]
to drive away (scare away)	a goni	[a go'ni]

to drop (let fall)	a scăpa	[a skə'pa]
to drown (ab. person)	a se îneca	[a se ine'ka]
to dry (clothes, hair)	a usca	[a uska]
to eat (vi, vt)	a mânca	[a min'ka]

to eavesdrop (vi)	a trage cu urechea	[a 'tradʒe ku u'rekɪa]
to emit (diffuse - odor, etc.)	a împrăştia	[a imprəʃti'a]
to enjoy oneself	a se veseli	[a se vese'li]
to enter (on the list)	a înscrie	[a in'skrie]

to enter (room, house, etc.)	a intra	[a in'tra]
to entertain (amuse)	a distra	[a dis'tra]
to equip (fit out)	a utila	[a uti'la]
to examine (proposal)	a analiza	[a anali'za]

to exchange (sth)	a face schimb	[a 'fatʃe 'skimb]
to excuse (forgive)	a scuza	[a sku'za]
to exist (vi)	a exista	[a ekzis'ta]
to expect (anticipate)	a aştepta	[a aʃtep'ta]

to expect (foresee)	a prevedea	[a preve'dɪa]
to expel (from school, etc.)	a exclude	[a eks'klude]
to explain (vt)	a explica	[a ekspli'ka]
to express (vt)	a exprima	[a ekspri'ma]
to extinguish (a fire)	a stinge	[a 'stindʒe]

233

to fall in love (with …)	a se îndrăgosti	[a se indrəgos'ti]
to fancy (vt)	a plăcea	[a plə'ʧa]
to feed (provide food)	a hrăni	[a hrə'ni]
to fight (against the enemy)	a lupta	[a lup'ta]
to fight (vi)	a se bate	[a se 'bate]
to fill (glass, bottle)	a umple	[a 'umple]
to find (~ lost items)	a găsi	[a gə'si]
to finish (vt)	a termina	[a termi'na]
to fish (angle)	a pescui	[a pesku'i]
to fit (ab. dress, etc.)	a plăcea	[a plə'ʧa]
to flatter (vt)	a flata	[a fla'ta]
to fly (bird, plane)	a zbura	[a zbu'ra]
to follow … (come after)	a urma	[a ur'ma]
to forbid (vt)	a interzice	[a inter'ziʧe]
to force (compel)	a forța	[a for'tsa]
to forget (vi, vt)	a uita	[a uj'ta]
to forgive (pardon)	a ierta	[a er'ta]
to form (constitute)	a forma	[a for'ma]
to get dirty (vi)	a se murdări	[a se murdə'ri]
to get infected (with …)	a se contamina	[a se kontami'na]
to get irritated	a se irita	[a se iri'ta]
to get married	a se căsători	[a se kəsəto'ri]
to get rid of …	a scăpa	[a skə'pa]
to get tired	a obosi	[a obo'si]
to get up (arise from bed)	a se ridica	[a se ridi'ka]
to give a bath (to bath)	a face baie	[a 'faʧe 'bae]
to give a hug, to hug (vt)	a îmbrățișa	[a imbrətsi'ʃa]
to give in (yield to)	a ceda	[a ʧe'da]
to glimpse (vt)	a vedea	[a ve'dʲa]
to go (by car, etc.)	a merge	[a 'merdʒe]
to go (on foot)	a merge	[a 'merdʒe]
to go for a swim	a se scălda	[a se skəl'da]
to go out (for dinner, etc.)	a ieși	[a e'ʃi]
to go to bed (go to sleep)	a se culca	[a se kul'ka]
to greet (vt)	a saluta	[a salu'ta]
to grow (plants)	a cultiva	[a kulti'va]
to guarantee (vt)	a garanta	[a garan'ta]
to guess (the answer)	a ghici	[a gi'ʧi]

254. Verbs H-M

to hand out (distribute)	a distribui	[a distribu'i]
to hang (curtains, etc.)	a atârna	[a atir'na]
to have (vt)	a avea	[a a'vʲa]
to have a bath	a se spăla	[a se spə'la]

to have a try	a încerca	[a intʃer'ka]
to have breakfast	a lua micul dejun	[a lu'a 'mikul de'ʒun]
to have dinner	a cina	[a tʃi'na]
to have lunch	a lua prânzul	[a lu'a 'prinzul]
to head (group, etc.)	a conduce	[a kon'dutʃe]
to hear (vt)	a auzi	[a au'zi]

to heat (vt)	a încălzi	[a inkəl'zi]
to help (vt)	a ajuta	[a aʒu'ta]
to hide (vt)	a ascunde	[a as'kunde]
to hire (e.g. ~ a boat)	a închiria	[a inkiri'ja]
to hire (staff)	a angaja	[a anga'ʒa]

to hope (vi, vt)	a spera	[a spe'ra]
to hunt (for food, sport)	a vâna	[a vi'na]
to hurry (vi)	a se grăbi	[a se grə'bi]
to imagine (to picture)	a-şi imagina	[aʃ imadʒi'na]
to imitate (vt)	a imita	[a imi'ta]

to implore (vt)	a ruga	[a ru'ga]
to import (vt)	a importa	[a impor'ta]
to increase (vi)	a se mări	[a se mə'ri]
to increase (vt)	a mări	[a mə'ri]
to infect (vt)	a molipsi	[a molip'si]

to influence (vt)	a influenţa	[a influen'tsa]
to inform (e.g. ~ the police about …)	a anunţa	[a anun'tsa]
to inform (vt)	a informa	[a infor'ma]
to inherit (vt)	a moşteni	[a moʃte'ni]
to inquire (about …)	a afla	[a af'la]

to insert (put in)	a pune	[a 'pune]
to insinuate (imply)	a face aluzie	[a 'fatʃe a'luzie]
to insist (vi, vt)	a insista	[a insis'ta]
to inspire (vt)	a stimula	[a stimu'la]
to instruct (teach)	a da instrucţiuni	[a da instruktsi'uni]

to insult (offend)	a jigni	[a ʒig'ni]
to interest (vt)	a interesa	[a intere'sa]
to intervene (vi)	a interveni	[a interve'ni]
to introduce (sb to sb)	a face cunoştinţă	[a 'fatʃe kunoʃ'tintsə]

to invent (machine, etc.)	a inventa	[a inven'ta]
to invite (vt)	a invita	[a invi'ta]
to iron (clothes)	a călca	[a kəl'ka]
to irritate (annoy)	a irita	[a iri'ta]
to Isolate (vt)	a izola	[a izo'la]

to join (political party, etc.)	a adera	[a ade'ra]
to joke (be kidding)	a glumi	[a glu'mi]
to keep (old letters, etc.)	a păstra	[a pəs'tra]
to keep silent, to hush	a tăcea	[a tə'tʃa]
to kill (vt)	a omorî	[a omo'ri]
to knock (on the door)	a bate	[a 'bate]
to know (sb)	a cunoaşte	[a kuno'aʃte]

to know (sth)	a şti	[a ʃti]
to laugh (vi)	a râde	[a 'ride]
to launch (start up)	a porni	[a por'ni]
to leave (~ for Mexico)	a pleca	[a ple'ka]
to leave (forget sth)	a lăsa	[a lə'sa]
to leave (spouse)	a părăsi	[a pərə'si]
to liberate (city, etc.)	a elibera	[a elibe'ra]
to lie (~ on the floor)	a sta culcat	[a sta kul'kat]
to lie (tell untruth)	a minţi	[a min'tsi]
to light (campfire, etc.)	a aprinde	[a a'prinde]
to light up (illuminate)	a lumina	[a lumi'na]
to limit (vt)	a limita	[a limi'ta]
to listen (vi)	a asculta	[a askul'ta]
to live (~ in France)	a trăi	[a trə'i]
to live (exist)	a exista	[a ekzis'ta]
to load (gun)	a încărca	[a inkər'ka]
to load (vehicle, etc.)	a încărca	[a inkər'ka]
to look (I'm just ~ing)	a privi	[a pri'vi]
to look for … (search)	a căuta	[a kəu'ta]
to look like (resemble)	a semăna cu	[a semə'na ku]
to lose (umbrella, etc.)	a pierde	[a 'pjerde]
to love (e.g. ~ dancing)	a plăcea	[a plə'tʃa]
to love (sb)	a iubi	[a ju'bi]
to lower (blind, head)	a lăsa în jos	[a lə'sa 'in 'ʒos]
to make (~ dinner)	a găti	[a gə'ti]
to make a mistake	a greşi	[a gre'ʃi]
to make angry	a supăra	[a supə'ra]
to make easier	a uşura	[a uʃu'ra]
to make multiple copies	a multiplica	[a multipli'ka]
to make the acquaintance	a face cunoştinţă	[a 'fatʃe kunoʃ'tintsə]
to make use (of …)	a se folosi	[a se folo'si]
to manage, to run	a conduce	[a kon'dutʃe]
to mark (make a mark)	a semnala	[a semna'la]
to mean (signify)	a avea sens	[a a'vʲa sens]
to memorize (vt)	a memora	[a memo'ra]
to mention (talk about)	a aminti	[a amin'ti]
to miss (school, etc.)	a lipsi	[a lip'si]
to mix (combine, blend)	a amesteca	[a ameste'ka]
to mock (make fun of)	a-şi bate joc	[aʃ 'bate ʒok]
to move (to shift)	a mişca	[a miʃ'ka]
to multiply (math)	a înmulţi	[a inmul'tsi]
must (v aux)	a fi dator	[a fi da'tor]

255. Verbs N-R

to name, to call (vt)	a numi	[a nu'mi]
to negotiate (vi)	a purta tratative	[a pur'ta trata'tive]

| to note (write down) | a însemna | [a insem'na] |
| to notice (see) | a observa | [a obser'va] |

to obey (vi, vt)	a se supune	[a se su'pune]
to object (vi, vt)	a contrazice	[a kontra'zitʃe]
to observe (see)	a observa	[a obser'va]
to offend (vt)	a jigni	[a ʒig'ni]

to omit (word, phrase)	a omite	[a o'mite]
to open (vt)	a deschide	[a des'kide]
to order (in restaurant)	a comanda	[a koman'da]
to order (mil.)	a ordona	[a ordo'na]
to organize (concert, party)	a organiza	[a organi'za]

to overestimate (vt)	a reevalua	[a reevalu'a]
to own (possess)	a poseda	[a pose'da]
to participate (vi)	a participa	[a partitʃi'pa]
to pass through (by car, etc.)	a trece	[a 'tretʃe]
to pay (vi, vt)	a plăti	[a plə'ti]

to peep, to spy on	a urmări pe furiş	[a urmə'ri pe fu'riʃ]
to penetrate (vt)	a pătrunde	[a pə'trunde]
to permit (vt)	a permite	[a per'mite]
to pick (flowers)	a rupe	[a 'rupe]
to place (put, set)	a instala	[a insta'la]

to plan (~ to do sth)	a planifica	[a planifi'ka]
to play (actor)	a juca	[a ʒu'ka]
to play (children)	a juca	[a ʒu'ka]
to point (~ the way)	a arăta	[a arə'ta]

to pour (liquid)	a turna	[a tur'na]
to pray (vi, vt)	a se ruga	[a se ru'ga]
to prefer (vt)	a prefera	[a prefe'ra]
to prepare (~ a plan)	a pregăti	[a pregə'ti]

to present (sb to sb)	a reprezenta	[a reprezen'ta]
to preserve (peace, life)	a păstra	[a pəs'tra]
to prevail (vt)	a predomina	[a predomi'na]
to progress (move forward)	a progresa	[a progre'sa]

to promise (vt)	a promite	[a pro'mite]
to pronounce (vt)	a pronunţa	[a pronun'tsa]
to propose (vt)	a propune	[a pro'pune]
to protect (e.g. ~ nature)	a apăra	[a apə'ra]

to protest (vi)	a protesta	[a protes'ta]
to prove (vt)	a dovedi	[a dove'di]
to provoke (vt)	a provoca	[a provo'ka]
to pull (~ the rope)	a trage	[a 'tradʒə]

to punish (vt)	a pedepsi	[a pedep'si]
to push (~ the door)	a împinge	[a im'pindʒe]
to put away (vt)	a ascunde	[a as'kunde]
to put in order	a pune în ordine	[a 'pune in 'ordine]
to put, to place	a pune	[a 'pune]

to quote (cite)	a cita	[a t͡ʃi'ta]
to reach (arrive at)	a atinge	[a a'tind͡ʒe]
to read (vi, vt)	a citi	[a t͡ʃi'ti]
to realize (a dream)	a realiza	[a reali'za]
to recognize (identify sb)	a recunoaşte	[a rekuno'aʃte]

to recommend (vt)	a recomanda	[a rekoman'da]
to recover (~ from flu)	a se vindeca	[a se vinde'ka]
to redo (do again)	a reface	[a re'fat͡ʃe]
to reduce (speed, etc.)	a micşora	[a mikʃo'ra]

to refuse (~ sb)	a refuza	[a refu'za]
to regret (be sorry)	a regreta	[a regre'ta]
to reinforce (vt)	a consolida	[a konsoli'da]
to remember (Do you ~ me?)	a ţine minte	[a 'tsine 'minte]

to remember (I can't ~ her name)	a-şi aminti	['aʃ amin'ti]
to remind of …	a aminti	[a amin'ti]
to remove (~ a stain)	a scoate	[a sko'ate]
to remove (~ an obstacle)	a înlătura	[a inlətu'ra]

to rent (sth from sb)	a închiria	[a inkiri'ja]
to repair (mend)	a repara	[a repa'ra]
to repeat (say again)	a repeta	[a repe'ta]
to report (make a report)	a raporta	[a rapor'ta]

to reproach (vt)	a reproşa	[a repro'ʃa]
to reserve, to book	a rezerva	[a rezer'va]
to restrain (hold back)	a reţine	[a re'tsine]
to return (come back)	a se întoarce	[a se into'art͡ʃe]

to risk, to take a risk	a risca	[a ris'ka]
to rub out (erase)	a şterge	[a 'ʃterd͡ʒe]
to run (move fast)	a alerga	[a aler'ga]
to rush (hurry sb)	a grăbi	[a grə'bi]

256. Verbs S-W

to satisfy (please)	a satisface	[a satis'fat͡ʃe]
to save (rescue)	a salva	[a sal'va]
to say (~ thank you)	a spune	[a 'spune]
to scold (vt)	a certa	[a t͡ʃer'ta]

to scratch (with claws)	a zgâria	[a zgiri'ja]
to select (to pick)	a lua înapoi	[a lu'a ina'poj]
to sell (goods)	a vinde	[a 'vinde]
to send (a letter)	a trimite	[a tri'mite]

to send back (vt)	a expedia destinatarului	[a ekspedi'ja destina'taruluj]
to sense (~ danger)	a simţi	[a sim'tsi]
to sentence (vt)	a condamna	[a kondam'na]
to serve (in restaurant)	a servi	[a ser'vi]
to settle (a conflict)	a aranja	[a aran'ʒa]

to shake (vt)	a scutura	[a skutu'ra]
to shave (vi)	a se bărbieri	[a se bərbie'ri]
to shine (gleam)	a străluci	[a strəlu'ʧi]

to shiver (with cold)	a tremura	[a tremu'ra]
to shoot (vi)	a trage	[a 'tradʒə]
to shout (vi)	a striga	[a stri'ga]
to show (to display)	a arăta	[a arə'ta]

to shudder (vi)	a tresări	[a tresə'ri]
to sigh (vi)	a ofta	[a of'ta]
to sign (document)	a semna	[a sem'na]
to signify (mean)	a însemna	[a insem'na]

to simplify (vt)	a simplifica	[a simplifi'ka]
to sin (vi)	a păcătui	[a pəkətu'i]
to sit (be sitting)	a şedea	[a ʃə'dʲa]
to sit down (vi)	a se aşeza	[a se aʃə'za]

to smell (emit an odor)	a mirosi	[a miro'si]
to smell (inhale the odor)	a mirosi	[a miro'si]
to smile (vi)	a zâmbi	[a zim'bi]
to snap (vi, ab. rope)	a se rupe	[a se 'rupe]

to solve (problem)	a rezolva	[a rezol'va]
to sow (seed, crop)	a semăna	[a semə'na]
to spill (liquid)	a vărsa	[a vər'sa]

to spit (vi)	a scuipa	[a skuj'pa]
to stand (toothache, cold)	a răbda	[a rəb'da]
to start (begin)	a începe	[a in'ʧepe]
to steal (money, etc.)	a fura	[a fu'ra]

to stop (for pause, etc.)	a se opri	[a se o'pri]
to stop (please ~ calling me)	a pune capăt	[a 'pune 'kapət]
to stop talking	a tăcea	[a tə'ʧa]
to stroke (caress)	a mângâia	[a mingi'ja]

to study (vt)	a studia	[a studi'a]
to suffer (feel pain)	a suferi	[a sufe'ri]
to support (cause, idea)	a susţine	[a sus'ʦine]
to suppose (assume)	a presupune	[a presu'pune]

to surface (ab. submarine)	a ieşi la suprafață	[a e'ʃi la supra'faʦə]
to surprise (amaze)	a mira	[a mi'ra]
to suspect (vt)	a suspecta	[a suspek'ta]
to swim (vi)	a înota	[a ino'ta]

to take (get hold of)	a lua	[a lu'a]
to take a rest	a se odihni	[a se odih'nɪ]
to take away (e.g. about waiter)	a duce cu sine	[a 'duʧe ku 'sine]

| to take off (aeroplane) | a decola | [a deko'la] |
| to take off (painting, curtains, etc.) | a scoate | [a sko'ate] |

to take pictures	a fotografia	[a fotografi'ja]
to talk to …	a vorbi cu …	[a vor'bi ku]
to teach (give lessons)	a învăța pe cineva	[a invə'tsa pe tʃine'va]

to tear off, to rip off (vt)	a smulge	[a 'smuldʒe]
to tell (story, joke)	a povesti	[a poves'ti]
to thank (vt)	a mulțumi	[a multsu'mi]
to think (believe)	a crede	[a 'krede]

to think (vi, vt)	a se gândi	[a se gin'di]
to threaten (vt)	a amenința	[a amenin'tsa]
to throw (stone, etc.)	a arunca	[a arun'ka]
to tie to …	a lega	[a le'ga]

to tie up (prisoner)	a lega	[a le'ga]
to tire (make tired)	a obosi	[a obo'si]
to touch (one's arm, etc.)	a se referi	[a se refe'ri]
to tower (over …)	a se înălța	[a se inəl'tsa]
to train (animals)	a dresa	[a dre'sa]

to train (sb)	a antrena	[a antre'na]
to train (vi)	a se antrena	[a se antre'na]
to transform (vt)	a transforma	[a transfor'ma]
to translate (vt)	a traduce	[a tra'dutʃe]

to treat (illness)	a trata	[a tra'ta]
to trust (vt)	a avea încredere	[a a'vʲa in'kredere]
to try (attempt)	a se strădui	[a se strədu'i]
to turn (e.g., ~ left)	a întoarce	[a into'artʃe]

to turn away (vi)	a se întoarce	[a se into'artʃe]
to turn off (the light)	a stinge	[a 'stindʒe]
to turn on (computer, etc.)	a conecta	[a konek'ta]
to turn over (stone, etc.)	a întoarce	[a into'artʃe]

to underestimate (vt)	a subaprecia	[a subapretʃi'a]
to underline (vt)	a sublinia	[a sublini'a]
to understand (vt)	a înțelege	[a intse'ledʒe]
to undertake (vt)	a întreprinde	[a intre'prinde]

to unite (vt)	a uni	[a u'ni]
to untie (vt)	a dezlega	[a dezle'ga]
to use (phrase, word)	a folosi	[a folo'si]
to vaccinate (vt)	a vaccina	[a vaktʃi'na]

to vote (vi)	a vota	[a vo'ta]
to wait (vt)	a aștepta	[a aʃtep'ta]
to wake (sb)	a deștepta	[a deʃtep'ta]
to want (wish, desire)	a vrea	[a vrʲa]

to warn (of a danger)	a preveni	[a preve'ni]
to wash (clean)	a spăla	[a spə'la]
to water (plants)	a uda	[a u'da]
to wave (the hand)	a flutura	[a flutu'ra]
to weigh (have weight)	a cântări	[a kintə'ri]
to work (vi)	a lucra	[a lu'kra]

| to worry (make anxious) | a nelinişti | [a neliniʃti] |
| to worry (vi) | a se nelinişti | [a se neliniʃti] |

to wrap (parcel, etc.)	a împacheta	[a impake'ta]
to wrestle (sport)	a lupta	[a lup'ta]
to write (vt)	a scrie	[a 'skrie]
to write down	a nota	[a no'ta]

Printed in Great Britain
by Amazon